A cognitive approach to performance appraisal

Performance appraisal is acknowledged as one of management's most effective tools for good employee motivation, satisfaction, and productivity. Not surprisingly then, there are plenty of books of the 'how to do' sort for managers, but are the methods described based on a sound theoretical knowledge? Do they correctly account for the biases and heuristics in memory, for instance?

A Cognitive Approach to Performance Appraisal is the account of a meticulous and extensive research program into rater cognitive processes and their effects on performance appraisal decisions. Angelo DeNisi has conducted over 30 experiments both in the laboratory and in real-life situations to investigate such important topics as the role of rater memory and the effect of liking some employees more than others. It is also the story of long-term research: the high and low points, the successes and the pitfalls, and the differences between work in the laboratory and the real world.

A Cognitive Approach to Performance Appraisal is relevant to all those researching in organizational psychology, especially in the field of appraisal. It will also be of interest to all psychologists whose work in the lab is criticized as of little use in applied settings, as it shows how the move from lab to field may be successfully undertaken.

Angelo DeNisi is Professor of Human Resource Management at Rutgers University. His primary research focus has been in the area of cognitive models of performance appraisal. He is an active member of the Society for Industrial and Organizational Psychology, and the Academy of Management, and he is the editor of the *Academy of Management Journal*. He has written numerous articles for the major journals in the field of industrial and organizational psychology.

People and organizations
Series editor: Sheldon Zedeck
Department of Psychology, University of California, Berkeley

The study of organizations has increased significantly in recent years. In recognition of the growing importance of behavioral science research to our understanding of organizations, *People and Organizations* is a new series devoted to advanced research in industrial and organizational psychology, and organizational behavior.

The books in the series are derived from empirical programmatic research on topics related to organizations and the ways in which people interact, respond to, and cope with the organization. Topics of special interest include: organizational culture, work and family, high technology, organizational commitment, careers, and studies of organizations in international markets. Books in the series are theoretically grounded and include specific guidelines for future research.

Already available:

Leadership and Information Processing
Linking Perceptions and Performance
Robert G. Lord and Karen J. Maher

Role Motivation Theories
John B. Miner

Volunteers
The Organizational Behaviour of Unpaid Workers
Jone L. Pearce

A cognitive approach to performance appraisal

A program of research

Angelo S. DeNisi

London and New York

First published 1996
by Routledge
11 New Fetter Lane, London EC4P 4EE

Simultaneously published in the USA and Canada
by Routledge
29 West 35th Street, New York, NY 10001

© 1996 Angelo S. DeNisi

Typeset in Garamond by
Pure Tech India Limited, Pondicherry
Printed and bound in Great Britain by
Redwood Books, Trowbridge, Wiltshire

British Library Cataloguing in Publication Data
A catalogue record for this book is available from the British Library

Library of Congress Cataloging in Publication Data
DeNisi, Angelo S.
    A cognitive approach to performance appraisal: a program of
research / Angelo S. DeNisi.
      p. cm. – (People and organizations)
    Includes bibliographical references (p.   ) and index.
    1. Employees–Rating of.   2. Psychology, Industrial.   3. Cognitive
psychology.   I. Title.   II. Series: People and organizations
(London, England)
HF5549.5.R3D46   1996
658.3' 125–dc20   96–353

ISBN 0–415–11251–6

Dedicated to Adrienne, Jessica, Rebecca, and "Luce"
— the women in my life

Contents

Illustrations

FIGURES

TABLES

Preface

This book had the most modest beginnings I can imagine. It all began with my need to write a Ph.D. dissertation that I could claim as being all my own, rather than another in a series of dissertations on the Position Analysis Questionnaire written under Ernest McCormick. My respect and admiration for Dr. McCormick (I never could call him "Mac") was never in question, and performance appraisal simply seemed like a reasonable alternative to job analysis for a topic. Yet, the decision to write a dissertation on performance appraisal and, specifically, to try to focus on how raters acquired information needed for appraisal decisions, started me down a path I am still traveling. Along the way, there were models, reviews, and a number of empirical studies, and a program of research which looks more systematic now than it ever seemed to be when I was in the middle of it. In fact, only when I was asked to write a volume for his series did I really step back and realize that the pieces did actually come together to form a picture.

In this book, I have tried to convey to the reader more than just a model, hypotheses, and a list of studies and results. There was a logic as we went from one study to another, and there were many disappointments, frustrations, and failures along the way as well. I feel that, too often, scholars present their research in a way that makes it seem like everything worked out exactly as planned at every step along the way. Maybe that is true for others, but it was not true for me, and I wanted to communicate some of the feelings as well as the ideas themselves that went into this program of research.

I have also tried to provide a realistic picture of what I and my colleagues accomplished. As I note several times in the book, there are other cognitive models of the appraisal process, and ours is not necessarily better than the others. Furthermore, there have been a number of other scholars working in this area, and many of them have published more and may have more to say than I do. So why did *I* write this book? I am associated with a model that did make a contribution to cognitive research in performance appraisal and, I have used this model and the results of earlier studies based on the model to guide a systematic approach to the study of appraisals. It is the systematic nature of the program of research and the perseverance over time that make these studies and this approach unique – it is not the genius of the ideas.

I have also tried to give proper credit to my colleagues throughout the years. I believe that I had (and have) a view of cognitive appraisal research that has been the driving force behind this program of study, but I also know that little of this would have actually been accomplished without the help of a great many people. I mention them throughout the book where they played a role, but Bruce Meglino, Tom Cafferty, Kevin Williams, Allyn Blencoe, Tim Summers, Tina Robbins, Larry Peters, and Arup Varma deserve as much credit as I can possibly give them for the studies and models I describe in this book.

I must also thank and credit my colleagues from other schools who have contributed ideas, critical feedback, and encouragement. Jack Feldman, Kevin Murphy, and Wally Borman spring immediately to mind because my association with them goes back quite a few years, and they have always been there with help and ideas. But there are many others, including Jan Cleveland, John Bernardin, Bob Lord, Steve Kozlowski, Greg Dobbins, Bob Cardy, and, of course, Dan Ilgen. Each one of these individuals provided encouragement, ideas, and critiques over the years, whether in classes, at professional meetings, or over a cocktail.

Finally I need to thank those individuals who have contributed in other ways to this book. First, on that list, is my wife, Adrienne Colella who has had to put up with lost weekends and even higher stress levels as I worked on this project. Without her understanding, support, and love, this book would never have been written. But I also need to thank my colleagues at Rutgers who took up the slack when I was busy working on the book, as well as those administrators, namely my department head, Jim Chelius, and Dean John Burton, who provided support and allowed me the flexibility I needed to get this done. Finally, of course, I need to thank Sheldon Zedeck, the Series Editor, for believing in me enough to invite me to write this book.

I wrote this book for several reasons. One was simply to tell a story about a research program and how such a program *really* progresses over the years. I also wrote this to make it clear that the cognitive approach to performance *could* and *did* make a contribution to both science and practice, and that it continues to make such a contribution. Contrary to many critics over the years, I believe this approach has had something to say and has had a profound impact on how we think about performance appraisal. Furthermore, I wanted to make it clear that this contribution is not over, and that there are a number of interesting directions for this research to take in the future.

Finally, I wanted to talk about the failures and frustrations that are part of any research program and of any researcher's career. I think that, overall,

I have been quite lucky in my career and have enjoyed some success, yet there have also been many failures and rejections. The grand plan for my dissertation, which started this program of research, never produced a published paper, and there were many mistakes along the way. Therefore, my final purpose was to tell others who have had papers rejected and who have come up against frustrations in their research that there is hope and that, at least sometimes, perseverance does pay off.

Chapter 1

Why a cognitive approach?

There are few decisions made in modern organizations that do not, somehow depend upon performance appraisals. Although it may be possible in a limited number of jobs to obtain objective performance information, more typically this is not the case. Instead, organizations are forced to rely upon some type of subjective evaluation of a person's performance. Systems that rely upon goals (e.g., MBO) still retain some aspect of subjectivity and judgment, even if it is just about what constitutes a meaningful goal. Given the subjective nature of these appraisals, it is not surprising that there have been volumes written about the errors, bias, inaccuracy, and inherent unfairness of most performance appraisals. What is perhaps more surprising, however, is that appraisals continue to be used, and used widely in most organizations.

For example, many, if not most compensation systems include some type of merit pay component where a portion of a person's pay is determined by their performance on the job. In fact, more recent views of managerial compensation (e.g., Gerhart & Milkovich, 1993; Gomez-Mejia & Balkin, 1992; Gomez-Mejia & Welbourne, 1988), adopting an Agency Theory perspective (cf., Eisenhardt, 1989), have recommended that *more* of the executive's compensation should be "put at risk" and made dependent upon performance. Although in some of these cases, compensation is tied to accounting measures (e.g., Return of Equity) or financial performance (e.g., stock price), these trends suggest that performance will be even more important for determining compensation in the future. Furthermore, since accounting and financial indices are less relevant for assessing the performance of middle- to lower-levels managers, and since few other objective measures are generally available to gauge their performance, merit-pay decisions, based upon a performance appraisal will only become more important over time. It is worth noting, however, that there is a different perspective which suggests that, in the future, compensation decisions will be based more on skill or knowledge acquisition than upon performance (see discussions by Dewey, 1994; Gupta, Ledford, Jenkins & Doty, 1992; Tosi & Tosi, 1986).

Needs analysis, as the basis for the design and implementation of training programs, is also usually based upon these subjective evaluations of performance. That is, organizations typically include a performance appraisal as a critical part of establishing where training is needed and what kinds of training are needed (cf., Wexley & Latham, 1981). Furthermore, after the training has been implemented, program evaluation is typically concerned with changes in performance, among other potential outcomes and, in most cases, this performance and any changes are measured by a performance appraisal.

Performance appraisals are used as the basis for taking disciplinary action, in many cases, where the perception of performance that falls short of a standard or expectation typically triggers the action (cf., Arvey & Jones, 1985) and, in extreme cases, this action can include the decision to terminate an individual. Of course, performance appraisals are a major part of performance management programs, including the various coaching and developmental activities that take place as part of the performance management process. Finally, in cases where organizations need to validate selection techniques such as tests, or to answer questions about the adverse impact of such techniques, the criterion measure involved is typically some measure of performance which, in most cases, is a performance appraisal.

Furthermore, since performance appraisals are usually the only measure of performance available, they are also used as the criterion measures for a wide range of organizational topics. Thus, for example, when we discuss things such as organizational commitment or job satisfaction, we usually try to establish relationships between these variables and performance – often measured using performance appraisal. Also, training efforts, as well as other types of interventions, are also usually aimed at improving performance and/or productivity (although see Goldstein, 1993, for a discussion of the importance of determining the proper criterion measure for evaluating training efforts), and so performance appraisals play a role in evaluating these interventions as well.

The fact that appraisals are so important, and yet so prone to problems, goes far to explain why performance appraisal has been the focus of so much research activity for so long a period of time. It is intolerable to many managers, used to making rational decisions and having control over situations, to have to depend so much upon a measurement technique that inspires little trust. Therefore, for almost seventy years, scholars have been studying performance appraisals to understand what makes them so poor as indicators of "true" performance. As we shall see, even the definition of what is meant by "true" performance is open for debate, and the problems of how we would know if we *did* measure true performance accurately are also considerable. Nonetheless, through it all has been the hope that, if we could understand what causes all the problems with performance appraisals, we could figure out what to do to make them work better.

This book is about a program of research which has adopted a cognitive, process-oriented focus on performance appraisal. But this approach is only one of the latest approaches to studying the problem. In order to understand how we came to adopt such an approach, it is necessary to understand the state of appraisal research up until the 1980s. The now classic paper by Landy and Farr (1980) marked the beginning of the "cognitive era" in performance appraisal research, and the program of research discussed here is one example of the kind of research that adopts a cognitive approach. But how did we come to this approach? Why did process-oriented research on appraisals become so popular? What kinds of research did people do before (and still do now), that was not process oriented, or concerned with cognition? In order to provide this background, I will begin with a brief history of the research on performance appraisal. Other such reviews can be found in Landy and Farr (1980) and Feldman (1994), as well as in the appraisal texts by Cardy and Dobbins (1994) and Murphy and Cleveland (1991), while slightly less exhaustive reviews are also presented with the cognitive appraisal model proposed by DeNisi, Cafferty, and Meglino (1984) and the model proposed by Feldman (1981).

This historical view will then provide the introduction to some of the better-known cognitive appraisal models that have been proposed. The second chapter will present our cognitive model (the DeNisi, Cafferty, & Meglino, 1984 model), as well as a number of the research propositions that were generated by that model. These propositions were the beginning of the research program described here, and Chapter 3 (especially) describes a series of studies that were designed to test some of these propositions. But over time, the research program was dictated by the results of some of the studies we conducted. Thus, in Chapter 4 I begin discussing studies dealing with reprocessing objectives and interventions designed to help raters organize performance information. These two themes were not part of the original set of research propositions, but the results of the studies designed to relate acquisition strategies to ratings suggested that these were important directions for our research to follow. Chapter 5 returns to some of the original research propositions, but also describes the studies that began with simple ideas about affect and bias (which were part of the original propositions), but which eventually moved the program further in those directions than had been anticipated. Chapter 7 traces the progression of the research program from the lab, where all the prior studies had been conducted, to the field, and demonstrates that this line of research *did* have external validity. Finally, the last two chapters provide discussions of what I think we have learned from this research, and some ideas about where we should go from here. I begin, then, with a brief history of research on performance appraisal to set the stage for everything else to come.

RESEARCH ON PERFORMANCE APPRAISAL: AN HISTORICAL PERSPECTIVE

Interest in the evaluation of performance probably goes back well over a thousand years (see Murphy & Cleveland, 1991), but published research on appraisals goes back at least to 1920 with Thorndike's (1920) paper on rating errors. This paper not only represents one of the earliest attempts to deal with appraisal problems, it also represents the beginning of a very specific orientation to these problems that has lasted almost until today. Why should we be concerned about an "error" that causes ratings on different scales to be correlated with each other? At the time these studies were conducted, it was generally assumed that, if we could reduce rating errors we would also increase rating accuracy. In fact, throughout much of the history of appraisal research, rating errors were seen as a proxy of rating (in)accuracy. Later in the book, this issue will be revisited, as there is no longer any real agreement that such correlations constitute an error at all. In fact, as we shall see later, there is disagreement over whether the relationship between these "errors" and accuracy is actually positive or negative, as well as disagreement over how accuracy should be operationalized, and even over whether accuracy should be the focus of our attention at all. But all of this was to come much later, in the 1920s there was general interest in reducing rating errors as a means of increasing rating accuracy.

It is also clear, in retrospect, that Thorndike's paper coincided with the widespread introduction of graphic rating scales, and that some of the "halo" being discussed was seen as resulting from the use of these scales (also see Rudd, 1921, for criticisms of graphic rating scales). Thus we were well down several paths that would influence (and perhaps hinder) appraisal research for many years to come: there was a focus upon rating errors; there was an assumption that reducing errors would result in an increase in rating accuracy; and there was the assumption that rating errors were due, at least in part, to the nature of the rating scale being used.

Of course, even early on in the process, there were voices that were fighting against this tide. Bingham (1939) argued that not all of what we called "halo error" should be considered "error," as some of the observed covariance could be attributed to "true" covariance. Similar arguments were voiced again much later, by Cooper (1981b), when they received more attention, but Bingham's (1939) protestations seemed to have little impact. Even more noteworthy, in 1952, Robert Wherry Sr. (Wherry, 1952) proposed a model of the appraisal process that was not only way beyond the simplistic views of appraisals and errors that were prevalent at the time, but also anticipated many of the "innovations" that came with the cognitive approach to performance appraisal of which our research program is part. We will discuss this model in more detail later, but, in the 1950s, this model was available only as an unpublished technical report, and it had little influence on the practice or research in performance appraisal. In fact, the paper was not even generally available until thirty years later, when a slightly abridged version was published (Wherry & Bartlett, 1982), and so this forward thinking model actually had little impact on the early cognitive models, even though those models drew much of their support from the same sources as were tapped by Wherry (1952).

For the most part, then, the focus was on reducing rating errors, and the preferred solution appeared to lie with the nature of the rating scale. Furthermore, this focus and preference seemed to stay with us for quite a while. As a result, research concentrated on the best ways to construct rating scales in order to reduce rating errors, emphasizing such things as the number of scale alternatives and the degree to which traits are defined (e.g., Barrett, Taylor, Parker, & Martens, 1958; Bayeroff, Haggerty, & Rundquist, 1954; Blumberg, De Soto, & Keuthe, 1966; Peters & McCormick, 1966; Taylor & Hastman, 1956). In one interesting study, Johnson and Vidulich (1956) suggested that we could minimize halo by having raters evaluate every ratee on one dimension, and then move to the next dimension and evaluate every ratee on that one as well. (The interested reader should compare this to the notion of "task-blocked" information, which will be discussed in the next chapter.) These authors suggested that this could reduce halo error, although a subsequent re-analysis of the data (Johnson, 1963) concluded that the differences in halo attributable to the two rating methods were non-significant.

There was some concern that it was mistaken to rely upon these subjective evaluations, regardless of the particular scale used. Instead, it was argued, evaluations should be based upon more objective measures of productivity and output such as scrap rates and time required to complete a task (e.g., Rothe, 1946a, 1946b, 1949, 1951, 1978). But such measures are not available for many jobs, and scholars who have correlated objective measures with more subjective evaluations have found the correlations to be modest to low (e.g., Gaylord, Russell, Johnson, & Severin, 1951; Severin, 1952). Of course, these findings may simply confirm the belief that subjective models do not really capture the essence of performance on the job, but there is an alternative explanation as well. Wexley and Klimoski (1984) have argued that there is no "true" performance. Instead, all we have are different indicators of true performance, and measures such as output and performance ratings simply tap different aspects of performance and reflect different models of performance, termed outcome and person models. If we want to focus on only outcomes and not be concerned with understanding how we got the outcomes we did, or how to improve performance, then an outcome model would make sense. But, if we want to also understand how we got the level of performance we did so that we can work to improve performance, then we must focus on the person model, and performance appraisals, subjective though they may be, become important.

But these were digressions. The main thrust of the research was still on developing better rating instruments so that we could reduce rating errors. It is true that several authors reported disturbing findings, such as the failure to find any one rating format superior to another (e.g., Taylor & Hastman, 1956), or the fact that rating format seemed to have less effect on halo than did rater training (Brown, 1968), but these only seemed to spur researchers even further to develop even better rating instruments.

In fact, the range of alternative proposals was fairly amazing (see Landy & Farr, 1980, for a complete review of these developments). For example, John Flanagan proposed an appraisal method (still very much in use today) which focused attention on the identification of incidents of especially good or especially poor performance, called critical incidents, rather than on the entire set of behaviors that a ratee might exhibit on the job (Flanagan, 1949, 1954; Flanagan & Burns, 1955). At about the same time, Sisson (1948) proposed that we adopt a methodology commonly used in personality measurement to performance appraisal. He demonstrated techniques for determining two (or more) descriptive items which were equally desirable or undesirable, but only one of which has been determined (empirically) to discriminate between good and poor performers on the job. This Forced Choice technique would then present raters with the pair of items and ask raters to choose the one which best described the ratee. Only if the rater selected the "discriminating" item did the ratee receive any credit for the rating. This was supposed to prevent raters from providing overly lenient ratings, but had the effect of communicating to the rater that he or she could not be trusted. Forced Distribution methods (which Schmidt & Johnson, 1973, argue are particularly effective with large numbers of ratees) force a rater to limit the number of ratees assigned to each rating category. Although any distribution could be "forced" in this way, it is most commonly used to ensure that ratings are normally distributed, eliminating leniency, central tendency, and any other distributional "error" (cf., Berkshire & Highland, 1953).

A major innovation came in the 1960s with *Behaviorally Anchored Rating Scales* (BARS; Smith & Kendall, 1963). Here, the raters were completely involved in the development of the scales and the anchors to be used, and those anchors were expressed in terms of specific behaviors rather than adjectives such as "poor" or "outstanding." These scales received a great deal of attention in the literature, as researchers proposed alternative ways to develop and implement these scales (e.g., Arvey & Hoyle, 1974; Bernardin, LaShells, Smith, & Alvares, 1976), and also presented a number of comparisons of these scales with other scale formats (e.g., Bernardin, Alvares, & Cranny, 1976; Campbell, Dunnette, Arvey, & Hellervik, 1973; Dickinson & Zellinger, 1980). There was also a variant proposed, called Behavioral Observation Scales (BOS; e.g., Kane & Bernardin, 1982; Latham, Fay, & Saari, 1979; Latham & Wexley, 1977) which required raters to observe and note behaviors rather than evaluate them. It will be interesting to think back to this proposal later, when in Chapter 6 I discuss the different definitions of rating accuracy, which include something called behavioral accuracy.

Other proposals over the years included Mixed Standard Rating Scales (Blanz & Ghiselli, 1972) which required raters to indicate whether a ratee performed below, above, or at the level of performance described by a series of statements, and which scatters the items relevant for a given dimension throughout the questionnaire, and a rather different approach called Performance Distribution Assessment (PDA; Kane, 1982a, 1982b) which is concerned that raters consider the variance in performance over time as well as the level of performance most typically displayed. All of these efforts led to a long line of studies dedicated to determining which format was superior. None of the studies actually compared all the formats, but the numerous comparative studies failed to reveal one clearly superior type of scale (see Landy & Farr, 1980, for a review). It is important to note here that the basis for these comparisons was usually the same – the level of psychometric errors present in the data, and perhaps some consideration of interrater reliability. Clearly, we were still willing to assume that the absence of rating errors indicated more accurate ratings. Thus, by the time Landy and Farr wrote their review paper, there had been a great deal of research on rating scale content and format, and the sum of this research was to note that no one scale was superior to others in terms of reducing errors or increasing interrater reliability.

Before discussing how appraisal research changed following the publication of Landy and Farr's paper, it is important to take note of another trend in the literature that was developing at the same time as the literature on rating scales. For much of the same time, research was also being conducted on the role of rater training. For the most part, rater training programs were designed to familiarize raters with the rating instruments and the jobs in question (e.g., Brown, 1968), but by the 1970s, this emphasis had shifted towards training programs designed to reduce the incidence of rating errors such as halo and contrast effects (e.g., Latham, Wexley, & Pursell, 1975; Wexley, Sanders, & Yukl, 1973). Following much the same logic as was driving scale format research, the design of training research was based on the premise that reducing psychometric errors was actually a proxy for improving accuracy, so that a program which successfully reduced the incidence of errors was assumed to also increase accuracy. But, as the emphasis in the field moved to one where there was more concern for rater decision making, and as scholars became more suspicious of the relationship between errors and rating accuracy, the focus of training research changed as well. In the "cognitive" era, training designed to make raters better raters by providing clear standards and instruction on their use (Frame of Reference Training; e.g., Bernardin & Buckley, 1981; Pulakos, 1984, 1986) became much more prevalent and we saw the appearance of programs designed to sensitize raters to errors in processing as well (e.g., Steiner, Dobbins, & Trahan, 1991), while the criteria for assessing the effectiveness of these programs moved away from rating errors and towards rating accuracy.

THE COGNITIVE SHIFT IN APPRAISAL RESEARCH

It is clearly the case that Landy and Farr's review paper shifted the focus of researchers away from rating scale format and error training, and towards a consideration of the decision making process that underlies all appraisal decisions. These authors concluded that past efforts had provided little progress, but this was because those efforts ignored the role of the rater in the process. Instead, they argued, we should focus on how raters obtain and use performance information to make the decisions they do, and that these processes, and not the nature of the training or the rating scale used, would be the most important determinant of appraisal accuracy. This amounted to a paradigm shift in the appraisal area, and changed appraisal research forever. Yet this shift was actually anticipated by several other models of appraisals, and there was even an earlier model that proposed appraisal research move off in a very different direction – and one that has more recently gained popularity.

Wherry's model of the appraisal process

In 1952 Robert Wherry proposed a model of the appraisal process that used a "true-score" approach to explaining the source of rating errors and inaccuracy. He relied heavily upon the already old concept of "schema" (Bartlett, 1932) to propose a series of research propositions dealing with conditions more likely to lead to accurate ratings. Since schema and related concepts are so critical to a cognitive perspective on appraisal, it might be worth clarifying them here.

Most views of social cognition begin by suggesting that we all make assumptions and judgments about other people. This allows us to interact with them because it allows us to anticipate their actions. But, since we begin by having little information about people we meet or encounter, and since we don t know enough about them to really predict their behavior, we must first determine what "type" of person an individual can be considered. Thus we consider salient characteristics of the person, and use these to match them with some pre-existing category we have for people. Once we have determined how to categorize the person, we can then use assumptions or beliefs we have associated with that category to predict behavior. Such a system is called a schema, and these systems subsequently guide and influence everything we acquire, store, and process about that person, as

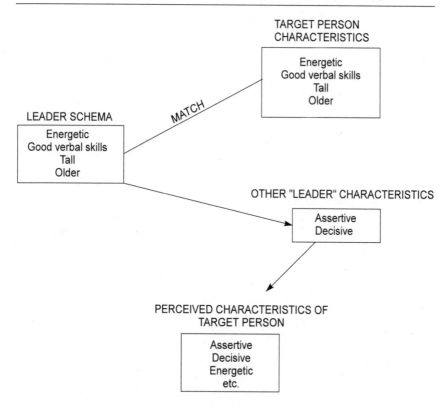

Figure 1.1 An illustration of how we use schemata in the evaluation of target persons. The characteristics of the target person represent a good match with our schema of a good leader. We therefore categorize the target person as a "leader." Since that schema also includes other characteristics, we assume that the target person possesses those as well, even though we have no real evidence for them.

well as the way we evaluate the person. In an appraisal context, once a ratee is categorized in some way, he or she will be evaluated and judged, based on our schema for that category. These processes are also illustrated in Figure 1.1, where we compare the characteristics for a target person to a number of possible schemata until we get a "match" with the leader schema. In other words, our perceptions of the target person are most consistent with the salient characteristics of what we consider a good leader. Notice, however, that leaders are also seen as having other characteristics, and once we categorize the target person as a "leader" we assume that he or she also has these other characteristics in addition to ones we have observed.

Basically, Wherry suggested that rating accuracy depended upon the performance of the ratee, the observation of the rater, and the recall of the observation by the rater. He also recognized that raters might always provide inaccurate ratings intentionally (the role of rater motivation has also become much more important in more recent views of the appraisal process), but his model was only concerned with unintentional errors. Therefore, his model described how accurate a rater *could* be, not how accurate that rater actually was when providing evaluations. His model is expressed in terms of an equation of a rating response, and he then developed a series of theorems and corollaries which followed from this basic equation. Wherry presented the equation in mathematical terms, but little is gained by reproducing the equation here. As noted above, he saw the ratee's behavior as the first determinant of a rating, but even here there was true performance (which was theorized to be due primarily to ability), as well as environmental factors (such as tools and machines), and a certain amount of error. Wherry also recognized that it was the rater's *perception* of that behavior that was more critical to the eventual rating, and so he included terms that represented the rater's opportunity to observe the ratee, bias specifically aimed at the given ratee, as well as a general bias on the part of the rater and another random error term.

Performance information would also have to be recalled, but again there would be bias in the recall. This bias could either be specific to the ratee (and this was where rater schema about the ratee came into play) or be more general to the rater, and there was also a random error term. Wherry further suggested that the bias in perception would be the same as the bias in recall, and that the difference between more and less accurate ratings was determined by the relative weights given to the various terms in his model, so that:

> The Rating of Person A = Behavior of Person A + Rater's Perception of the Behavior of Person A + Rater's Recall of the Perceived Performance of Person A + Random Error

Furthermore:

> Behavior = True Behavior (due to ability) + Environmental Factors + Random Error
> Perception = Behavior + Bias Specific to Person A + General Rater Bias + Random Error
> Recall = Perception + Schema About Person A + General Rater Bias in Recall + Random Error

Thus Wherry proposed that rating errors (or inaccuracy) resulted primarily because we either placed a ratee into the wrong category and so used the wrong schema to predict and rate his or her behavior, or because we relied too heavily upon the schema even though there was other information available that contradicted it. It is amazing how well Wherry's work foreshadowed later work in cognitive processes. For example, Wherry noted that raters would have an easier time evaluating behaviors that occur more frequently, as opposed to those which occur rarely, since the raters would have more opportunity to observe those behaviors and so would rely more upon "true" behavior than upon any bias. This same idea was echoed twenty-five years later by Kane and Lawler (1970) suggesting the use of Behavioral Discrimination Scales to deal with the potentially confounding effects of different behaviors occurring with different frequency.

Wherry also suggested that raters *not* be trained to avoid errors, but instead they should be trained to know what to look for when observing performance and how to observe that performance more objectively, since he believed that this would naturally lead to increased accuracy. Thirty years later, Pulakos published several papers comparing rater error training and Frame of Reference Training, which emphasized providing raters with information about what to observe and how to evaluate what they observed. Her work (Pulakos, 1984, 1986) clearly supported the superiority of Frame of Reference Training. Wherry also suggested that raters should be provided with rating instruments prior to the observation of performance, so that they could use the categories present in the rating scale as a way of organizing the information they encountered (see DeNisi, Robbins, & Summers, 1995; and DeNisi & Summers, 1986, for more recent adaptations of this idea); that raters may be reluctant to give low, but accurate ratings when they are required to justify those ratings to ratees (see Fisher, 1979; and Sharon & Bartlett, 1969, for later discussions of this problem, and see Murphy & Cleveland, 1991, for a discussion of rater motives and ratings); and that rater diary keeping would aid recall and lead to increased rating accuracy (see subsequent studies by Bernardin & Walter, 1979; and DeNisi, Robbins, & Cafferty, 1989).

Thus, thirty years before Landy and Farr's paper appeared, Wherry proposed a model that included many of the processes and variables that became part of the cognitive models that will be discussed later in the chapter. Of course, the Landy and Farr paper was based on a comprehensive review of the literature, which made a stronger case for *why* we needed to change the focus of our research. The former paper was pure conceptual development, and was not even published until after Wherry's death (Wherry & Bartlett, 1982). Furthermore, although most of the propositions presented by Wherry are based on cognitive processes, not all of them are, and, in truth, Wherry's "model" is more a series of propositions and theorems than a conceptual framework. It was Wherry's ability to see and present the various implications of his mathematical equation that led to the various propositions he generated. Nonetheless, although Landy and Farr (1980) changed how we studied appraisals, it was Wherry (1952) who first developed a cognitive model, and presented ideas and directions for future research that are still useful today.

Other early "cognitive" approaches

While Landy and Farr were developing their model, other researchers were beginning to move in the same direction. DeNisi (1977) proposed and provided a rudimentary test of rater cognitive processes, emphasizing the importance of rater observation and later recall of relevant performance information. Borman (1978) also focused on rater cognitive processes in proposing a model dealing with how accurate ratings could be under optimal conditions. He provided a test of this model, but found only limited support for its usefulness, leading Borman to suggest that other (cognitive) processes were probably more important. In both these cases, the "models" consisted of little more than flow charts suggesting that raters systematically acquire, store, and then recall performance information, and that they later combine the bits of information they recall to form a judgment that becomes a rating. Thus these authors proposed frameworks for studying appraisals rather than fully developed models of any cognitive processes.

Although his focus was a bit narrower, Cooper's (1981b) approach to the study of halo error was developed independent of the Landy and Farr model, and also emphasized cognitive processes as the source of halo error. Cooper specifically cited issues of observation and the transfer from short-term to long-term memory as important sources of halo in ratings. His view of halo error, and subsequent empirical tests (Cooper, 1981a) emphasized the importance of decision making and memory, and noted that, at every step in the cognitive process, error can be introduced into an appraisal. This paper also marked the beginning of the debate about the nature of rating "errors," especially halo. Cooper's work made it clear that not all the observed halo could be attributed to errors as we had usually considered them, and led other researchers to begin looking more closely at valid versus invalid halo.

Meanwhile, on the rater training front, Bernardin and his colleagues had begun accumulating data to show that rater training programs, designed to reduce rating errors, actually *reduced* rating accuracy (Bernardin, 1978, 1979; Bernardin & Buckley, 1981; Bernardin & Pence, 1980). These ideas would eventually lead to proposals for Frame of Reference Training, and would also help fuel the still-to-develop debate over the relationship between rating accuracy and rating error. But at the time their major contribution was to suggest that reducing rating errors might actually *reduce* rating accuracy in settings where raters were being trained to reduce errors. In these cases, the training was simply substituting one response set (i.e., ratings should *not* be correlated) for another (i.e., ratings are correlated), but there was no reason to believe this new response set was any more accurate and, by leading raters to avoid correlated rating, the training actually reduced accuracy since raters would not provide correlated ratings even if they truly believed a ratee was good (or bad) on a number of dimensions.

DeCotiis and Petit's model

DeCotiis and Petit (1978) proposed a process-oriented model of performance appraisal which took a somewhat different tack. Their model proposed three major determinants of rating accuracy: (1) rater ability; (2) rater motivation; and (3) the availability of judgmental norms. Their proposals concerning rater ability focused primarily upon rater training, the presence of standards, and the opportunity to observe relevant performance, and were probably not as sophisticated as some of the subsequent models in this area, but many other scholars tended to focus exclusively on ability and ignore the other two aspects of the process. Although the models proposed by DeNisi, Cafferty, and Meglino (1984), Feldman (1981), and Ilgen and Feldman (1983), all consider rater motivation, this is not a major part of their discussions of the appraisal process, nor does it play a big role in Landy and Farr's model (although they do discuss the purpose of the appraisal as being important). Their proposals concerning judgmental norms were concerned primarily with the congruence between rating scale content and job content, as well as the availability of clear rating standards. The notions about congruence were developed further some years later by Ostroff and Ilgen (1986), and were developed still further by Feldman (1986) who discussed jobs in terms of their analyzability and the ambiguity of outcomes, and then related the jobs to different types of appraisal processes that were consistent with different types of appraisal instruments. Their model is presented in Figure 1.2.

It was their proposals about rater motivation, however, that probably represented DeCotiis and Petit's (1978) greatest contribution. They proposed that the adequacy of appraisal instrument, and the presence of clear

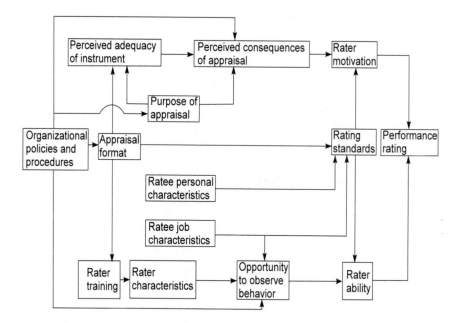

Figure 1.2 The DeCotiis and Petit (1978) appraisal model

standards could influence rater motivation to provide accurate appraisals. But they primarily viewed rater motivation in terms of the perceived consequences of the ratings. Thus, the purpose of the appraisal was seen as critical (raters would be *most* likely to provide accurate ratings when the ratings were used for experimental purposes or for feedback only), as was the need to provide face-to-face feedback to the ratees (this would reduce rater motivation to be accurate). But their work was somewhat overshadowed by the Landy and Farr paper appearing two years later, and their contribution had been overlooked for some time. More recently, though, Murphy and Cleveland (1991) proposed a view of the appraisal process where rater motivation plays a critical role. In fact, Murphy and Cleveland are careful to distinguish between performance judgments and performance ratings. The latter, they note, are the final product of the appraisal process, but are a function of both rater ability and rater motivation. Furthermore, Robbins and DeNisi (1994) have attempted to integrate some of the ideas concerning rater–ratee interactions, and the notion of rater affective reactions to ratees, into some of the more typical cognitive models of the appraisal process. Thus, although the DeCotiis and Petit (1978) model did not generate a great deal of research directly, it has nonetheless contributed to what we later discuss as the "hot" approach to cognitive processing performance appraisal, by emphasizing the role of rater motivation. Aspects of this approach have been integrated into our later work, and I believe rater motivation will become even more important for appraisal research in the future.

Landy and Farr's model

Despite the merits of these various models and proposals, it took Landy and Farr's (1980) paper to really change the way people did appraisal research. The "model" they proposed did not go far beyond the frameworks proposed by Borman (1978) or by DeCotiis and Petit (1978), but the impact of their review and model has been substantial. The model itself, presented in Figure 1.3, is based on their comprehensive review of some sixty years of literature, and specifies a number of sub-systems of the rating process. This model is the result of that literature review, which led Landy and Farr to conclude that, although it was clear that performance appraisals were far from perfect, it was *not* clear if any of the proposals from those years had noticeably improved appraisals. Instead, they called for a shift in the focus of appraisal research. They suggested that the rater was the ultimate "instrument" in the appraisal process, and that future research should focus on the rater. Specifically, they suggested that raters engaged in cognitive processes closely related to the decision making process and that, if we could come to fully understand how raters made appraisal decisions, we would be more likely to develop means to improve those decisions.

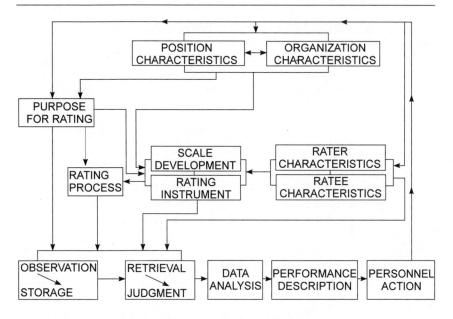

Figure 1.3 Landy and Farr's (1980) proposed process model of appraisals

As can be seen, their model proposes that there are characteristics of both the rater and the ratee that are brought to the appraisals setting. On the rater's side, these include race, sex, age, and experience, while the ratee brings in similar characteristics, as well as other, non-performance-related factors which might influence the way in which a rater reacts to him or her. Landy and Farr also discuss the importance of organizational and contextual factors such as the policies of the organization and the culture of the organization, and they recognize that the purpose of the appraisal is also important. The rating instrument is also seen as playing a role, but part of this role is a function of the process through which the rating instrument is developed. For example, a rating instrument developed with the input of the raters would be likely to produce different ratings (and different rating problems) than would an instrument developed by upper management or consultants, and then imposed upon the raters. Finally, the Landy and Farr model considers the actual rater cognitive processes that played a role in the frameworks proposed earlier by DeCotiis and Petit (1978), Borman (1978), and even DeNisi (1977).

Landy and Farr's paper marked the real beginning of the cognitive approach to performance appraisal. It also focused research on rating accuracy rather than rating errors, and this too had a major impact on appraisal research for the next twenty-five years. But mostly, the Landy and Farr paper spurred scholars to think about rater cognitive processes as determinants of the ratings they provided. As a result, a number of cognitive models of the appraisal process were developed (some of which are discussed below), and a number of tests of components of the Landy and Farr model, as well as these other models, were also generated. Of course, one of the models that followed is the one that the research program discussed here is based upon, and which will be discussed in much more detail.

COGNITIVE MODELS OF PERFORMANCE APPRAISAL

The Landy and Farr paper brought a focus to various efforts to develop cognitive models of the appraisal process. These models did not focus on the properties of ratings, *per se*, nor on the properties of rating instruments. Instead, they focused upon the rater, as decision maker, as the key to understanding what really happened in performance appraisals. Furthermore, these models focused on the entire decision making process, rather than just the final assignment of ratings. The underlying assumption, whether explicit or implicit in all of these models was that ratings could be made more accurate if we could understand, and eventually influence, rater cognitive processes. In order to do so, however, we needed models which described which cognitive processes were important, what factors influenced those processes, and how these processes were related to rating accuracy.

Three models have emerged that have tended to guide the research in this area, including ours, but there have been other scholars who have either stopped short of proposing formal models, or developed models that came later and moved beyond cognitive processes. For the sake of completeness, all of these will be discussed, although the DeNisi, Cafferty, and Meglino model (1984) will be the focus of the next chapter, and further refinements of that model will be discussed at several later points in the book. For now, we turn to the other two major cognitive models of the appraisal process.

The Feldman model

Landy and Farr (1980) ended their paper with a fairly simple cognitive model of the appraisal process, but, as noted above, it was not that model they proposed that was so influential, it was their proposed new emphasis on cognitive processing that was critical. It remained, then, for someone to develop a more elaborate cognitive model, and to build the rationale for such a model, not based on earlier non-cognitive research, but by integrating appraisal research with the more general research on social cognition. Feldman proposed such a model in a highly influential paper published in 1981 (Feldman, 1981). He built upon a growing body of literature in social cognition to develop a model that was as much a person perception model as a performance appraisal model, and this model set the tone for the others to follow. It should be noted, however, that although this clearly was a "model," there was no series of boxes and arrows proposed in the paper, and so I shall simply describe the major aspects of the model as presented.

Feldman (1981) characterized the appraisal environment as uncertain, and "noisy," and imposing many non-appraisal-related demands upon the rater. Feldman's basic approach posited that raters must: (1) recognize and attend to relevant information; (2) organize the information in memory for later access; (3) recall this information in a way that it is useful when ratings are required; and (4) integrate this information into a summary judgment. Thus Feldman focused squarely on rater cognitive processes, and upon information that was incomplete or not immediately available (as opposed to simpler attributional models which focused on complete and available information).

An important aspect of Feldman's model is his consideration of automatic and controlled processing of information (Schneider & Shiffrin, 1977; Shiffrin & Schneider, 1977). In this view, when raters encounter stimuli with which they are familiar, or have had experience with, that information can be processed "automatically" without conscious awareness on the part of the rater, and without interference with other ongoing mental activities (e.g., Posner & Snyder, 1975). Thus, a rater would engage in automatic processing whenever he or she encountered information that was clearly relevant to performance on the job; that was easy to evaluate as good or poor; or that was consistent with the rater's prior expectations about the ratee. According to Feldman (1981), under automatic processing, all information processing is based on categories and prototypes, and very little cognitive energy is expended. Only when information is acquired that is inconsistent with the established category (and beyond some threshold of discrepancy), does a rater need to engage in controlled processing. Here, according to Feldman (1981), cognitive effort is expended, the rater engages in various attributional processes but, in the end, in both cases, Feldman suggests that the rater ends by putting ratees into categories, and subsequent processing of information is all based upon those categories (cf., Rosch, 1975, 1977).

Thus, Feldman's model suggests that raters develop expectations about a ratee and encounter information consistent with those expectations, engaging, all along in automatic processing. As a result, the rater is able to assign the ratee to some predetermined category such as "good/poor worker," or "lazy/ambitious" worker. Once a ratee is assigned a category, information that is inconsistent with this category is screened out, or reinterpreted in a way that *is* consistent with the category. This goes on until the rater encounters a piece of information that is *so* inconsistent or troubling that it requires more purposeful, "controlled" processing. As a result, the rater may decide to reassign the ratee to a new category, and the process continues as before, except for the new category.

Feldman's model is the most widely cited of the cognitive models, and his work has influenced researchers working in many areas outside performance appraisal. Many appraisal scholars have been guided by his work as well, although his model has had more influence on the conceptual development of other models and views of the appraisal process than on specific studies, since some notions, such as those associated with automatic and controlled processing in appraisals, are relatively difficult to test. Nonetheless, Feldman's model has had an influence on every subsequent cognitive model of the appraisal process, and Feldman himself further refined some of the ideas from the model concerning the role of rating instruments and category accessibility into a more fully articulated approach to the design of appraisal instruments and rater training (Feldman, 1986) that has itself had a great impact on thinking in this area.

The Ilgen and Feldman model

Feldman's (1981) model was refined and more fully specified by Ilgen and Feldman (1983). This newer model also expanded the earlier work by giving serious consideration to the work context. Here the authors considered such factors as the intended function of the appraisal, the problems with opportunities to observe relevant performance, the difficulties associated with performance appraisal in group settings, and the role played by limited opportunities to reward performance. The newer model also included suggestions that feedback and decision making roles for performance appraisals should be separated (echoing a much earlier suggestion by Meyer, Kay, & French, 1965), and they suggested that raters would engage in purposeful search for information (as opposed to simply encountering information as it came) as part of the shift from automatic to controlled processing. Thus, the Ilgen and Feldman model was more clearly an appraisal model, while Feldman's original model, as noted earlier, was as much a person perception model as an appraisal model.

Specifically, the role of categorization (as discussed earlier) in the appraisal decision making process is probably the most influential aspect of the Feldman, and Ilgen and Feldman models. The reliance upon automatic and controlled processing in an appraisal setting, on the other hand, has been somewhat disputed (e.g., Bargh, 1982), and has largely been supplanted by the distinction between memory-based and on-line processing (Hastie & Park, 1986). This latter processing model has played a greater role in influencing appraisal researchers, but both the Feldman (1981) and the Ilgen and Feldman (1983) models continue to guide and influence researchers in performance appraisal and other areas where cognitive decision making activities are important.

Other models

Although these two models, along with the DeNisi, Cafferty, and Meglino (1984) model have generated a great deal of the cognitive research in the appraisal area, there are two other models that must be acknowledged as well, since they have also been quite important in this area. Robert Lord and his associates have developed and tested a cognitive model of leadership and leadership perceptions (e.g., Foti & Lord, 1987; Lord, 1985a, 1985b; Lord & Maher, 1991; Nathan & Lord, 1983). This model relies heavily upon the notions of leadership schema and the salience of prototypical leadership behaviors. Subordinates, or observers, encounter behaviors and then determine how closely these behaviors match their own view of the prototypical effective leader. Strong matches result in the leader being more likely to be perceived as a leader in general, and an effective leader specifically. The implication here is that the evaluation of leadership behaviors relies less on whether or not those behaviors are objectively effective, but more upon whether they match an observer's schema of what an effective leader does.

Not only have Lord and his associates actually applied this model to appraisal settings (especially Foti & Lord, 1987; Nathan & Lord, 1983), but their work has also influenced other appraisal researchers who have developed "folk models" of effective performance on the job. Borman (1987) demonstrated both the existence and variance of these models in a field setting, while Blencoe (1984) demonstrated, in a laboratory setting, that the extent to which, when observed performance matched schematic "good worker" performance, evaluations of subordinates were higher, regardless of how good or bad those behaviors actually were. I will return to a discussion of these models and the role they might play in Chapter 7, but the nature and importance of these models may represent one of the most interesting directions for cognitive research to take in the future.

The final model or approach that must be discussed was proposed by Murphy and Cleveland (1991) in their book. Although the authors call it a model, it is different from the other models I have discussed. There are only four components to the model : (1) context; (2) judgment; (3) rating; and (4) evaluation. Context includes all the external factors that might influence performance ratings. These range from factors based on the economy and culture of a country, through strategic organizational considerations, and include even things like time pressures and conflicting demands faced by raters. Judgments are the evaluative decisions raters come to hold about ratees. These are private, and are less sensitive to some contextual factors than are ratings. Ratings are the public statement of evaluations, but they often reflect other concerns and pressures facing raters in addition to reflecting evaluations. Evaluation, here, refers to the assessment of whether the rater is communicating to the ratee what he or she wants to communicate. This also includes the rater's goals in conducting performance appraisals, which are often different from the organization's goals in having an appraisal system. In this view, a discrepancy between "true" performance and rated performance may not reflect an error, or a rater's inability to evaluate that performance. Instead, it may simply reflect the rater's unwillingness to provide a given rating in a given context.

Since the model was proposed fairly recently, and since it provides a broad framework for studying appraisals rather than a specific model, it would not seem to have had a major impact upon appraisal research. This may be deceptive however, because this simple model *does* propose a different set of factors to consider in appraisal research, and much of it *is* based on work the authors have already done. In any case, this model and view are likely to become more important as researchers become more aware of the role of rater goals and motives.

SUMMARY

Performance appraisal research has had a long history. For most of that history, research has taken a psychometric orientation, and has focused on the development of better rating instruments. Furthermore, for most of that history, researchers have focused on the absence of rating errors as a proxy for rating accuracy, and have implemented programs and systems designed to reduce rating errors. With the publication of Landy and Farr's (1980) review paper, researchers began focusing on the rater as a decision maker, and upon the cognitive processes engaged in by a rater making an appraisal decision. Although there had been some earlier efforts to develop such models, the most influential models were developed in the few years following the Landy and Farr paper.

These cognitive models represent a radical departure from the earlier approaches to studying performance appraisal. They also represent a view that, by understanding rater cognitive processes associated with appraisal decisions, we will be able to design interventions that will somehow improve those processes and so produce more accurate appraisals. Thus there is surely a fair amount of overlap among these models, but they do differ in their emphases. That is, although all the models discussed deal with rater cognitive processes at some level, the models differ in terms of which aspects of those processes they are most concerned with. These differences, though, represent differences in emphases and perceived importance more than basic differences in how appraisal decisions are made, and the simple overall framework, provided in Figure 1.4, allows us to see some of the areas where those differences occur.

Two of those major models (Feldman, 1981; Ilgen & Feldman, 1983) focused on categorization and the distinction between automatic and controlled processing. A model developed by Lord, in the leadership area (Lord, 1985b), has also influenced appraisal research and focuses on the match between observed behaviors and behaviors prototypical of effective leaders (performers). Thus, these models are more concerned with the ways in which information is encoded and processed by the rater to form judg-

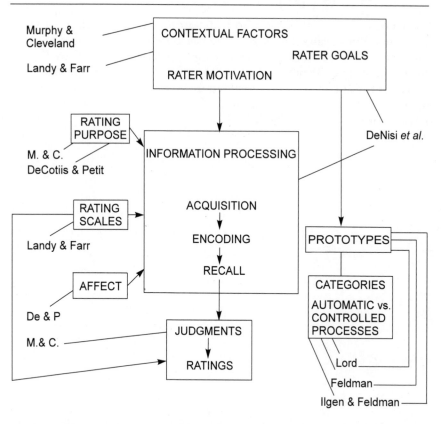

Figure 1.4 Areas of overlap and differences in emphases among cognitive appraisal models. All the models described in this chapter are concerned with basic cognitive processes, but they emphasize different aspects of the appraisal process, and focus on different variables.

ments, rather than on how information is acquired. Landy and Farr also considered all processing activities, but did consider contextual factors as well, and remained interested in the nature of the rating scale. DeCotiis and Petit also considered the full gamut of processing activities, but their emphasis was on rater motivation. Finally, Murphy and Cleveland's (1991) model is much more concerned about the role of context on this process than any other model has been. This model also distinguishes between private judgments and public ratings, as well as the factors that determine the discrepancies between the two.

The remaining cognitive model was proposed by DeNisi, Cafferty, and Meglino (1984). It has been the major driving force behind the research program described in this book, although the conceptual and empirical work of others has surely played a role as well. As noted in Figure 1.4, this model pays relatively more attention to information acquisition and encoding, and also considers a host of factors that might influence those processes. But, again, this is really just a difference in emphasis, not a difference in the fundamental view of the appraisal process. Thus, I want to end this chapter by noting that our model receives all the attention in this book not because there is any reason to think it is superior to other models discussed. For better or worse, it is simply the model that guided the research program I am going to discuss.

Chapter 2

A cognitive model of the appraisal process

As noted in Chapter 1, for many years the research in performance appraisal tended to focus upon rating scale formats and rater training – usually aimed at reducing psychometric errors. The rater was viewed as a fairly passive participant in this process, or so it would seem most researchers assumed. The relevant information was based on the performance of the ratee, and the rater was simply the depository of this information. Furthermore, for the most part, the information that was acquired by the rater was seen as being an accurate representation of the behavior exhibited by the ratee. Finally, the rater was viewed as being motivated to be as accurate as he or she could be in the evaluations provided, and so willing to exert effort to improve rating accuracy. No other specific goals were attributed to the rater in the appraisal process.

Thus, the emphasis was on developing techniques that would allow the rater to do a better job of rating the performance of subordinates, such as "better" rating instruments, or training to help the rater avoid rating errors. Of course, raters are now seen as being more active players in this process than even we thought at the outset, but, for the most part, at the beginning of the 1980s, raters were still cast as rather passive participants in the appraisal process.

As I noted in the previous chapter, this view of raters began to change with the publication of the Landy and Farr (1980) paper, and several cognitive models of the appraisal process soon appeared. These were presented and discussed in the previous chapter, and I will touch on some of them again briefly here, but the primary focus in this chapter is on one particular cognitive model of the appraisal process. That model, proposed by two colleagues at the University of South Carolina and myself (DeNisi, Cafferty, & Meglino, 1984), is given special attention in this chapter because it was the impetus for, and much of the driving force behind, the research program described in this book. But that model was also the result of an evolution that took place over seven or eight years, and it was truly a collaborative effort among the three of us. The original "model" that got me started on cognitive appraisal, however, was mine alone, and was rather less sophisticated. I will begin then with earlier manifestations of this model and trace its development to the published form that was the focus of much of the research program I will describe.

EARLY VERSIONS OF THE MODEL

The DeNisi *et al.* (1984) model was published some time after the models of Feldman (1981) and Ilgen and Feldman (1983), but was first proposed, in a very rudimentary form, in my dissertation (DeNisi, 1977). Although social cognition was already developing as a field at that time, I was unaware of it, and there was no review paper by Landy and Farr to put the previous years of research into perspective. What there was, though, was a legacy of research on rating errors, but most especially on halo error. It was this literature, as well as some work on decision making, upon which I relied most heavily in developing my original model. Although this work had not been labeled as "cognitive," I found a great deal of thinking about rater decision making processes that did, in retrospect, seem rather cognitive in orientation.

For example, I had noted that Johnson and Vidulich (1956) had proposed arguments similar to those put forward by Guilford (1954), in approaching halo error from an analysis of variance perspective. They suggested that halo (here defined as correlations among trait ratings) could be due to any one of three possible explanations:

1 The correlations could be true, in other words, the traits were actually correlated in the world and someone who performed well in one area also performed well in another. Thus, the observed halo reflects the real state of affairs.
2 The rater's observations might be correlated so that, regardless of the true correlations among traits, the information obtained by the rater indicates that someone is performing well (or poorly) in each of several areas. Thus, the observed halo reflects the information available to the rater at the time she/he must make ratings.
3 The rater may be mistaken, so that the observed halo reflects an error in judgment rather than true correlations or correlated observations.

Note that only in the third case would halo really be seen as an error, but it would be this case that we would want to minimize. Of course, William Cooper developed a much more sophisticated view of halo along much the same lines some years later (Cooper, 1981b), and even provided some empirical evidence concerning the origin of halo (Cooper, 1981a), but the earlier views of halo were enough to stimulate some thinking about the role of the rater in appraisal decisions.

Other stimuli for focusing on rater cognitive processes also came from the appraisal literature, but from studies dealing more with decision making rather than with halo error. For example, Wright (1974) had described how raters facing time pressures and distractions tended to provide less accurate ratings because they focused on fewer relevant performance cues, and relied upon simple heuristics for combining those cues. Several studies also examined the role of profiles of performance, and had demonstrated how raters processed profile information in making appraisal decisions. For example, Scott and Hamner (1975) studied ratings and attributions made by raters, observing ratees performing at the same overall level of performance, but displaying different patterns of performance. They reported that, although overall performance ratings did not vary as a function of performance patterns or variability, evaluations of ability and motivation did vary as a function of both. In this study, raters had available to them objective measures of true performance (ratees were stacking cans on the shelf in a grocery store, and the appraisal was focused upon the number of cans put on the shelf), and so probably found the overall rating task fairly simple, but the other results reported suggested that raters were active processors of information in appraisal decisions. They did not simply take what we gave them or what they saw and report it directly – they actively processed that information to make their decisions.

In fact the Scott and Hamner study, as well as an earlier study (Jones, Rock, Shaver, Goethals, & Ward, 1968) had examined the impact of profiles of performance where there was not an objective measure of performance available, and they found much more widespread effects for patterns and variability than had been reported by Scott and Hamner (1975). Furthermore, Jones et al. (1968) reported that ratings and expectations differed depending upon whether they were obtained from the raters (observers) or the ratees (actors). At the time, this suggested the possibility that the way raters gathered or obtained (or attended to) information would also affect evaluations. Others had, of course, discussed information sampling as well, but had not fully integrated it into a larger model of rater information processing. Whitlock (1963), though, reported reliable relationships between the number of performance incidents a rater observed for a given ratee, and the ratings he/she would give to that ratee. In one final piece of data that I drew upon, Gordon (1970) had reported that raters were able to more accurately rate behavior that was "correct" relative to job requirements, than behavior that was incorrect. All of these studies suggested to me, some form of active processing on the part of the rater.

Finally, general treatments of attribution theory (e.g., Jones & Davis, 1965) led me to argue that judges would not consider all pieces of information as equally useful. Instead, they would actively seek the kinds of information they felt they needed to evaluate performance and to make attributions for that performance. The exact role attribution theory played in the development of our appraisal model will be discussed later in this chapter. For now, though, it is enough to say that the goal in attribution research is for the observer to be able to attribute a behavior to a stable and internal cause. Thus a rater observing a ratee performing some aspect of the job, would want to attribute that performance to ratee ability (or perhaps ratee motivation). I saw the information acquisition process as an attempt to obtain the missing information needed to make such an attribution (I will discuss this again later, as a basis for specific research propositions in the model).

Thus, in 1977, I proposed a simple model of rater decision making focusing on the *active* acquisition of performance information by raters, and the processing of that information by raters. Dependent variables included a crude measure of rating accuracy (the ability of the rater to differentiate "good" from "poor" performance based on pilot ratings of videotaped ratees), and the degree of intercorrelation among ratings (i.e., halo). The model was very simple. It posited that rating errors (which would indicate rating inaccuracy) could stem from three potential sources:

1 Poor information gathering strategy on the part of the rater. That is, the rater might simply not collect enough or the right kind of information about the person being rated. The rating might be perfectly accurate given the information that was collected, but would still not accurately reflect the ratee's true performance.
2 Inadequate information processing activities on the part of the rater. That is, the rater may have collected the right kind and amount of information, but cannot process it properly to arrive at an accurate evaluation. This is seen as an error of judgment.
3 A constraint operating on the rater that simply keeps the rater from correctly recording the evaluation decided upon. Although this constraint may be organizational in nature, my primary focus was upon some aspect of the rating scale that does not allow the rater to express the rating properly, or at least makes it too easy for the rater to deviate from that rating.

The emphasis in my dissertation, however, was on information acquisition. This was due to my belief that information acquisition might turn out to be more interesting and a more unique area of contribution, as well as my inability to actually measure any processing variables. Unfortunately, this emphasis led to a design where raters chose which performance segments to observe (there were three grocery clerks performing each of seven tasks). The raters were constrained, however, to choose *one* ratee performing each task. Thus, each rater observed seven performance incidents, but they differed in terms of whom they observed performing which tasks. The results were largely unsupportive of my hypotheses, and, although I was able to identify some patterns of search and relate them to ratings, the results were also largely uninterpretable, since it was difficult to compare the ratings of raters who based their evaluations upon different information.

Nonetheless, the fact that I believed I had identified some patterns of information acquisition (these were based on cluster analysis, and not any theory), and that I found these patterns to be related to overall ratings of performance (although again, there was no theory to guide this, the means for overall performance were simply different depending upon the acquisition pattern a rater had followed) convinced me that the pattern in which raters acquired information, and the information itself, might be important for appraisal decisions.

I should note, though, that the decision to constrain rater choices in observation was actually based on some thinking about the cognitive demands facing a rater on the job. It seemed that past research had not only ignored the fact that raters were *active* processors of information, but it also overlooked the fact that raters who used different information acquisition strategies might actually be making decisions based on different information (this simple fact was overlooked by my colleagues and I in a later stage of this research). Raters were typically supervisors who had other competing tasks (i.e., they operated in a cognitively busy environment), and so they would not be able to observe all the relevant information available. I had argued that raters would therefore have to make choices (and suggested that they would actually formulate reliable sampling strategies) about whom to observe and when, but all raters would be operating with incomplete, and non-identical information.

Later, Lord and his colleagues worked from a similar notion, and developed it much further, suggesting that rating accuracy could only be assessed relative to what was observed (Lord, 1985a; Lord & Alliger, 1985; Lord, Foti, & DeVader, 1984; Lord, Foti, & Phillips, 1982). That is, rating accuracy should be computed as a function of a rater's ability to accurately evaluate those performance incidents she/he observes, and *not* consider other ratee performance if it was not observed. This again emphasized the importance of the rater as an active player in the appraisal process by recognizing that rater observation or acquisition activities would actually define the limits of rating accuracy. This led to a definition of rating accuracy known as observational accuracy (Murphy, 1991), and acknowledged that ratings could be no more accurate than the information upon which they were based. I will return to these and other ideas concerning the calculation and importance of rating accuracy in Chapter 6, but, at the time, the idea of constraining choices seemed reasonable, even if it did subsequently present problems for interpreting the results of my study.

OUR MODEL OF THE APPRAISAL PROCESS

Several years were spent trying to publish both the early version of the model and the limited empirical findings, but these efforts were in vain. After moving to the University of South Carolina (from Kent State

University), I began working with Bruce Meglino and Thomas Cafferty, both of whom also had interests in appraisal processes. Together, we began to refine the rudimentary model upon which I based my dissertation, which now began to integrate aspects of social cognition (this was largely Tom Cafferty's contribution). Feldman's model (Feldman, 1981), and the modification of that model (Ilgen & Feldman, 1983) appeared in print, but these authors actually helped us in developing our arguments and in differentiating the model we were developing. As the model was developed further, we submitted a grant proposal to the National Science Foundation to fund a program of research based on this model and we received a grant from them at about the same time that our model was accepted for publication. The DeNisi, Cafferty, and Meglino (1984) model was the basis upon which we began the research program I will describe.

The DeNisi *et al.* model is presented in Figure 2.1. The model went far beyond the simple model that guided my dissertation, but information acquisition still played a prominent role, and in fact at this time we still thought of information acquisition primarily in terms of raters actively seeking or sampling performance information. Attributional processes were included as well, but much of the cognitive processes theorizing was based on the work of Srull and Wyer (e.g., Srull & Wyer, 1979, 1980; Wyer & Srull, 1981). A number of ideas from Wherry's (1952) model (described in the previous chapter) were also integrated into our model.

The model reflected a view that "performance appraisal is an exercise in social perception and cognition embedded in an organizational context requiring both formal and implicit judgment" (DeNisi *et al.*, 1984: 362). The proposed process begins with the job-relevant behavior, or performance, exhibited by the ratee, and then suggests the following steps:

1 the behavior is observed by the rater;
2 the rater forms a cognitive representation of the behavior;
3 this representation is stored in memory;
4 stored information is retrieved from memory when needed;
5 retrieved information is integrated, along with other information, to form a decision about the ratee; and
6 a formal evaluation is assigned to the ratee using the appropriate rating instrument.

The model continued to recognize that raters could not observe every job-relevant behavior exhibited by a ratee, and so began with raters sampling the job performance of a ratee. The accuracy of any evaluation would always be dependent upon the information available to the rater, and so this first step was seen as critical to the appraisal process and, in fact, it is this emphasis on information acquisition, more than any other single feature, that has distinguished our model from the other cognitive models proposed and tested.

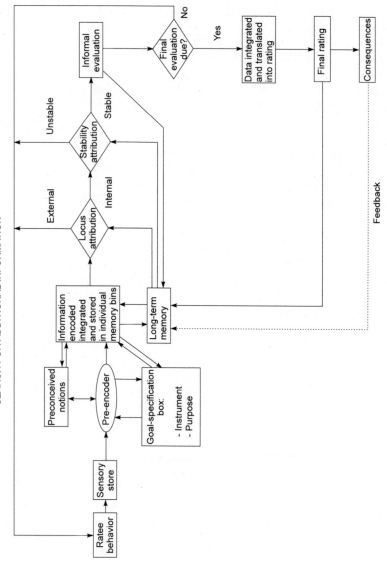

Figure 2.1 The DeNisi, Cafferty, and Meglino (1984) cognitive appraisal model

Our model also recognized the fact that, in most organizations, formal appraisals are relatively infrequent events. Thus, not only did a rater have to observe a ratee's performance, and be able to characterize that performance as "effective" or "ineffective," the rater also had to accurately represent that evaluation in memory. Note that our model suggested from the outset, that "The representation of the behavior is stored, and not the behavior itself" (p. 364). Thus, we always believed that it would be relatively difficult for a rater, unaided, to recall the actual behaviors or performance incidents that led to her/his evaluation of a ratee. Later, Hastie and Park (1986) drew a distinction between "on-line" and "memory-based" processing in social judgments (I will discuss the role of this distinction in performance appraisal more fully in subsequent chapters), but our position on what was accessible in memory would have placed us on the side of arguing for on-line processing in performance appraisal. Subsequent data, discussed later, suggests to me that memory-based processing is actually more prevalent in appraisals, but that is not the position advocated in our model.

Also, our model proposed a relatively modest *direct* role for the appraisal instrument itself. This was, in part, a reaction to the decades of research on developing "better" appraisal instruments that had yielded little, but the appraisal instrument was viewed as playing a potential role in how performance information was categorized. Although Feldman's models (Feldman, 1981; Ilgen & Feldman, 1983) better discussed the role of categorization in the appraisal process, we were suggesting that the content of the appraisal instrument might well prime certain categories to make them more likely to be used by the rater. Thus, the rating instrument had a more critical indirect effect as a partial determinant of categories to be used in storing and organizing information (as we shall see later, the evidence to support such a role has been mixed, cf., DeNisi & Summers, 1986; Ostroff & Ilgen, 1986). Its direct effects did not enter the process until the rater moved to translate his/her judgment to a formal rating. Our model, therefore, also suggested that judgments and ratings were not isomorphic. This distinction, though, was much better developed and discussed in the later work of Murphy and Cleveland (1991), who also proposed political and motivation processes that intervened in the translation from judgment to rating, and went far beyond the simple distinction made in our model.

As noted above, Feldman's model of the appraisal process was much more detailed in its discussion of the role of categorization, but our model also considered how raters categorized their ratees and the information they collected about those ratees. We relied upon Wyer and Srull's (1981) work, and their "bin" model for trying to understand this process (this model conceptualizes memory as a series of "bins," in which information is stored; what we find in memory depends on which "bins" we search through, and some information may never be "found" if we don't search through the correct bins), but this model is really not very different from other schema-based processing models and, in fact, "bins" are generally seen as being "labeled" according to prototypes.

We also recognized that motivational forces were at work here, since ratings had consequences for both raters and ratees. Although we did not go nearly as far as Murphy and Cleveland (1991) eventually did in developing the potential role for rater motivation, we did recognize that raters might not be willing to provide accurate ratings (even if they could) under certain circumstances. Finally, our model was basically a "cold" model, as opposed to a "hot" model where affect plays a critical role (cf., Robbins & DeNisi, 1994), but we did attempt to consider the earlier work of DeCotiis and Petit (1978) among others, in our cognitive model, so that there was some role specified for affect, even if it was limited.

Although this discussion provides a reasonable overview of the major features of the DeNisi, Cafferty, and Meglino model, it is important to discuss the various components in more detail, and to present some of the research propositions that were derived from this model. Although we never did test all of them, and in fact subsequent findings caused a rethinking of a number of them, and sent the research program off in other directions, these research propositions provide a good framework for understanding how we went about empirically testing the role of cognitive processes in performance appraisal, and help put all subsequent discussions into context.

Observation of behavior

As noted above, the emphasis on the observation of behavior, expanded to consider the more general acquisition of performance information, is an important defining characteristic of this approach to studying cognitive processes in performance appraisal. Basically, the decision making process in performance appraisal begins with raters acquiring information, and the outcome of this process (i.e., the performance information available to the rater) will determine the evaluation made. Since we assume that raters cannot observe all aspects of the performance of each ratee because of conflicting demands on their attention, or simply because of physical constraints, raters will make decisions based only upon samples of the ratee's performance. Even if two raters are observing the same ratee then, if they engage in different information search or acquisition activities, they will have different information available to them, and so will likely arrive at different evaluations.

The information in question might be in the form of actual behavior, products, or outcomes, or it might consist of evaluations provided by others. We noted that a number of scholars (e.g., Einhorn & Hogarth, 1981; Slovic & Lichtenstein, 1971) had pointed out that much of the research in decision making had been focused on how decision makers integrated information, but had ignored how they acquired information. We also noted that Crocker (1981), among others, had proposed that information acquisition was critical for decision making in social cognition contexts, and that, in fact, judges consciously decided what kinds of information to seek and acquire.

At the time, we stressed purposeful acquisition of information (as opposed to more passive encounters that might also be informative), and used an attributional framework (i.e., Kelley, 1967) to try to understand what kinds of information a rater might seek. That is, consistent with some other research at the time in both social cognition (e.g., Garland, Hardy, & Stephenson, 1975; Major, 1980) and consumer behavior (e.g., Capon & Burke, 1980; Jacoby, Chestnut, Weigel, & Fisher, 1976; Payne, 1976; Payne, Braunstein, & Carroll, 1978) we discussed three types of information: distinctiveness information, consistency information, and consensus information. Using familiar models from attribution theory, we argued that raters tried to make stable, internal attributions for the performance information they observed and this determined the types of information they would seek, as illustrated in Figure 2.2.

Rater observes Ratee A performing well on Task 1.

Problem: Before rater is willing to give the ratee credit for this good performance, the rater must determine if the performance can be attributed to an internal characteristic of the ratee. Before the rater is willing to predict the ratee will perform at this level in the future, the rater must determine if the performance can be attributed to a *stable* internal characteristic of the ratee.

Types of information:

1. Distinctiveness: does the ratee perform as well on other tasks? Helps determine if the performance was specific to Task 1 only.
2. Consistency: does the ratee perform well on Task 1 on other occasions? Helps determine stability of performance.
3. Consensus: do other ratees perform well on Task 1? Helps determine if performance was a function of Task 1 being an easy task.

Solution: Rater will observe Ratee A and others perform Task 1 and other tasks in order to answer these questions.

Ratee performance is likely to be attributed to the ratee (and so the ratee given credit for the performance) *if* Ratee A performs well on other tasks as well, and other ratees do not also all perform well on Task 1.

Rater is likely to give credit to Ratee A, *and* predict that Ratee A will also perform well in the future, *if* Ratee A performs well on other tasks, if all other ratees do not also perform well on Task 1, and if Ratee A performs well on Task 1 on other occasions.

Figure 2.2 Relationship between types of information and raters' ability to attribute performance to ratees

This framework also led to several general research propositions concerning information acquisition and the observation of behavior, including:

> The rater is more likely to search for more information about a target ratee when performance is attributed to an external cause. . . . . When an observed incident of performance is attributed to an unstable cause the rater is more likely to search for more information about the target.
>
> (DeNisi *et al.*, 1984: 375)

Both these propositions were derived from our view that raters would always try to make internal attributions for performance observed, because only then did it make sense to give the ratee credit (or penalize the ratee) for the observed performance. Clearly, if the observed performance was not "caused" by the ratee, she/he should neither benefit nor suffer for the performance. In addition, we believed that this would extend to the rest of the cognitive processes such that:

> Incidents of performance attributed to stable, internal causes are most likely to be retained in memory, recalled, and considered in the final decision.
>
> (p. 376)

As we shall see later, we never fully developed this line of research, and eventually dropped the strong reliance upon attribution theory in information acquisition. In part, this was due to the fact that we were chastised for using attributional terminology where we couldn't be sure anyone was trying to make attributions, and we adopted alternative ways of dealing with the types of information raters sought in making appraisal decisions. Furthermore, as our research findings began to suggest different directions for our studies to take, we pursued those directions instead of the propositions related to attributions. That is not to say, though, that these ideas do not make sense, and it would still be worthwhile to test some of them.

In addition, our model proposed that there would be four factors influencing information search activities. Specifically, we argued that the nature of the information sought and acquired by a rater would be influenced by: "(1) preconceived notions the rater had about a given ratee; (2) the purpose for which the appraisal is conducted; (3) the nature of the rating instrument used; and (4) the time pressures operating on the rater" (p. 367).

Preconceived notions

Although we never generated very specific hypotheses about the nature of the relationship between preconceived notions and information acquisition, we argued that these initial impressions would make a difference. These preconceived notions were seen as coming from either prior interaction with the ratee in other contexts, earlier evaluations, or information obtained from others about the ratee. These preconceived notions were seen as establishing a schema for the ratee, which would then guide the acquisition of subsequent information as well as all other cognitive processes (Fiedler, 1982, provided an excellent review of this literature), but we noted somewhat conflicting suggestions for what kinds of information would be sought following the activation of a schema.

Several researchers (e.g., Ebbesen, 1981; Snyder, 1981; Snyder & Cantor, 1979; Swann, Stephenson, & Pittman, 1981; Wong & Weiner, 1981) had argued that judges, or raters, would seek to confirm their expectations and schemata, and so raters would be expected to seek information consistent with however the ratee was initially categorized (e.g., the rater would seek positive information about a ratee who was categorized as being a "good performer"). But others (e.g., Trope & Bassok, 1982) suggested that judges tended to seek diagnostic information which would best enable them to categorize persons, regardless of whether it confirmed prior expectations or not. Yet others suggested that judges would always seek negative information (whether this was consistent or not; Hamilton & Huffman, 1971) *because* negative information was the most diagnostic in that it produced the greatest reduction in uncertainty (e.g., Jones & Thibaut, 1958); but again there was disagreement, with some scholars arguing that extreme information in *either direction* resulted in the greatest reduction of uncertainty (e.g., Fiske, 1980; Hastie, 1981).

As a result of this conflicting research we were only able to generate a fairly broad research question concerning the nature of the information sought as a result of preconceived notions, but it seemed that these should make a difference. As we shall discuss below, we tried to be more specific about the role of preconceived notions on information integration, and in fact there were several studies, conducted by us and others, which looked at the role of expectations or past performance on subsequent performance evaluations (e.g., DeNisi, Cafferty, Williams, Meglino, & Blencoe, 1982; Murphy, Balzer, Lockhart, & Eisenman, 1985). Nonetheless, we proposed the following, consistent with the research on the role of schemata in determining the type of information sought (cf., Ebbesen, 1981; Weiss, Ilgen, & Sharbaugh, 1982): "A rater encountering information inconsistent with expectations will be more likely to seek additional information in order to confirm those expectations" (p. 375).

Purpose of the appraisal

We were on somewhat more solid ground when we discussed the relationship between appraisal purpose and information acquisition. DeCotiis and Petit (1978) had already proposed that appraisal purpose played a role in the appraisal process, and there was considerable evidence to back up their assertion. But most of the earlier research had focused on rater motivation, noting that raters would be more willing to provide negative (and presumably more accurate) ratings when the ratings were not being used for administrative decision making (such as for merit-pay increases), or when the rater would not learn about the ratings (e.g., Bartlett & Sharon, 1969; McCall & DeVries, 1976; McGregor, 1957: Meyer, Kay, & French, 1965).

These forces would presumably influence the kinds of information a rater would seek, but we were proposing an expanded role for appraisal purpose, where purpose was seen as determining rater goals in the appraisal process. Such rater goals had been found to affect information acquisition in social cognition judgments (e.g., Chaiken, 1980; Cohen, 1981a; Crockett, Mahood, & Press, 1975; Fisher, 1979; Hoffman, Mischel, & Mazze, 1981; Jeffrey & Mischel, 1979; Ross, Lepper, Strack, & Steinmetz, 1977; Wyer, Srull, Gordon, & Hartwick, 1982), and we believed that similar effects would be found in the appraisal context. From these various arguments, we were able to put forward several research propositions, including:

> Raters will be less likely to search for negative information when evaluations are to be used for administrative purposes, or when the rater must personally give feedback to the ratee; but they will be more likely to search for negative information when evaluations are to be used for counseling, or when they are to be kept confidential. . . .
> Appraisal decisions requiring comparative judgments about ratees (e.g., whom should we promote) will result in a search for consensus information, while decisions requiring relatively absolute judgments (e.g., how large a raise to give a worker) will result in a search for distinctiveness information.
>
> (p. 374)

As we shall see in the next chapter, we did design a study to test these propositions in somewhat modified form.

Time pressures

There was a fairly well-established literature to support the notion that the time pressures facing a rater would also influence information acquisition processes. Studies in consumer behavior (e.g., Staelin & Payne, 1976), as well as in decision making (e.g., Christensen-Szalanski, 1980; Wright, 1974) suggested that decision makers facing time constraints tended to search for (and use) fewer cues, and tended to rely more heavily upon negative information. Of course, given our view of a rater as someone who had to balance conflicting demands on her or his time, there would always be time pressures, but these would be more severe at some times than at others. Nonetheless, the continuing demands would mean that raters would always tend to rely upon less rather than more information, and would be wary "consumers" of information, seeking the most diagnostic information they could find so as to maximize the return on their time investment (this line of reasoning was developed much more fully by Stigler, 1961, in his discussion of the economic cost of collecting information for decision making).

Since we also argued that negative information was generally more diagnostic, this led us to propose:

> Raters facing time pressures will consider fewer pieces of information and will be more likely to search for negative information, as well as be more likely to rely upon the results of past evaluations.
>
> (p. 374)

Nature of the rating instrument

The final factor we hypothesized to influence information search was the nature of the rating instrument. Here we suggested that the content of the rating instrument (i.e., the areas in which ratings were required) would be prime categories that would be used to organize incoming information, but would also cue the rater as to what kinds of information to seek. Thus, for example, scales that required raters to make judgments about ratee traits, would guide the rater to seek information that could be used to infer something about those traits. Scales that required judgments about task performance, on the other hand, would guide raters to look for opportunities to observe performance on those tasks. These arguments were consistent with research in social cognition indicating that what raters were told to look for determined the ways in which they perceived a situation (e.g., Press, Crockett, & Delia, 1975; Ross, Lepper, Strack, & Steinmetz, 1977), as well as how they segmented that information into behavioral incidents (e.g., Newtson & Ridner, 1979).

We also suggested that the type of ratings required would influence search processes. For example, since both Behaviorally Anchored Rating Scales (Smith & Kendall, 1963) and Behavioral Observation Scales (Latham & Wexley, 1977) require raters to simply observe, rather than evaluate ratee behavior, using these scales may cause the rater to simply seek and store behaviors which are not evaluated, and which are not pre-encoded. Rating scales requiring more evaluative judgments might require raters to seek additional information so that they can judge the behavior, instead of simply note it. This led us to suggest the following broad proposition:

> The type of rating scale used will influence the way performance is perceived by the rater.
>
> (p. 373)

We also suggested a more specific proposition as follows:

> Scales which require ratings in broad general categories of performance will lead individuals to perceive larger segments of performance than scales which call for ratings in finer, more distinct categories.
>
> (p. 373)

Finally, we argued that these effects would be stronger for more experienced raters. These raters would be more familiar with the rating scale and the categories of judgments required, and so presumably would more readily perceive information in ways consistent with these categories. As I shall discuss later, we actually operationalized this a bit differently when we tried to test this proposition, but the argument remained that just handing a rater a scale might not guarantee that he or she would use it to guide information acquisition. At some level, the rater had to internalize the categories before they would have an effect. In any event, at this time, we argued that:

> Individuals who had more experience with a particular rating scale are more likely to perceive ratee performance in terms of the dimensions called for on the scale.
>
> (p. 373)

Thus, although we began thinking about the observation of behavior as the result, primarily, of active information seeking by the rater, this was expanded to consider any method that would result in a rater observing a ratee at work. We realized at this point (and this became much more important to subsequent thinking and research on the model) that raters acquired much of the information they used in making appraisal decisions much more casually. That is, a great deal of information would simply be encountered rather than be the result of active search. Nonetheless, we believed that the processes we outlined and stated propositions about would still hold. We believed that, in the case of more casual acquisition, the mechanisms we discussed would operate instead as filters, and would help determine, of the information encountered, what would actually be perceived, consistent with the discussion of unconscious, pre-attention filters discussed as far back as Miller (1956) and later by Bargh (1982).

As will be discussed in later chapters, a great deal of effort went into devising technology to allow us to examine information acquisition activities (some of those studies will be discussed later) and the results of those studies had a great deal of influence on our subsequent thinking. Finally, as I stated earlier, I believe that it has been this attention paid to information acquisition that has most separated our model from the other cognitive appraisal models. Nonetheless, we did discuss and put forward propositions concerning other cognitive processes as well.

Encoding, storage, and retrieval of performance information

In most organizations, performance appraisal is a relatively infrequent event. Therefore, over a considerable period of time, raters observe ratee behavior, but must then store it until the actual appraisal is due. At that time they recall the information stored in memory, but knowing exactly *what* is stored in memory, as well as knowing *how* it is stored, is important for understanding the appraisal process. Encoding refers to the rater's translation or interpretation of the information he or she observes, and it is this representation that is typically stored in memory and so subsequently recalled and used. The encoding and subsequent storage processes are extremely important determinants of a performance appraisal, since these processes will affect what *can be* recalled and ultimately used in making a decision. It shouldn't be surprising then, that this is where we focused most of our attention.

Our view of the encoding process was not much different from that suggested by Feldman (1981) or by Ilgen and Feldman (1983). We relied upon the notion of categories, and suggested that raters assign a piece of information to a category they see as appropriate. Over time, the strength of the category assignment builds and, in most cases, it is the category information that is eventually stored in memory, rather than the actual behavior that triggered the category (I will discuss this process when raw behavior is actually accessible in much more detail in later chapters). The categories we proposed are those which are known as schemata.

Schemata are interpretative frameworks used by raters to categorize ratee behavior. They have been widely studied and it is proposed that they operate in a variety of settings (see reviews by Hastie, 1981; Ostrom, Pryor, & Simpson, 1981). More complete treatments of the role of schemata in performance appraisal are also available in either model paper mentioned above, or in a more recent work by Feldman (1994). For our purposes though, it was important to note that, once a schema category is activated, it not only provides a means for interpreting incoming information but there is evidence that raters may eventually come to rely upon schemata instead of actual information when making decisions, and the schema may also be a direct source of information about a ratee that is "recalled" (e.g., Ajzen, Dalton, & Blyth, 1979; Cohen, 1981b; Kuiper & Rogers, 1979; Lord, Foti, & Phillips, 1982; Press, Crockett, & Delia, 1975; Snyder & Uranowitz, 1978; Taylor & Crocker, 1981). What was especially troubling was the further suggestion that raters would continue to rely upon schema-based information even though they encountered information that contradicted the schema (Anderson, Lepper, & Ross, 1980; Hamilton, 1979). In fact, a number of researchers had presented data to suggest that there was a systematic bias to recall information consistent with initial schemata (e.g., Hamilton, 1979; Howard & Rothbart, 1980; Rothbart, Evans, & Fulero,

1979; Rothbart, Fulero, Jensen, Howard, & Birrell, 1978; Sentis & Burnstein, 1979). Although others (Hastie & Kumar, 1979; Lingle & Ostrom, 1979; Smith, 1973) suggested that information *inconsistent* with a schema was more salient, and was more likely to be recalled (Taylor, Crocker, Fiske, Sprinzen, & Winkler, 1979), probably because it was deeply processed (Craik & Lockhart, 1972; Craik & Tulving, 1975). Either way (and authors such as Kanouse & Hansen, 1972; and Fiske, 1980; suggested that all information that was extreme in any direction was actually inconsistent with a schema and so more salient), the schema held by a rater concerning a ratee was seen as extremely important.

Furthermore, as noted above, there was evidence that, once an observed behavior is encoded in terms of a schema, raters would recall *only* the representation of the behavior using the schema, and not the actual behavior itself (Greenwald, 1968; Higgins, Rholes, & Jones, 1977; Ostrom, Lingle, Pryor, & Geva, 1980; Schank & Abelson, 1977). To make this matter more critical, Srull & Wyer (1980) had reported that the tendency to rely upon the schema-based representation rather than the actual behavior, actually increased over time. This would mean that, if an appraisal was done only once a year (which is probably the modal frequency for formal appraisals), raters would have little actual behavior to rely upon in making decisions and giving feedback. Instead, they would be forced to rely upon a representation of that behavior, derived from the schema-based category they were using for a particular ratee. Later, Hastie and Park (1986) proposed a distinction between on-line and memory-based processing that substantially clarified when raw behavioral information would and would not be available to a rater, and this played an important part in our research program, but, at the time we proposed the model, it seemed that the role of schemata in encoding was critical to appraisal process.

We therefore generated a number of research propositions, concerning the role of schemata in the encoding and recall of performance information, which included:

> Raters will be more likely to recall overall impressions of ratees and the evaluations associated with those impressions, than the specific behaviors which gave rise to those impressions and evaluations.
>
> (p. 381)

> Behavior inconsistent with a rater's schemata will be better recalled than behavior which is consistent.
>
> (p. 381)

Thus, on this last point, we came down on the side of inconsistent behavior requiring deeper processing because it was more salient, and so more likely to be recalled. Furthermore, we suggested that preconceived notions, the purpose of the appraisal, and the nature of the rating scale would all influence *which* schema a rater might activate and use for categorizing a ratee, thus, based on the work of Mischel and his associates (Hoffman, Mischel, & Mazze, 1981; Jeffrey & Mischel, 1979), we also proposed:

> Behavior is more likely to be perceived in terms of ratee goals when the purpose of the evaluation is primarily for the benefit of the ratee (e.g., counseling and feedback).
>
> (p. 373)

We also had specific propositions that simply stated that all three of the factors listed above would affect schemata used by the rater.

Notice that we focused our attention on the encoding of performance information, and suggested that this would have a direct effect on what was recalled. It is worth noting here that, when we got around to testing some of these notions, we really never directly measured how information was encoded. Instead we assessed recall, and from the recall information inferred how the information was encoded and stored in memory. Although this was, and continues to be a common practice, it is reasonable to argue that the content and structure of recall is related to encoding processes, but they may not be exactly the same thing. This is potentially a limitation to our research.

One last note about our model and research propositions dealing with recall of information, is worth discussing. We had proposed that recall would be unduly (perhaps) influenced by the schema used by a rater for a ratee. As noted above, there was reason to believe that reliance upon a schema would distort what information would be recalled, and could even lead to information not really observed being recalled, if it was consistent with a schema. We suggested that this reliance upon schema was potentially harmful to the ultimate accuracy of the appraisals provided, and further suggested that some of this bias in recall could be ameliorated if we could help raters have access to observed information without reliance upon their biased memories. We therefore proposed (consistent with Wherry's 1952 model, as well as the work of Bernardin & Walter, 1977) that:

> Diary keeping, critical incident files, or other types of records may result in less biased recall.
>
> (p. 383)

This proposition is interesting because, as our research program developed, we began to envision a very different role for diary keeping, and several studies exploring this expanded role were conducted. Nonetheless, in a later study (Varma, DeNisi, & Peters, 1996) we reported that diary keeping was related to bias in recall *and* ratings, but that using diaries to record performance information actually *increased* the effects of bias! I will return to this study, and discuss it in more detail in Chapter 6.

Information integration and rating

The final portion of our model deals with the integration of the information, retrieved from memory, to form a judgment, which is then translated into a rating. For the most part, we considered the judgment and the rating to be essentially the same, and proposed only factors relating to the appraisal instrument as influencing the translation. But in this we were wrong. Murphy and Cleveland (1991), most clearly distinguished these two, noting that judgments are private evaluations, based more closely on the behavior observed, while ratings are more public, and are dependent upon anticipated outcomes of ratings and organizational norms among other factors (cf., Murphy & Cleveland, 1991: 20–22). Similar distinctions have been made by others as well (e.g., Banks & Murphy, 1985; Mohrman & Lawler, 1983), but we did not. Thus, in the discussion that follows, the reader must accept our apologies for not being more perceptive concerning these differences, and realize that, for the most part, we are talking about judgments and not ratings.

Thus, we drew heavily upon the literature concerned with decision making in performance appraisals (e.g., Zedeck & Kafrey, 1977) in forming our arguments and developing research propositions. One issue, then, was the relative weight assigned to different bits of information retrieved from memory, in determining an overall evaluation. It seemed clear that the literature suggested that negative information was given more weight in decision making than was positive information (Hamilton & Huffman, 1971; Hollman, 1972; London & Hakel, 1974; London & Poplawski, 1976; Wyer & Hinkle, 1976), and the notion that negative information would be given more weight *because* it was seen as having greater diagnostic value, was also consistent with the theory of correspondent inference in attributions (Jones & Davis, 1965; Jones & McGillis, 1976). But, we also argued that negative information was more likely to be inconsistent with our generally positive schemata about people, and so more deeply processed and more easily retrieved from memory. Thus, we proposed the following:

> Raters will give the greatest weight to pieces of information most easily retrievable from memory. . . .
> Negative or unfavorable information will be given more weight than positive, or favorable information in an overall evaluation.
>
> (p. 386)

We also drew upon the literature from social psychology and attribution theory, dealing with the utilization of consensus, or base-rate information. Some basic ideas from attribution theory were discussed in Chapter 1 and, as I noted earlier, we eventually moved away from testing propositions stemming directly from attribution theory. Nonetheless, this theory played an important role in the initial development of our model, as a way of categorizing the types of information a rater might seek and use in making appraisal decisions. Thus, in the context of performance appraisal, if a rater observed a ratee performing a task at some level of performance, consensus information would be information about how other ratees performed on the same task. Clearly, one would expect a rater to evaluate a level of performance differently for an easy task as opposed to a difficult task, and consensus information would help provide information about how difficult the task was. But the literature on attribution theory suggested that judges did *not* give much weight to consensus information in their decisions (e.g., Kahneman & Tversky, 1973; McArthur, 1972; Nisbett & Borgida, 1975). Other scholars argued that judges *did* utilize base-rate information, but only when they believed it to be truly representative of the population (Wells & Harvey, 1977). Even under those circumstances, though, they might under-utilize the base-rates (Borgida, 1978). Furthermore, others (Hansen & Donoghue, 1977; Hansen & Lowe, 1976) argued that judges used a type of base-rate information, but this information was generated on the basis of how they believed *they* would behave in a situation. Although there was surely disagreement on the role of base-rate information in attributions (and much of this debate was summarized by Manis, Dovalina, Avis, & Cardoze, 1980), we thought that raters might well rely on their own performance standards for making judgments (also, see the review by Bobko & Colella, 1994), rather than consensus or base-rate information. They would, we believed, be willing to rely upon consensus information, when the rater was inexperienced or, for some other reason, did not have clear performance standards, so that we proposed:

> Consensus, or base-rate information, will be utilized (i.e., given a non-zero weight) in performance appraisals, only when the rater does not have clear standards against which to compare performance.
>
> (p. 386)

We also took up the problem of how biasing information might be used in decision making for performance appraisal. The literature has identified a number of personal characteristics that have been considered as sources of bias, including ratee race (see review and meta-analysis by Kraiger & Ford, 1985) and ratee gender (e.g., Dobbins, Cardy, & Truxillo, 1986, 1988), as well as interpersonal affect towards the ratee (again, see the review and study by Robbins & DeNisi, 1994). These and other factors had long been associated with bias in appraisals (cf., Landy & Farr, 1980), but there had been little consideration of the process by which these factors might influence ratings.

Much of our discussion revolved around the question of the salience of the biasing information. There was literature to suggest that biasing factors became less important as more relevant performance information became available (e.g., Dipboye, Fromkin, & Wiback, 1975; Renwick & Tosi, 1978;

Rose & Andiappan, 1978). In these cases, it would seem, the performance information is the most salient information available, and the biasing information gets less attention. On the other hand, anything that would make the biasing information more salient, such as the lack of clear performance information, unexpected performance (see Leventhal & Michaels, 1971), or "solo status" (e.g., one woman in an otherwise all-male work group; Taylor & Fiske, 1978), will result in this factor playing a bigger role in the evaluation.

We also proposed studying the potential effects of such biasing factors through some type of policy-capturing research, such as that used by Zedeck and Kafrey (1977), or Naylor and Wherry (1965), although we never did follow this route. In any case, consideration of how these biasing factors might be integrated into appraisal decisions led to the generation of several research propositions including the following one, based on the idea that biasing factors might have an effect on ratings by leading to the activation of a schema for the ratee that could not be included in some other schema, active for the ratee, such that:

> Biasing factors, such as ratee race and sex, will be considered (i.e., given a nonzero weight) in the final evaluation only to the extent that these variables cannot be integrated into other schema activated for a worker.
>
> (p. 387)

Finally, we considered the role of rater training in processing of information to make a decision. At the time, rater training had been suggested, primarily as a means of avoiding rating "errors" (e.g., Latham, Wexley, & Pursell, 1975; Levine & Butler, 1952; Stockford & Bissell, 1949). Reviews of these programs were generally favorable (cf., Spool, 1978), but there was already an awareness that these training programs did not appear to improve rating accuracy (e.g., Borman, 1975), and Bernardin (1979) had further argued that these rater training programs actually served to *reduce* rating accuracy. Instead, we proposed that rater training would only be successful if it helped raters to better acquire and integrate performance information. We further suggested that the latter goal could be accomplished by training raters to abandon incorrect schemata they were using in their decision making, and to adopt more "accurate" schemata (or at least modify the schemata they had to make them more accurate). We never pursued research on the training programs, but it is interesting to note that similar ideas about training (expressed in much more specific terms) were later developed into Frame of Reference Training (e.g., Pulakos, 1986), and Feldman (1986) even proposed a schema-based training program for improving rating accuracy.

As I noted at the beginning of this section, we considered judgments and ratings as more or less interchangeable in our model. Nonetheless, we did consider the idea that the rating instrument might play a role in the final translation from decision (judgment) to rating. Earlier, Atkin and Conlon (1978) had proposed studying rating scale format from this perspective, but there had been no real research on a "cognitive" role for appraisal instruments. As noted earlier, the instrument was proposed to play a role in the entire process and, although we stated no specific propositions for the role of the rating instrument at this stage of the process, we did continue to pursue learning more about how the rating instrument might influence cognitive processes in performance appraisal.

CONCLUSIONS

The cognitively oriented model proposed by DeNisi, Cafferty, and Meglino (1984) set the stage for some ten years of research aimed at trying to understand how raters acquired the information they used, and how they processed, stored, and eventually recalled that information to make appraisal decisions. As I noted at the beginning of this chapter (and in the previous chapter), ours was not the first cognitive model of the appraisal process although, in its most basic form, the model had its "birth" before the publication of the other models. This model *is* unique to the extent that it has emphasized the role of information acquisition, but it is more important because it guided our research program for some years to come (see Feldman, 1994: 350–351, for an excellent comparison of our model and Feldman's model).

Most of the remainder of this book describes the studies that were conducted in a program of research that was based on this model. But, as will become clear, these studies did not proceed in linear fashion from the model. A number of the research propositions that were part of the paper (and there were twenty-eight in total) were tested, but others were not. When the research program began it was our intent to test every one of these propositions, but findings from some earlier studies suggested to us that things were more complex than we had originally believed, and our research began to broaden beyond the ideas in this model. Thus, for example, our work on patterns of strategies of information acquisition, and the role of appraisal purpose, eventually brought us to the realization that information was often acquired for one purpose but later used for another. This, in turn, led to several experiments dealing with the *reprocessing* of information – a topic we never really considered when the model was being proposed.

Finally, research based on this model led us to consider rating accuracy as the proper dependent variable in our studies. We were not alone in this, and in fact discussions and debates arose over the "best" measure of rating accuracy (and these continue, cf., Day & Sulsky, 1995). But, rather than leading to a decision over the best measure of accuracy, these discussions led to a better understanding of what rating accuracy was and was not. As a result, more recently, there is evidence of a complete coming around to a view that, perhaps, rating accuracy should *not* be the focus of appraisal research (e.g., Ilgen, 1993; DeNisi & Peters, 1995). These are all quite serious and important issues, but they will be discussed in more detail in Chapters 6, 7, and 8.

Again, the point is that, over time, the research program moved far beyond anything we anticipated when we proposed the DeNisi *et al.* 1984) model. Our research agenda shifted as a function of the findings of some of our studies, but it also shifted in response to the findings that other scholars were reporting in the area of performance appraisal, or in social cognition. Thus, for example, some of the ideas about the appropriateness of trait-based evaluations and rater models of effective performance come from Borman's work, and that of his colleagues (Borman, 1978, 1983, 1987, 1991; Borman, White, Pulakos, & Oppler, 1991), while Murphy's work on rating accuracy (e.g., Murphy, 1991; Murphy & Balzer, 1989) was also influential in the conceptualization and design of some of our later studies.

Clearly, not all the research on cognitive process in performance appraisal has been the result of our model, and not even all of our work has been the result of this model. Nonetheless, a considerable amount of research on cognitive processes in performance *has* been the result of this model. In any case, this model provides a good framework for discussing the larger body of research as well as my own program of research. Furthermore, the model provides a good point of departure for discussing the directions that cognitive appraisal research has taken, as well as some thoughts on the directions that research might continue to take over the coming years.

Chapter 3

Research on information acquisition processes

As I noted in the previous two chapters, a distinguishing characteristic of the DeNisi, Cafferty, and Meglino (1984) model, was the emphasis we placed on the acquisition of information raters would use in making appraisal decisions. It followed from this that we should spend a considerable amount of effort in trying to understand how raters acquired information they used, and the implications of these acquisition activities for subsequent evaluations. In fact, much of our effort in this program over the first years was focused on questions of information acquisition strategies, their determinants, and implications.

SOME BACKGROUND

Traditionally, performance appraisal research took the actual information used to make decisions as a given. This is not to say that no one had noted that performance information, as displayed by a ratee, might not have a one-to-one correspondence with the information used by the rater, but this was simply not a major consideration in most of the studies conducted. Wherry (1952; Wherry & Bartlett, 1982), though, had already suggested that information acquisition might be a factor. His model included a term p which referred to the "number of perceptions which contribute to recall at the time of rating" (Wherry & Bartlett, 1982: 532), and his Theorem 4 stated:

> Raters will vary in the accuracy of ratings given in direct proportion to the number of previous relevant contacts with the ratee.
>
> (Wherry & Bartlett, 1982: 532)

From this theorem he further suggested that ratings would be more accurate for ratees where the rater had more frequent contact, and thus more chances to observe relevant performance. It is interesting to note, though, that this also led Wherry to suggest that ratings would be *more* accurate for close job associates, even though others had suggested that proximity might be a source of rating bias (e.g., Hausmann & Strupp, 1955; Kipnis, 1960).

But Wherry was concerned more with the opportunity for observation than with purposeful information acquisition, or even differential attention to information. In fact, others had also noted that performance ratings could be no more accurate than the information upon which they were based (e.g., Guion, 1965), but here too the emphasis was on the availability of information about ratees. Furthermore, long before the "invention" of 360° appraisals (see Tornow, 1993), other researchers had noted that there was rarely convergence among ratings obtained from different sources (i.e., peers, supervisors, subordinates), and many suggested that this was a function (in part) of the information each rater had available upon which to base ratings (e.g., Heneman, 1974; Kavanagh, MacKinney, & Wollins, 1971; Lawler, 1967).

We focused, instead, upon the rater as a more active participant in the process. The rater was seen as someone who needed to make a decision about the performance of a subordinate. Raters clearly encountered performance information as part of their other duties, but we believed that the raters would then evaluate the information they had and decide upon what other types of information they needed to make good evaluations. Much of the idea for this came, not from research on performance appraisal or similar decisions, but from research in consumer behavior.

Specifically, I became familiar with the work of Jacoby and his associates (e.g., Jacoby, Chestnut, Weigel, & Fisher, 1976), dealing with the choices consumers made in areas such as breakfast cereal, and focusing upon the kinds of information consumers sought. In the mid to late 1970s, the U.S. Federal Trade Commission had begun pushing ideas about truth in packaging, and were prompting manufacturers to include detailed information about contents and nutrition on the package. Did consumers actually read and use all this information to make their decisions? Could they process the myriad items of information presented to them? These were the questions driving Jacoby's work, as well as the work of other consumer behaviorists (e.g., Capon, & Burke, 1980; Payne, 1976; Payne, Braunstein, & Caroll, 1978).

The specific methodology used by Jacoby and associates seemed well suited for the study of performance appraisal. They had set up a trailer outside local supermarkets and presented consumers with an information board, as illustrated in Figure 3.1. As noted above, this research was concerned with the purchase of breakfast cereal, but later studies dealt with the purchase of margarine as well. As can be seen in the figure, consumers were presented with a list of brand-name cereals across the top of a large board. Along the side were categories of information about those cereals, including the amount of sugar and the number of calories per serving. The board itself contained cards, so that each "cell" in the "matrix" contained information about one brand of cereal on one attribute.

Consumers were asked to indicate the brand they usually purchased, and asked why, and then were asked to select as many cards as they wished,

	Kellogg's Corn Flakes	Post Raisin Bran	Cheerios	Wheaties
Calories per serving	110	120	125	115
Fat per serving	5 g	7 g	8 g	6 g
Percentage sugar	23%	30%	15%	10%
Per cent of RDA for vitamin C	5%	10%	3%	3%

Figure 3.1 Brand × product attribute information board for breakfast cereal
Note: All entries are fictitious and are meant to be illustrative only.

until they believed they had enough information. The results suggested that consumers were brand loyal, and tended to search within a brand for the most part, although they also sought comparative information about critical characteristics. Some brands were not searched at all, and some categories were largely ignored. (For example, I believe that for the margarine study, very few consumers sought information concerning whether the spread was kosher, but subsequent interviews indicated that "kosher" was not a salient category of information for many of the consumers in West Lafayette, Indiana, at the time.)

It seemed that a reasonable parallel could be drawn to the rater trying to make an appraisal decision. The rater was faced with several ratees (usually), and potential information about a number of tasks. Raters *could* search for as much information as they needed, but searching for information came with a cost, especially since raters typically had many tasks to carry out, and performance appraisal was probably not even the most important of these on a day-to-day basis. Therefore, I concluded that raters would search for only a limited amount of information (this was the finding of the consumer behavior studies as well, and the few studies dealing with performance ratings, such as Wright, 1974; had also found that raters searched for relatively little information before making a decision). This also suggested that we should impose some limitations on the search activities we allowed raters in our experiments, as will be discussed below.

In fact, relying upon the attribution framework discussed earlier, it seemed reasonable to expect raters to search for information in some systematic way, and so, a search for acquisition strategies seemed to follow. But even if such strategies could be identified (and they were), the big question remained whether or not different strategies resulted in different ratings. Specifically, we needed to demonstrate that raters employing one strategy would produce ratings that were more accurate than those employing some other strategy. Such a finding would not only demonstrate the importance of information acquisition activities for the accuracy of ratings but, we hoped, would point to a type of training that focused on the optimal search strategies for raters. These goals were generally met, but, as will be discussed, other factors became clear as well, and the idea of training raters to become better acquirers of information was never pursued. Instead, research on information acquisition strategies led to the realization that the organization of information in memory was perhaps more critical for rating accuracy, and so we turned instead to studying factors that would enable raters to better organize that information.

But all of that came later. In the beginning were simple experiments, mimicking the consumer behavior research. Eventually we employed newer, and hopefully better technologies, and we were able to identify reliable strategies. The quest to relate those strategies to rating accuracy was more illusive, but, eventually, we were able to establish this link as well. We turn, then, to a discussion of those early experiments.

EARLY INFORMATION SEARCH EXPERIMENTS

As noted above, many of the ideas for the study of information search came from the consumer behavior studies being conducted at the time. In my dissertation (DeNisi, 1977) I tried to emulate those studies, but using more interesting technology. I was able to videotape three grocery clerks, employed at a local supermarket, performing a series of eight tasks, including stocking shelves and helping customers. The clerks worked from scripts prepared by me, with their help, so that each exhibited different levels of performance on the tasks. I pilot tested the videotapes, to ensure that subjects (undergraduate students) could distinguish among different levels of performance when they were given performance standards.

For the actual experiment, a subject was seated in a booth, and was given information about the three grocery clerks (simple background and identifying information), performance standards to help them evaluate what they saw, and several questionnaires. On these questionnaires, each subject was asked to rank-order the eight tasks in terms of their relative importance (in the subject's opinion); to rate the relative interpersonal attractiveness of the three clerks (after initial warm-up observation, and again after the observation was complete); and, after the observation was complete, to rate the performance of the three clerks. In order to simulate the constraints that might operate on raters, the subjects could only observe one ratee perform each task, so that each subject observed only eight performance segments, and was asked to rate all three clerks on all eight tasks, as well as provide an overall rating of performance for each. At the beginning of each task, a subject was asked (by me, sitting in a control booth), which clerk they wished to see performing the next task. I could transmit one clerk's performance to each of three booths at a time, so that a subject would see only the clerk he or she requested perform that task.[1]

As I suggested in the previous chapter, the results of that experiment were inconclusive. As it turned out later, the design presented problems for analyses, and in any case no clear patterns of performance emerged. Raters seemed to sample almost randomly, although some random strategies seemed to produce more accurate ratings than others. Interpersonal attractiveness was not a strong determinant of information search, although I noted with interest that ratings of attractiveness changed from the beginning to the end of the study and that, by the end of the study, attractiveness seemed to be a function of observed performance (this general pattern of results became more important in later studies, when interpersonal affect seemed to be a function of observed performance, rather than a biasing factor, e.g., Varma, De-Nisi, & Peters, 1996). But, for the most part, any interpretation of the results seemed unclear given the unreasonable constraints put on the raters, which forced them to make most of their ratings without any clear information.

Despite my disappointment in the results, I continued to believe that rater acquisition was an important process. I wanted to continue to examine information acquisition strategies but, when I went to the University of South Carolina, I found that the facilities needed to replicate the methods used in my dissertation were not available. I therefore needed to identify some alternative technology to use in presenting performance information to raters and the use of information boards, similar to those used by Jacoby on his consumer behavior studies, seemed promising. In a series of experiments with Cafferty and Meglino, we used the job of "Administrative Assistant," and provided information on four ratees (Anne, Betty, Cathy, Dianne) performing four tasks (budget preparation, typing memos, answering customer phone inquiries, and file clerk supervision). Thus we constructed a matrix with sixteen cells, and each cell represented information about a ratee's performance on a task.

As we began to work on this, our thinking moved in the direction of attribution theory. Perhaps the matrix format for information presentation helped this but, as described earlier, we began to conceive of the task facing a rater as similar to that facing someone trying to make a causal attribution for the behavior of a target. Such a view required a third dimension to our matrix, however. We had information about persons and tasks, but we needed to have information about *multiple* incidents of performance for each person on each task. Thus, we included four incidents (i.e., four cards) of performance, so that each ratee performed each task well sometimes, but badly at others. Now we had an array of sixty-four total incidents, and we could begin to study information acquisition from an attributional framework. Figure 3.2 presents a version of our array, indicating how we hoped to portray the consensus, consistency, and distinctiveness information used to make attributions.

Our earliest experiments with this information board began with asking raters to indicate which task they felt was the most critical to the job. We

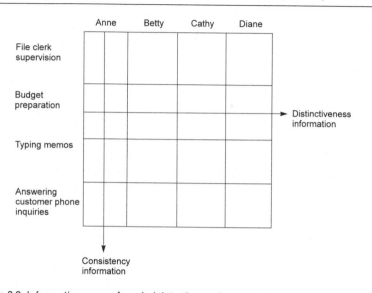

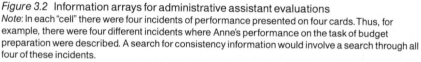

Figure 3.2 Information arrays for administrative assistant evaluations
Note: In each "cell" there were four incidents of performance presented on four cards. Thus, for example, there were four different incidents where Anne's performance on the task of budget preparation were described. A search for consistency information would involve a search through all four of these incidents.

rotated the order of the ratees across trials, but *not* the order of the tasks. This was, as it happened, a serious mistake. Our initial results indicated that most raters believed that the "file clerk supervision" was the most important task in the Administrative Assistant's job and we found that most raters also searched most extensively from this category before making appraisal decisions. We let raters acquire as much information as they wished before making ratings but found that, although some raters searched through almost all of the information, others searched through only a handful of incidents, and, on average, raters acquired about thirty pieces of information (just less than half) before making a decision. We reported the results of these preliminary experiments in 1982 (DeNisi, Cafferty, Meglino, Williams, & Blencoe, 1982), and thought we had begun to understand how raters searched for the information they used in making appraisal decisions.

But, as I noted, we never varied the position of the various tasks, and information about supervision was always in the upper left corner of the information board. When we realized that this category was searched most frequently in part because it was the *first* category searched, we were concerned that this position effect might explain our results. We then searched for an alternative method for presenting the information that would eliminate position effects, by eliminating "the upper left hand corner." After some thought, we began replicating the earlier experiments with the information presented on a cylinder (actually, a plastic trash barrel, with the information in pockets that were taped to the side). Fortunately, we continued to find that raters searched most heavily from the category they felt was most important, and clearer patterns of information search were beginning to emerge.

NEW TECHNOLOGY AND NEW DIRECTIONS

The results with the trash barrel were never published, since they were simply meant to rule out position effect explanations for our earlier results. Although the barrels eliminated some of the problems of presentation, they seemed a distraction to the subjects, and so we searched for alternative means for information presentation. Two Ph.D. students (Kevin Williams and Allyn Blencoe) joined our project, and with their help and the money from the National Science Foundation, we decided that we needed to produce a new set of videotapes that could serve as stimulus material for information acquisition studies, as well as for other studies we might conduct in the future. We began the process of developing and producing those tapes (which will be described later), but we also sought an interim solution to replace the trash barrels. Our two students supplied that solution by writing and installing a program for a micro-computer which presented an array of information to the subject, who was then asked to select a "cell" (identified according to person, task, and incidence). Subjects could be shown the information on the computer screen, and the program could keep track of which choices the subject made.

Two experiments on information acquisition were designed to employ the computers (DeNisi, Cafferty, Williams, Blencoe, & Meglino, 1983). In both experiments, just as in the previous studies, we presented information on four file clerks, performing four tasks, on four separate occasions. Also, in Experiment 1, as previously, raters were allowed to request as many pieces of information as they wished, but the mean was thirty pieces of information. This time, however, we used the information contained in the computer to try to characterize the specific strategy employed by the subject in searching through the information. As illustrated in Figure 3.3, we started with the first choice the subject made. For example, let us suppose the subject chose to see Anne typing on one occasion. If, on the next trial, the rater chose to see Anne typing again, the rater was scored as making one choice for consistency information. If, instead, the rater chose to see Anne doing a different task, the rater was scored as having made one choice for distinctiveness information; and a choice to see a different target person typing was scored as a choice for consensus information.

These were, of course, the three types of information considered in attribution research, and so these were the major focus of our study. Specifically, we wanted to see if some types of information were favored over others, and we had predicted that, in the case of Experiment 1, there

Choice 1:   Anne typing memos
Choice 2:   Anne typing memos (second incident)
Score: 1 choice for consistency information

Choice 1:   Anne typing memos
Choice 2:   Anne supervising file clerks
Score: 1 choice for distinctiveness information

Choice 1:   Anne typing memos
Choice 2:   Betty typing memos
Score: 1 choice for consensus information

Choice 1:   Anne typing memos
Choice 2:   Betty supervising file clerks
Score: 1 choice for "mixed" information

Figure 3.3   Scoring scheme for search strategies study

would be a preference for "distinctiveness information". This prediction was based on the work of Hansen (1980), who suggested that an "economic" decision maker might not really need all three types of information to make attributional decisions. Instead, he argued, if a rater gathered distinctiveness information, he or she would learn how well the ratee performed in a number of situations, which would allow the rater to draw an inference about the ratee's ability, which would make other judgments easier. Hansen (1980) also suggested that a good, but less effective, alternative would be to search for consensus information, and therefore we predicted that consensus would be the second preferred information type (given that these raters would probably *not* have clear performance standards).

But, before moving to the results, it is important to recognize that there is another "type" of information that a rater might seek in our study (illustrated in the fourth case in Figure 3.3). If we think about the information types in terms of changes between choices, this should become clear. After an initial choice, if a rater changes the target person, but keeps the same task, she or he is searching for consensus information; a change of task, but not ratee, indicates distinctiveness information; and a change of occasion only, while keeping with the same ratee *and* task, would indicate a search for consistency information. But what if the rater chose to change *both ratee and task*? This type of comparative information does not correspond to any of the types of information considered in attribution research, but was a viable alternative here as well. We called this a search for "mixed information."

The results for our 140 undergraduate raters, indicated that distinctiveness information was sought 44% of the time, followed by consensus information (30%), consistency information (18%), and "mixed" information (8%). We transformed the percentages, analyzed the data using analysis of variance and post hoc (Scheffe) tests, which, together, told us that each mean was significantly different from the others. Thus we found that raters did seem to prefer distinctiveness information for making appraisal decisions, although these *were* rather naive raters, and they were able to acquire all the information they wished.

Therefore, in Experiment 2, we replicated the study but now imposed a limit on the amount of information a rater could acquire. This time, sixty undergraduate subjects were studied, using similar procedures to those described above. A few changes were made, however. First, the number of ratees was increased to five, and the number of tasks was increased to five as well (preparing written reports was added). Next, since consistency information had been sought relatively infrequently in Experiment 1, and since there was no basis for expecting the frequency to increase under constraints, we eliminated multiple occurrences and presented just one occurrence per ratee per task. Finally, we constrained the number of choices a rater could make to nine (in fact, somewhat arbitrary, but equal to the number of ratees + the number of tasks − 1). We also collected information about the perceived relative importance of the tasks, since we thought this might help explain some choices under such harsh constraints.

Since all subjects chose exactly nine pieces of information, we analyzed the absolute frequency for each type of information, using the same scoring procedures as described above. Still relying upon Hansen (1980) we predicted that, given the constraints, raters would seek more consensus type information than any other type, and that the task selected to make the comparisons would be the task seen as most important. In fact, we found that "budget preparation" was rated as the most important task, and it was also the task where information was sought the most often (142 choices vs. 106 for the second most important task).

But, counter to prediction, consensus information was *not* the most frequently requested type of information. Instead, "mixed" information was requested 58% of the time, followed by consensus information (34%), and distinctiveness information (8%), and these frequencies were significantly different from each other.

With the results of these two studies, then, we had established that raters did seek information related to the type of information used in making attributions; that their choices of information type could be predicted from attribution theory; and that putting constraints on information acquisitions had a significant impact on search behavior. This latter finding supported the role of time constraints in our model as well. But the most intriguing finding, for us, was the importance of the "mixed information" when choices were constrained. This type of information did not correspond to any type of information studied in attribution research, but it *did* seem to be an efficient strategy. A rater seeking primarily mixed information, recall, would switch *both* ratee and task from one choice to the next. Thus, given a limited number of choices, a rater employing this as a primary strategy would maximize the number of *both* ratees and tasks she or he observed.

There would not be much depth of information on any one person or task, but the rater would get to sample all ratees and all tasks. This trade-off of breadth for depth seemed quite reasonable, and so it was not surprising that, eventually, we became *most* interested in information acquisition following this pattern – but we will return to this a bit later.

THE NEXT STEP AND NEW PROBLEMS

With the results reported in the DeNisi, Cafferty, Williams, Blencoe, and Meglino (1983) paper we had begun to understand search activities in the appraisal process but, unless we could also relate those activities to appraisal decisions, this would be just an academic exercise. Before discussing the efforts to establish the link between search and rating, though, there are a few other developments worth mentioning. In the discussions above, as in our discussions and writings at the time, we had tied ourselves to attribution theory, and to approaching the appraisal process primarily from an attribution framework. This is why, in part, we labeled types of information as consensus, consistency, and distinctiveness information. When we presented these data, however, some members of the audience objected to our use of the labels from attribution theory. They argued that we could not be sure raters were actually looking for distinctiveness information. All we could be sure of was that they were searching for information in a pattern that resembled someone looking for distinctiveness information.

In response, we dropped the labels from attribution theory and began using more generic labels, which were also being used in the social cognition literature. As a result, searching for information for ratee no. 1 on a task, followed by information for ratee no. 1 on a second task, etc. (formerly labeled as a search for distinctiveness information), was labeled as searching for "person-blocked information." Searching for information on ratee no. 1 performing a task, followed by information for ratee no. 2 on the *same* task (formerly labeled as searching for consensus information) was termed searching for "task-blocked information," and our "mixed" category was now termed "unblocked information." Since, in all the experiments we had conducted at this time, no one had searched for much information across occasions (i.e., "consistency information"), we didn't worry about a new label for this type of information and, in fact, this type of information is generally not prominent in social cognition research either.

We also began trying to identify individual differences that might predict preferences for search strategies. That is, we wanted to know if we could identify any such variables that might predict a preference for person-blocked, task-blocked, or unblocked acquisition strategies. It seemed as though cognitively oriented variables might relate to preferences for different types of information and/or ability to process more or less complex sets of information, and so this is where we began to look. For example, Stone

(1979) had demonstrated that field dependence–independence was related to how persons perceived task characteristics, and it seemed that this might be related to information acquisition as well. In a series of experiments, we used the same information acquisition design as we did earlier, but examined how field dependence might be related to search strategies. We operationalized field dependence by using the Group Embedded Figures Test (Oltman, Raskin, Witkin, & Karp, 1971), and even by using some measures we developed ourselves, but found no relationships between field dependence and any search or acquisition activities.

There was also some discussion in the literature about the importance of cognitive complexity in the appraisal process (see Schneier, 1977) and so we examined this possibility as well. We used a measure based on the Grid Repertory and, again, found no relationship between cognitive complexity and search activities (Bernardin, Cardy, & Carlyle, 1982, eventually concluded that cognitive complexity was not a useful individual difference in appraisal decisions). At this point we gave up trying. We could not identify an individual difference that determined search activities, but we did go back to our model and think about another potential determinant of search activities – the purpose of the appraisal.

As our model suggested, the appraisals conducted for different purposes might cause raters to search for different types of information, resulting in different acquisition activities. The policy capturing results reported by Zedeck and Cascio (1982) suggested that appraisal purpose might influence what information a rater attended to, and, of course, this was part of our appraisal model as well. But we faced a problem in trying to figure out a way to operationalize appraisal purpose in a meaningful way in a laboratory setting.

If we think about the dimensions of appraisal purpose that would be relevant for affecting information acquisition (or any cognitive processes) they would have to include the consequences of the decision for both the rater and the ratee (these would be a major factor in rater motivation to be accurate as well). But this is difficult to capture in a laboratory because, for the most part, everyone understands that appraisal decisions made in the lab have no consequences for either party, and so we weren't sure it would make much difference if we told raters that their ratings would be used for salary decisions (when no one was being paid) or disciplinary decisions (when no one was being disciplined).

In order to deal with these difficulties and yet capture some aspects of appraisal purpose, we decided to operationalize purpose along two dimensions. One was consistent with the traditional idea of purpose, and meant telling raters that their ratings would be used for salary decision, discipline, feedback, etc. But the other dimension was concerned with whether the raters were asked to single one person out for a treatment, or to rate how *deserving* each ratee was of a treatment. For example, if we told raters they were making salary decisions, we asked them either to select one ratee for a 15% salary increase (a "designation decision") or to tell us the extent to which each ratee deserved a 15% salary increase (a "deservedness decision"). We conducted two experiments – one dealing with how purpose affects acquisition and one dealing with how purpose affects processing, but we found significant effects only on acquisition.

Specifically, Williams, DeNisi, Blencoe, and Cafferty (1985) presented information about five administrative assistants performing five different tasks as before. Raters were either told that they would rate how deserving of an outcome each ratee was, or that they would select one ratee for that outcome. As noted above, the outcomes included a 15% pay increase, a promotion, disciplinary action, or remedial training. We again had subjects make requests for information via a computer and analyzed their choice strategies. Overall, we found that raters exhibited a continued preference for person-blocked information (similar to distinctiveness information) in all conditions. But we did find effects for appraisal purpose on the search for task-blocked information (similar to consensus information). Raters who were asked to make deservedness decisions were more likely to search for task-blocked information than were raters asked to make designation decisions. Although both tasks required comparisons, apparently raters believed that providing ratings for all ratees required comparative information on all ratees. Finally, it was interesting to note that this tendency was even stronger when raters were asked to rate the deservedness of all ratees for a pay increase. The results for this experiment are summarized in Table 3.1.

Table 3.1 Proportion of covariance information requested by appraisal purpose and outcome

Appraisal outcome	Appraisal purpose								
	Promotion			Salary increase			Training		
	Consistency	Distinctiveness	Consensus	Consistency	Distinctiveness	Consensus	Consistency	Distinctiveness	Consensus
Deservedness	.14	.45	.34	.29	.52	.15	.11	.55	.28
Designation	.18	.48	.26	.16	.28	.47	.14	.46	.28

Thus, we found that the purpose of the appraisal did seem related to the kinds of information raters would seek, even in a laboratory study. With the addition of this study, we also had considered three potential influences on information acquisition activities. We had found that raters did respond to constraints on the number of pieces of information they could seek by moving towards an unblocked search strategy. We also found that neither cognitive complexity nor field dependence were related to search strategies. And we found that raters who were asked to make deservedness decisions were more likely to seek comparative information (i.e., task-blocked information) than were raters asked to make designation decisions.

Despite these successes, we still needed to establish the link between these search and acquisition activities and appraisal decisions. Unfortunately, repeated attempts to establish such a relationship failed. In each case we had raters request information via computer, as before, tracked their acquisition strategy, asked them to rate the administrative assistants, and then we tried to relate search strategies to ratings. We varied the instructions to the raters for acquiring information; we reduced, and then increased, the numbers of ratees and tasks; we looked at specific dimensional ratings as well as at overall performance, but none of these efforts produced the results we were looking for. As frustrating as these failures were, we could not give up because, if we could not establish this link, the importance of all our other efforts would be diminished.

It is somewhat ironic that the solution to the problem was related to an issue that I had faced in trying to interpret my dissertation results. That is, two raters engaging in different information acquisition strategies are also going to have available to them different information upon which to base ratings. Therefore, given a single ratee being observed by two different raters (along with other ratees), each of whom was employing a different information acquisition strategy, we were interested in whether the pattern in which the information was acquired would make a difference. The two raters in the example would surely differ in these patterns, but they might also differ in terms of the actual information available to them, since they might well be observing different behaviors. By allowing raters to freely access the available information, our various raters were each making appraisal decisions based on different information. When we then looked for relationships with search strategies we were confounding the patterns of information acquisition with the actual information acquired, and the differences in ratings *due to* differences in information acquired were masking any differences due to patterns of information acquisition. It became clear that, in order to detect any effects for acquisition pattern on ratings, we would have to control for actual information, and just allow pattern to vary. When we came to this realization and designed a study to examine the link once more, we had also begun to realize that memory processes (encoding of information) played a role in this relationship. Therefore the study we designed not only overcame our problems with controlling for information, it also examined the role of information storage in memory, in determining the link between acquisition strategy and ratings.

LINKING ACQUISITION WITH RATINGS

Our 1986 study (Cafferty, DeNisi, & Williams, 1986) finally established the link we were looking for. We conducted two studies which, together, would establish that information acquisition patterns influenced the way in which information was stored in memory which, in turn, influenced the accuracy of both recall and ratings. We drew upon our earlier work as well as the social cognition research of the time, but our study also marked a departure from much of that social cognition research.

A number of studies had examined patterns of information organization in memory, and how these patterns were related to subsequent recall of that information (e.g., Hernstein, Carroll, & Hayes, 1981; Ostrom, Pryor, & Simpson, 1981; Pryor & Ostrom, 1981; Pryor, Ostrom, Dukerich, Mitchell, & Hernstein, 1983; Srull, 1983; Srull & Brand, 1983). These authors had generally concluded that: (a) in order to facilitate recall of information, that information had to be stored in memory in some pattern; and (b) information presented to subjects (or acquired by them) in a pattern, was more likely to be stored in memory according to that pattern. That is, raters who were presented (or who acquired) information blocked by persons (ratees) would be more likely to organize that information in memory according to persons. This organization should then facilitate subsequent recall of that information, compared to a rater who was not able (for whatever reasons) to organize information in memory in any meaningful pattern.

Referring again to the work of Hansen (1980), we suggested further that presenting information blocked by persons would induce memory organization by persons, which would lead to more accurate recall, and more accurate evaluations, than would any other organizing pattern. We began to diverge from the social cognition researchers in our emphasis on rating accuracy, but a more critical divergence was based on the nature of the information we were presenting.

Typically, in a social cognition experiment, subjects were presented with *individuated* information. That is, the information presented about each target person involves a unique set of attributes or activities that tends to accentuate the individuality of the target. Thus, they might be told that Tom Hanks is an actor, Tony Bennett is a singer, and Anne Rice is an author. But, in an appraisal setting, raters would typically be presented with non-individuated information, where each target would be described relative to the same attributes or activities. Thus, to continue with the example, they might be told that Tom Hanks, Paul Newman, and Jack Nicholson are all actors, but be told something about recent performance for each and be asked to rate their acting ability. Pryor and Ostrom (1981) had actually suggested that this type of information was not conducive to any organization in memory, and so we had to determine if non-individuated information *could* be organized in memory, and whether this information followed the same rule for organization as did individuated information.

Thus we set out to identify, again, patterns of information acquisition, and then to relate these patterns to patterns of organization in memory, which were then to be related to recall and rating accuracy. In the first of two experiments we conducted as part of this paper, we looked at patterns of acquisition. Subjects (forty-one undergraduates) were asked to search (via computer) through sixty-four performance vignettes describing four administrative assistants, each performing four different tasks, on four separate occasions. The target persons and the tasks were the same we had used earlier, and the subjects could search for as much information as they wished. They were told that the ultimate purpose of their search was to provide information they could use to rate the performance of the four administrative assistants. In fact, after acquiring the information, each subject rated the performance of the four ratees, even though we could not analyze these ratings data because of the problems I described earlier with ratings based on unique information.

We analyzed the data for information acquisition much as we had previously (i.e., by examining transitions), but we also analyzed these data by computing Adjusted Ratio of Clustering (ARC) scores based on patterns of search. These indices (Roenker, Thompson, & Brown, 1971) were typically used for analyzing information organization in recall (e.g., Murphy, 1979; Srull, 1983), and required a priori stipulation of categories for clustering.[2] we also used these indices for analyzing the acquisition data, which allowed us to express both search and organization in memory in common terms. The two methods yielded comparable results and, although we classified subjects according to their dominant search strategy, the results basically confirmed our earlier findings. In situations of unconstrained search, most raters sought information blocked by persons, followed by information blocked by tasks, and followed further by information blocked by occasion, and information acquired in the "mixed" pattern described earlier (i.e., unblocked).

With these results, the stage was set for the second experiment where subjects (125 undergraduate students) were presented (using a large screen overhead projector) with information pertaining to the same four administrative assistants performing the same tasks on separate occasions. Pre-testing and practical considerations led to each subject seeing sixteen performance vignettes, consisting of four incidents each for four target ratees. Although we counterbalanced order of ratees and tasks in each condition, every rater saw one target performing well on three tasks and poorly on one (75% effective performance), two targets performing well on two tasks and poorly on two (50% effective performance), and one target perform well on one task and poorly on three (25% effective performance). Approximately one-third of the subjects were presented with the information blocked by person (all the incidents for one target followed by all the incidents for a second target, etc.); one-third were presented with the information blocked by task (all ratees performing one task followed by all ratees performing a second task, etc.); and one-third were presented with the information in an unblocked format (neither ratee nor task were repeated from one incident to the next), as illustrated in Figure 3.4.

Condition 1: Person-blocked presentation

> Anne performing typing task
> Anne performing supervision task
> Anne performing telephone inquiry task
> Anne performing budget task
> Betty performing telephone inquiry task
> Betty performing supervision task
> Betty performing typing task
> Betty performing budget task
> Cathy performing supervision task
> etc.

Condition 2: Task-blocked presentation

> Cathy performing typing task
> Dianne performing typing task
> Anne performing typing task
> Betty performing typing task
> Dianne performing telephone inquiry task
> Cathy performing telephone inquiry task
> etc.

Condition 3: Unblocked presentation

> Betty performing budget task
> Cathy performing typing task
> Dianne performing telephone inquiry task
> Anne performing supervision task
> Cathy performing budget task
> Betty performing typing task
> Anne performing telephone inquiry task
> Dianne performing supervision task
> etc.

Figure 3.4 Design for information presentation (Study 2)
Source: Cafferty, DeNisi, and Williams (1986)

Subjects viewed each incident for approximately 30 seconds, but were *not* told that they would be asked to either recall the information they saw, or rate the performance of the targets (this, as we shall discuss later, may have been a problem since it would likely reduce the incidence of person clustering and would increase the level of memory-based processing). After completing the viewing, subjects were given an interpolated task (an embedded figures task), before we asked them to write down all the incidents they could recall, in any pattern they wished. After we collected these data, we asked the subjects to rate the performance of each ratee on each individual task, as well as on their overall performance using 7-point rating scales.

We first examined the pattern of clustering in memory, by computing ARC scores based on the recall data. We computed scores for organization by persons, tasks, and by performance level (good vs. poor performance), and the mean ARC scores for each clustering type, under each presentation pattern, are presented below in Table 3.2. The results of an ANOVA on these scores indicated that there was significantly less clustering by performance level than by either person or task; that there was significantly less clustering of any type when information was presented in an unblocked format, but that there was significantly more person clustering when information was presented blocked by persons (there was not a corresponding significant effect when information was presented blocked by task), suggesting that the pattern of information presented did influence how the information was organized in memory.

Table 3.2 ARC clustering scores under three presentation patterns

Clustering format	Presentation pattern		
	Person-blocked	Task-blocked	Mixed
Person ARC score	.60	.00	−.13[a]
Task ARC score	−.14[a]	.49	.10
Performance level ARC score	.06	−.02[a]	−.11[a]

Note: [a] ARC scores are not interpretable if they are negative. Although this can happen as a result of computational procedures, negative ARC scores are usually interpreted to mean there is no evidence of clustering of the type under consideration.
Source: Cafferty, DeNisi, and Williams (1986: 680)

We next examined the recall data themselves, noting the number of incidents recalled in each condition as well as the number (and per cent) of incidents recalled correctly and incorrectly. In addition, we analyzed the number of correct recalls and errors simultaneously, using an adaptation of a memory improvement score suggested by Graesser, Woll, Kowalski, and Smith (1980), which allowed us to compute the extent to which accurate recall was improved over chance levels.[3] These results, presented in Table 3.3, indicated (based on ANOVAs and post-hoc tests following significant effects) that the presentation pattern was important for recall (explaining 22% of the variance in recall), and that person-blocked presentation resulted in more incidents recalled than the other two conditions (which did not differ significantly from each other), and more incidents correctly recalled than in the other conditions, but that this condition also resulted in more incidents recalled *incorrectly* than in the other conditions (presentation pattern explained 28% and 14% respectively, of the variance in correct recall and incorrect recall). Finally, memory improvements scores differed only to the extent that mixed presentation produced poorer memory improvement than either person- or task-blocked presentation, which did not differ significantly from each other.

Finally, we examined the ratings themselves – for us the most critical aspect of the results. These results, presented below in Table 3.3, indicated

Table 3.3 Recall data under three presentation patterns

| | Presentation patterns | | | | | |
| Number of items recalled | Person-blocked | | Task-blocked | | Mixed | |
	Number	*%*	*Number*	*%*	*Number*	*%*
Total	9.72	100	6.87	100	7.50	100
Correct	6.02	62	4.74	69	3.97	53
Incorrect	3.69	38	2.13	31	3.53	47
Memory improvement score		.18		.20		.04

Source: Cafferty, DeNisi, and Williams (1986: 680)

that subjects in the three conditions could *all* distinguish among overall levels of performance. That is, there were no differences across condition in raters' ability to differentiate the 75% effective performer from the 50% effective performer from the 25% effective performer. There were, however, differences in subjects' ability to distinguish between different levels of performance exhibited by the same ratee on different tasks. Specifically, only those subjects who were presented the information blocked by tasks were able to discriminate between the good and poor performance incidents for a given ratee (post hoc tests all indicated that means differed significantly from each other, $p < .05$), and this was true for all three levels of overall performance.

Thus we had established that the pattern of information presentation (or acquisition) had an effect on the way information was stored in memory, and that these differences in memory organization resulted in differences in

Table 3.4 Mean performance ratings for overall performance, and good and poor performance incidents at each level of effectiveness under three presentation patterns

| Overall target performance effectiveness | Presentation patterns | | |
	Person-blocked	Task-blocked	Mixed
25% effective target			
Good incidents	3.53	4.30	3.33
Poor incidents	3.65	3.50	3.79
Overall performance	3.75	3.53	3.79
50% effective target			
Good incidents	4.21	4.26	4.22
Poor incidents	3.85	3.56	3.82
Overall performance	4.13	3.96	4.25
75% effective target			
Good incidents	4.84	4.83	4.59
Poor incidents	4.08	3.55	4.02
Overall performance	4.89	4.83	4.79

Source: Cofferty, DeNisi, and Williams (1986)

the accuracy of recall and ratings. Although the results indicated that *task*-blocked presentation was superior to person-blocked information, which was contrary to what we had predicted (and what had been suggested in the literature), we did find evidence that rater information search strategies were a factor in the accuracy of their ratings. Our suspicions about why the results turned out as they did, rather than as we had predicted, are discussed below. This had been the linkage we were struggling to establish, and our findings vindicated the importance we had placed on information acquisition in the appraisal process. But although we were pleased with this development, there were several aspects of this study that need further discussion. In addition, these results helped move our research in a direction that will be discussed in the next chapter.

FURTHER CONSIDERATION OF THE RESULTS AND A NEW DIRECTION

The first important issue about these results, other than the fact that our link had been established, was related to the failure of person-blocked presentation (and organization in memory) to produce the most accurate ratings. At the time, we thought that our results had deviated from what we had predicted (i.e., task-blocked organization produced more accurate ratings than person-blocked organization) because we had examined non-individuated information. Perhaps, we argued, person-blocked information acquisition resulted in halo error (i.e., the *inability* to discriminate among different levels of performance exhibited by the same ratee on different tasks). This would not have been evident in studies employing individuated information, and this would constitute a limitation of social cognition research for studies of the appraisal process (see Ilgen & Favero, 1985, for a fuller discussion of these limitations).

But, as we shall discuss later, in subsequent studies, we consistently found that person blocked information and/or organization in memory according to persons produced the most accurate recall and ratings. Instead, in hindsight, the problem seemed to lie with our instructions (or lack thereof) to the subjects. Recall that subjects were not told that they would be asked to either recall or rate the performance they observed. Subsequent work (Hastie & Park, 1986) which will be discussed later, suggested that, by not alerting subjects to their need to later recall and rate performance, we forced the subjects to engage in memory-based information processing. Since raters in the field would always know that performance appraisal would be one purpose behind their observation of ratee performance, this was not an accurate approximation of the field conditions we wanted to emulate. Furthermore, by then asking for recall and ratings, we were also forcing raters to reprocess the information they had collected for a different purpose. We did not know, of course, what purpose subjects had in mind when they were observing the performance incidents, and some of them may have suspected that the ultimate goal was evaluation, but this was a problem in generalizing our results. Thus, although we had established that the pattern of information acquisition was related to ratings, we could not be sure that person-blocked acquisition was, in fact, the preferred pattern, and in fact it turned out not to be.

In any event, these results led us to reconsider some of the directions our research had been taking. We saw a need to consider the role of reprocessing objectives (i.e., information acquired for one purpose which later had to be used for a different purpose), and we began to explore how this might influence cognitive processing. Perhaps more critically, though, we began to see an extremely important role in these processes for information acquired in an unblocked pattern. The results of this study, and the earlier search studies, had indicated that raters often *did* purposefully acquire information in an unblocked format. In fact, especially under conditions of constrained search, this even seemed to be a reasonably smart strategy for a rater to employ. But we had realized all along that, even though we were concentrating on purposeful acquisition, a great deal of the information a rater would acquire for making appraisal decisions would be acquired more casually. That is, just by performing other job duties, a rater would be likely to encounter performance information about ratees. This information was likely to be encountered almost at random, and so was unlikely to be blocked. Thus, we reasoned, a significant proportion of the information that raters would acquire, either through purposeful search or through less purposeful encounters, would be unblocked. Unfortunately, the results of our study (i.e., Cafferty, DeNisi, & Williams, 1986) had indicated that information acquired in this way could not easily be organized in memory, making it less accessible for recall and resulting in less accurate ratings.

Instead of continuing to study the information acquisition process and other factors that might influence how information was acquired, then, we realized that how information was organized in memory might be more important for determining rating accuracy. Furthermore, we realized that much of the information used to make appraisal decisions probably had been collected for some purpose other than appraisal, and so needed to be reprocessed before it could be used for evaluations. Finally, we realized that, in our 1986 study, we had used a very specific definition of rating accuracy – one that seemed closely linked to the absence of halo error – an issue that will be discussed further later. In any event, in the next chapter, I will discuss how the realization that information must be organized in memory according to some pattern, if raters are to be capable of making accurate ratings, led to a series of studies which examined the effectiveness of different interventions designed to impose order and organization to unorganized information acquired by raters.

NOTES

1 I was able to follow these procedures only because the Krannert Graduate School of Management at Purdue University allowed me to use their Behavioral Laboratories for my dissertation. They also allowed me to draw upon the technical assistance of Ben Mayes, the director of those labs.

2 The formula for the Adjusted Ratio of Clustering is as follows:

$$ARC = \frac{R - E(R)}{Max\,R - E(R)}$$

Where R = total number of observed repetitions,
Max R = N − k (where N = number of recalled items; k = number of target categories
$E(R) = (\varepsilon m(l)^2/N) - 1$. Values for ARC can range from 0.00 (no clustering) to 1.00 (perfect clustering).

3 Corrected score = [p (recalled) − p (errors)] / [1 − p (errors)].

Chapter 4

Reprocessing objectives and interventions designed to impose organization in memory

The Cafferty, DeNisi, and Williams (1986) paper marked the end of the first part of our research program and the beginning of the second. Specifically, the first phase of the research program had been concerned with the development of a model and the testing of several research propositions from that model, all dealing with the importance of the acquisition of performance information. After the studies demonstrating that there were identifiable patterns of acquisition, our attention moved to tying those patterns to actual appraisal decisions. But once that relationship was established, we did not continue to test other research propositions from our model. Instead, the second "phase" of the research program involved testing propositions and ideas that had been generated by the findings of the various studies we carried out in the earlier phase.

As I noted in the previous chapter, one important thing we learned was that information organization was critical for the success of the appraisal process. It had been clear all along that, since formal appraisals were typically infrequent events in organizations, it was critical that we understand how raters stored information in memory, so that they could later recall it and use it to make ratings. Furthermore, we were able to establish a relationship between acquisition activities and ratings only by recognizing the importance of the intervening step of how information was organized in memory. The critical realization, though, was that *most* of the information raters used for making appraisal decisions had to be acquired in a way that would make it difficult for that information to be organized in memory. Whether the information was acquired through purposeful search using an unblocked strategy, or through more casual encounters with ratees on the job, raters needed to deal with a great deal of performance information that was inherently unorganized, and which might be difficult to organize. Thus it seemed clear that we should therefore turn our attention to interventions that could be carried out by the rater or by the organization, which would allow the rater to impose some structure and organization on that information.

Also, as noted in the previous chapter, it became clear that, since a great deal of information would be acquired more casually, it was probably acquired for some reason other than a performance appraisal. For example, a rater/supervisor might ask a ratee/subordinate about work schedules, problems with other employees, possible training, or even last Saturday's college football game and, in doing so, might acquire performance information. This information would probably not be structured, and might not even be stored in memory with the goal of later using it for appraisal decisions. Perhaps there would be an attempt to somehow restructure, or at least reschedule work, and the rater would be collecting performance information to aid her or his decisions about how best to do that. This information might be stored in some pattern that would aid in those decisions, such as organized according to task or the sequence of performance, as opposed to a pattern that might make appraisal decisions easier, such as organization according to persons. In any case, the rater who was then faced with making appraisal decisions would have to reach back into memory, recall the information, and then reprocess it to make it more amenable to those appraisal decisions. Studying the role of reprocessing objectives also brought us into closer contact with the importance of on-line and memory-based processing as suggested by Hastie and Park (1986).

The present chapter will describe those studies conducted to examine interventions, as well as those designed to examine the importance of reprocessing objectives. In the process, I shall also discuss how the consideration of on-line vs. memory-based processing played a role in the research project. The material in this chapter is important for another reason as well. As the research program moved in other directions, much of that work was based on the findings reported here. For example, these studies led to a more serious consideration of the definition of rating accuracy. As I noted earlier, there has been considerable debate over the definition and measurement of accuracy, and this put us in the middle of that debate that led some of us to question whether or not rating accuracy is really the proper goal of appraisal research. Also, much of the field research that will be described in Chapter 6 has been an attempt to generalize the findings of studies discussed here to field settings. Finally, as I close the book with some thoughts about where this research might lead me and others in the future, many of the ideas follow from the results of the studies to be described in the present chapter. Therefore, I see this as a critical juncture in the program and so we turn, first, to a series of studies dealing with the role for reprocessing objectives, and next to studies dealing with possible interventions that could help raters impose structure on information in memory. Before we move to the studies, however, there was an additional technological advance that is worth discussing, as it provided new stimulus material for the other laboratory experiments we conducted.

VIDEOTAPED PERFORMANCE INCIDENTS

In describing the earliest experiments conducted on information acquisition, I told of our use of information boards and even plastic trash barrels to present information to raters. Eventually, we were able to present the performance information via computer, but we were still missing an important part of the appraisal process. Since the information was presented in textual form, the rater had no ambiguity about what she or he was "seeing." For example, when describing an administrative assistant performing a typing task, the card (or computer file) might say that she made five errors, or that she made no errors. In both cases the rater has a clear picture of how good the performance was. Recall that, in my dissertation, I used videotapes of grocery clerks which did require the rater to make a judgment about the level of performance displayed, but producing enough videotaped vignette to conduct the subsequent studies I described (usually sixty-four available incidents) was prohibitively costly. When we received our grant from the National Science Foundation, though, we had access to the funds we needed to produce enough videotapes to make their use viable.

The first problem, though, was to decide what job we would use in the videotapes. We thought first of the administrative assistant, since that was the job we had used in the previous studies. But we realized that it would be very difficult to *show* a person making typing errors without being too obvious. We needed a job where performance was visual, and where, without calling too much attention to the error (or absence of errors), we could portray different levels of performance. Furthermore, we needed to find a job where we could actually find people who could perform it well and who would allow us to videotape them.

At the time, Tom Cafferty was enrolled in a beginners' carpentry course at a local technical college, and he suggested that carpentry tasks might provide the job setting we needed. These tasks could be separated into definable segments, and the skills required to perform each segment were relatively simple and easy to explain. Furthermore, specific errors could be described for each segment of each task, and it was relatively easy to show when a worker was making one of these errors. It was also relatively easy to explain (and show) how each of these errors would affect the final product, and we thought that a videotaped presentation of various carpentry tasks might be more interesting than some other tasks we might have used. We therefore contacted Tom's instructor (John Scullion) and, after several meetings, arranged for a group of more advanced students to appear in our videotapes, performing five carpentry tasks related to the construction of three common objects. The objects were a tool chest, a work bench, and a bookcase, and the tasks were sawing pieces of wood, sanding the wood, fastening the pieces together (i.e., nailing one board to another), and staining the finished project. Short scripts were then written, describing each carpenter performing each task several times, both correctly and incorrectly.

So, for example, we videotaped each carpenter sawing boards several times. They each sawed boards of different sizes correctly, and then sawed each size board portraying a different error. In each vignette, the carpenter would begin by measuring a length of board, and then drawing a line to mark the desired length. The errors portrayed here were sawing on the wrong side of the line (one should saw on the "waste side" of the line), not sawing straight, not holding the saw at the proper angle (the saw should be held at a 45° angle to the board), and not holding the waste side piece of board when completing the sawing task (which causes the piece of wood to splinter off). In each case, the carpenter committed only one error per vignette, and we had vignettes showing each carpenter working on each of a variety of boards, performing all aspects of the given task correctly or committing an error.

All vignettes were pilot tested with other carpentry students, as well as with undergraduate students. We prepared written standards to enable undergraduate students to judge the performance portrayed, and re-shot some vignettes until pilot ratings indicated that we were successful in portraying the levels of performance we wanted. In all subsequent laboratory studies, we used some subset of these vignettes as stimulus materials, although no subsequent studies involved information search activities, which would have required the additional technology of a random-access video-cassette player. Having established the medium for presenting performance information, it is time to turn to the studies in the "second" phase of the research program.

THE ROLE OF REPROCESSING OBJECTIVES

One area which emerged from our initial studies as needing further investigation involved the role of reprocessing objectives in appraisal decisions. As noted earlier, much of the information that is used for appraisal decisions was initially acquired for other purposes, or for no specific purpose at all. If certain patterns of organization are more suited for some purposes than for others, performance information obtained for other purposes is likely to be organized in a way that is not optimal for making appraisal decisions. In these instances, a rater must first reprocess the information before it can be used effectively for appraisal decisions. The first step in understanding this process, then, was to determine how much of a problem reprocessing really presented to a rater. Williams, DeNisi, Meglino, and Cafferty (1986) designed an experiment to assess the nature of the problem.

The first stages in any cognitive model such as ours include acquisition and encoding of information in memory. Our findings (Cafferty, DeNisi, &

Williams, 1986), as well as the work of others in the area of human memory (e.g., Bransford & Franks, 1971; Craik & Lockhart, 1972; Horton & Mills, 1984), established the importance of initial encoding of information in memory for its eventual recall. For example, Craik and Lockhart (1972) discussed the importance of the depth of processing of information. They suggested that some incidents are processed more deeply (i.e., require or involve more processing) than others, and that these incidents will be more easy to recall later. Furthermore, Tulving's (1974) work suggested that the initial purpose for which information is encoded determines how it will be encoded, and how easily it will be recalled. Closer to our own work, Hamilton, Katz, and Leirer (1980) found that instructing subjects to form impressions about people resulted in a greater likelihood of organizing information in memory around persons.

Thus, it seemed clear that decision purpose would play a role in how information was organized in memory, which would affect its accessibility. But other research also indicated that initial decisions might also play a role in subsequent decisions (e.g., Higgins & McCann, 1984; Lingle & Ostrom, 1979; Wyer, Srull, & Gordon, 1984). Therefore, if performance information acquired initially for a purpose other than appraisals, this might not only affect the way the information would be organized in memory, but the decision for which the information was originally collected, once made, would also influence impressions and subsequent evaluations of a target person.

In this first study, we returned to the dimension of appraisal purpose that had been used in an earlier study of ours (Williams et al., 1985), and so focused on designation and deservedness decisions. The primary focus of this study, then, was to determine if having raters acquire blocked information for one purpose (deservedness or designation decisions) influenced later decisions for a different purpose (deservedness or designation, whichever one was *not* the initial purpose). Subjects were recruited from undergraduate classes (for extra credit) to participate in the study, and were told that, in order to receive credit, they would have to come to two sessions, two days apart. One hundred and one students reported for the initial session, but only seventy returned for the second session. At that first session, half the raters were told that they would be viewing the performance of four carpenters, each performing four tasks, for the purpose of rating how deserving each worker was for outside contracting work, while the other half were told they were to designate *one* carpenter for outside contracting work. Note that all subjects in this study received the information in a blocked format since we now knew that presenting information in an unblocked format made it more difficult to organize. Half the subjects in each condition saw the vignettes blocked by person, and half saw the vignettes blocked by task. Finally, one worker performed three of four tasks without error (75% proficient), two workers performed two tasks without error (50% proficient), and one worker performed only one task without error (25% proficient).

Raters watched the videotaped vignettes in groups and made their initial decisions immediately after viewing the tapes. After they made their ratings, the subjects were dismissed and told to return in two days. They were led to believe that, upon their return, they would be asked to perform a different task altogether. Instead, when they returned, the subjects were asked to rate each carpenter's performance, from memory, both for the individual tasks, as well as for overall performance. We analyzed the data for the initial decisions first and, not surprisingly, we found that initial designation and deservedness decisions were based primarily upon proficiency level. Proficiency explained 25% of the variance in deservedness ratings (with no effect for blocking pattern, nor a significant interaction), and, across the blocking conditions, the 75% proficient worker was designated for outside work in 35 of 50 cases. But the real test involved the subsequent decisions, which required some reprocessing.

The results for the individual task ratings indicated that raters were not able to reliably discriminate between incidents of good and poor performance regardless of initial purpose or blocking pattern. We interpreted this to mean that reprocessing was a difficult task and that these raters could not reprocess the information well enough to make fine distinctions among ratees. The results for the overall performance ratings, which are presented in Table 4.1, indicated that when raters made initial designation decisions, they were unable to make these grosser distinctions among ratees either. This was true whether they had viewed the vignettes blocked by person or by task. In each case, these raters were able *only* to differentiate the highest performing ratee (i.e., the 75% proficient ratee) from the other two, but could not differentiate between the 50% and the 25% proficient ratees. Only when the raters made initial deservedness decisions *and* viewed the information blocked by persons, could they distinguish reliably among the three levels of proficiency.

We concluded that the initial processing objective did influence the way the performance information was encoded in memory, and thus the ability

Table 4.1 Overall performance ratings as a function of initial purpose and blocking presentation

| Ratee performance | Initial: designation | | Initial: deservedness | |
	Person-blocked	Task-blocked	Person-blocked	Task-Blocked
75% proficient	5.33	6.05	5.06	5.15
50% proficient	4.29	4.28	4.25	3.77
25% proficient	4.58	4.05	3.28	4.08

Source: Williams, DeNisi, Meglino, and Cafferty (1986)

of the raters to reprocess that information and use it for a different purpose later. Since designation decisions require the identification of one "best" candidate for a treatment, and since, in the majority of cases this was the 75% proficient ratee, raters who encoded information for making designation decisions could only effectively separate the highest performer from the other three. Deservedness decisions, on the other hand, required raters to form some cognitive impression of all four ratees and, even though they were subsequently asked to make a somewhat different evaluation, this allowed them to better differentiate among the three levels of proficiency. These results suggested to us that the more congruent the initial and the subsequent purposes for observing performance information, the easier it would be for raters to reprocess the information they needed to make appraisal decisions. In fact, Barnes-Farrell and Couture (1983) had found much greater problems with reprocessing when they asked raters to make initial decisions that were quite different from performance appraisal.

These results also reinforced our belief that the way information was organized in memory was critical for appraisal decisions. In our earlier studies we focused on cases where the purpose of observation was always performance appraisal, but we were aware of the fact that this was not always the purpose for which raters initially acquired performance information. Given some tendency to acquire performance information in an unblocked format *and* given the likelihood that information would need to be reprocessed before it could be used for appraisal decisions, it seemed clear that raters would often not be able to accurately recall the information they needed to make accurate appraisal decisions, and that we would need to find ways to help raters organize information to make it more accessible to them. The results of this study also suggested some other issues regarding reprocessing that needed to be explored. The studies that were designed to address these issues, though, drew upon a distinction which I think will continue to prove to be important for understanding appraisal decisions – the distinction between on-line and memory-based processing. Therefore, before discussing those studies, it would help if I discussed the meaning and importance of these two processing models.

ON-LINE VS. MEMORY-BASED PROCESSING

Hastie and Park wrote:

> There ought to be a relationship between memory and judgment. Our intuition tells us that we should be able to generate more arguments and information in support of a favored position than against it, that evaluations of people should be related to the amounts of good and bad information we have about them.

> (Hastie & Park, 1986: 258)

They go on to point out that the support for such a relationship is inconclusive and mixed. In fact, they note that there has been support reported for three different positions on this relationship: (a) there is a direct relationship between memory and judgment such that we give higher evaluations for persons about whom we remember more positive information (e.g., Coombs & Slovic, 1979; Gabrielcik & Fazio, 1984; Lichtenstein, Slavic, Fischoff, Layman, and Coombs, 1978; Ross & Sicoly, 1979; Tversky & Kahneman, 1973); (b) there is no direct relationship between memory and judgments (e.g., Anderson & Hubert, 1963; Reyes, Thompson, & Bower, 1980); and (c) there is a relationship between the two, but it is the opposite to that described in (a) such that incidents *inconsistent* with an evaluation are the most likely to be recalled (e.g., Hastie, 1984; Hastie & Kumar, 1979; Srull, 1981).

The implications of this discussion for cognitive models of performance appraisal are quite sweeping. If there is no relationship between memory and performance ratings, then why should we be concerned about how information is stored in memory, or about ways to aid the organization of information in memory to facilitate its recall? Furthermore, since most organizations conduct performance appraisal *both* to aid in decision making *and* to provide performance feedback to ratees, if memory and ratings were unrelated, how would a rater provide the feedback necessary to help a ratee improve? Where would the specific incidents of performance come from, *or*, alternatively, would any such incidents that were recalled be related to the evaluations given? As we shall discuss later, some of these issues are related to different definitions of rating accuracy that are also critical for appraisal research, but for now we are concerned mostly with the relationship between memory and ratings.

Hastie and Park (1986) reviewed several different processing models and theoretical perspectives, but they finally come upon the distinction they term "on-line versus memory-based judgment tasks." Memory-based judgments are those which require the judges to go back into their memories to draw upon concrete incidents of performance or behavior upon which to form an impression. Thus, in these cases, the rater does not have an impression or evaluation already accessible. On-line decisions are those where the judge does have a readily accessible impression or evaluation. This evaluation may be updated as more information is acquired, but it does not require the judge to scan his or her memory for specifics. Only in the case of memory-based decisions, then, should there be a relationship between memory and ratings, but Hastie and Park also discussed the conditions which would favor one model over the other.

They suggested that people typically make spontaneous judgments about others, even without being instructed to do so. Therefore, all other things being equal, they would usually have some judgment accessible to them and, when asked to provide an evaluation, would give one that would be independent of what specific incidents of behavior they could recall about the target person. What would induce memory-based processing? They note that the most reliable means to invoke this mode would be to surprise raters. That is, similar to our arguments about reprocessing objectives, when a rater believes she or he is gathering information for one purpose, but is then asked to use that information to make a different type of judgment, memory-based judgment is likely to occur. Also, anything that would interfere with a person's natural tendencies to form impressions and evaluations (such as competing cognitive tasks or simply too many tasks) might necessitate memory-based judgments.

They argue that we can determine which processing mode is in operation by computing the correlation between the number of positive incidents recalled and the evaluation given. In their paper, cases where they believe on-line processing should be occurring result in correlations that are close to zero, and non-significant, while cases where memory-based processing should be occurring result in correlations that are fairly large in magnitude (mean close to .50) and statistically significant. Which processing mode is most prevalent in performance appraisal settings? This is clearly an important question for understanding the appraisal process and the role of memory in appraisal decisions. Our second paper dealing with reprocessing objectives (Williams, Cafferty, & DeNisi, 1990), which will be discussed shortly, actually addresses this issue and produced some interesting results. However, in general, there has been more speculation than data concerning which processing mode predominates in appraisal settings. One argument has been that most cognitive appraisal studies have taken place in the lab where artificial demands on raters favor memory-based processing, and so these studies over-estimate the role of memory in appraisal decisions made in the field where, presumably, on-line processing is more likely. Another argument, though, is that lab studies actually *increase* reliance upon on-line processing over memory-based processing relative to field settings because lab studies typically place fewer cognitive demands upon raters, allowing them to more easily form the impressions they need to use on-line processing.

At one point we actually tried to assess the reliance upon on-line and memory-based processing by combining the results of a series of lab studies we had conducted for various purposes. In this study (DeNisi, Robbins, & Williams, 1989) we combined the results of any study where we had collected recall data and evaluations, and correlated the number of positive incidents recalled with ratings. In general, we found results that fell somewhere in between those reported by Hastie and Park (1986) for their two processing modes. Most of the correlations were significant, indicating memory-based processing, but their magnitude was much smaller than those correlations reported by Hastie and Park (1986) for conditions favoring memory-based processing. But these individual experiments differed in some important ways. In several experiments, we had given raters a competing task to complete while they were observing and evaluating performance. Typically, this was a scheduling task, or an in-basket, and these were included to try to increase external validity by not allowing raters to focus all their attention on the appraisal process. We found that the mean correlation between the number of positive incidents recalled and ratings was .28 ($p < .05$) for those experiments where raters had been given a competing task, and the mean correlation was .12 ($p < .05$) when there was not a competing task. Furthermore, these correlations were significantly different ($p < .05$) from each other. Thus, our results indicated some evidence of both types of processing going on, but that there was evidence of more memory-based processing when raters were given competing tasks. This seemed to suggest that, in the field, where there are many competing tasks, raters would be more likely (not less likely) to engage in memory-based processing, although even then, we suspect, there will be considerable on-line processing as well.

With this discussion, we can return to the reprocessing studies. The next paper also helps shed light on the distinction between on-line and memory-based processing and, as I noted above, this distinction probably plays a role in the debate over the best accuracy measures. Nonetheless, the primary purpose for this study was to determine how raters processed information when it was not clear at the time the information was acquired that it would be used for appraisal decisions.

APPRAISAL SALIENCE AND REPROCESSING

The results of the earlier reprocessing study, as well as a consideration of the importance of the distinction between on-line and memory-based processing, led us to design two more studies where appraisal salience was explicitly manipulated. Williams, Cafferty, and DeNisi (1990) conducted two experiments into the relationship between appraisal salience and both information processing and actual ratings. The situation seemed quite simple. The literature suggested that the processing objective, operational at the time information was acquired, affected the organization and subsequent retrieval of that information (Hamilton, Katz, & Leirer, 1980; Hastie & Carlston, 1980; Hastie, Park, & Weber, 1984). Although appraisal researchers typically assume that appraisal decisions represent *the* processing objective for raters, this may not always be the case (Bernardin & Villanova, 1986; Williams, DeNisi, Meglino, & Cafferty, 1986). Furthermore, two other studies had demonstrated that, when raters must divide their attention between appraisal and non-appraisal tasks, their ability to attend to and retain appraisal-relevant behaviors is limited (Balzer, 1986; Barnes-Farrell & Couture, 1983). This led us to propose that, when appraisal purpose was salient, raters would engage in on-line processing of information and ratings would be based upon strong impressions formed by raters. In these cases, raters should organize information in memory according to person categories, and so ratings should be more accurate. When appraisal purpose was less salient, on the other hand, raters were predicted to engage in memory-based processing, and ratings would be based on weaker impressions and/or information recalled from memory. Both Posner and Snyder (1975) and Schul (1983) had described cognitive operations under conditions of heavier cognitive demands that might provide some basis for global impression formation, but these impressions would likely be weaker. Furthermore, since appraisal purpose was not salient, raters would be less likely to form person-based categories in memory and resultant ratings were likely to be less accurate.

The first experiment in this paper examined these issues, but also considered the role of a structured recall task in the process. Using Cohen's (1981b) taxonomy of observational goals, raters (eighty undergraduate students participating for partial course credit) were told they were observing behavior to either rate the performance of the ratees involved (four carpenters performing four woodworking tasks), or to rate the difficulty of the four tasks involved (sawing, sanding, hammering, and staining). Actual performance levels differed for the four carpenters as it had in our previous studies (i.e., one at 75% proficiency, two at 50%, and one at 25%). After observing the videotaped performance (presented in an unblocked format), raters were given a 30-minute interpolated task (the Group Embedded Figures Test, Oltman et al., 1971, to clear out any short-term memory traces) and then were either asked to provide ratings, followed by a recall task, or were asked to complete a recall task prior to ratings. In all cases, the recall task was a "free recall" task in which raters were given 20 minutes to write down, in a booklet provided, all the incidents they could recall from the videotape. They were further instructed to write down the incidents in a format that would name a ratee performing a specific task and would note whether the task was performed correctly or incorrectly.

Regardless of the initial instructions, all raters were asked to rate the performance of the four carpenters on each of the four tasks, and to provide an overall performance rating for each. All ratings were made on 7-point scales. For the raters who were given instructions to observe the tasks in order to evaluate the difficulty of the tasks, this represented a reprocessing objective, and these raters were given several minutes to reconsider the behavior they had observed from this new perspective, prior to completing either the rating or the recall tasks.

We analyzed the ratings, of course, as well as the recall data. In the case of the recall data we examined the degree of organization in memory by computing person and task ARC scores as we had previously. We also looked at the absolute number of performance incidents recalled, regardless of whether a specific rater or performance level were mentioned (termed "recalled items"), as well as the number of incidents where a rater and a level of task performance were paired (termed "recalled performance"), and finally we looked at the number of incidents recalled where ratee, task, and performance level were all present and correct (termed "performance correctly recalled").

The results for the clustering indices indicated that, as expected, raters for whom appraisal purpose was salient engaged in significantly more person clustering than did raters for whom appraisal salience was less salient, while these latter raters engaged in greater task clustering (appraisal salience explained 31% of the variance in clustering). The results for the recall data are presented in Table 4.2, and indicate that overall recall (items recalled) was greater when appraisal salience was higher, but there were no effects for salience on either "performances recalled" or "performance correctly recalled". There were, however, significant salience × order interaction effects on all three recall indices and, in all three cases, we found that when appraisal salience was low, subjects who performed the recall task first scored higher on the recall measure than raters who performed the rating task first, and that these subjects' recall did not differ significantly from that of the subjects in the high salience conditions. Thus salience did have some effect on recall, but introducing a free recall task prior to ratings canceled any advantage held by raters who always knew that the purpose of the exercise was performance appraisal.

Table 4.2 Recall indices as a function of appraisal salience and order of recall and rating

Appraisal salience	Order	Items recalled	Performances recalled	Performances correctly recalled
High salience				
	Recall first	6.95	4.25	2.80
	Rate first	8.52	5.68	3.58
Low salience				
	Recall first	8.26	5.42	3.75
	Rate first	4.35	3.20	1.85
	Means	6.99	4.62	3.00

Source: Williams, Cafferty, and DeNisi (1990: Study 1)

The results for the ratings data were not as clear. We found a significant effect for rater performance level (proficiency) on overall performance ratings, but post hoc tests indicated only that raters (in all conditions) could differentiate the best ratee from the other two. Turning to the task ratings, all raters were able to discriminate between tasks performed correctly and those performed incorrectly, and there was only a marginally significant ($p < .10$) effect to indicate that this discriminability was higher for raters for whom appraisal salience was high. Finally, when appraisal salience was high, the correlations between the proportion of positive incidents recalled and overall performance ratings was non-significant ($rs = .20$ and $.21$ ns, for the rate first and recall first conditions respectively), but these correlations were significant when appraisal salience was low ($rs = .46$ and $.43$, $ps < .05$ for the two conditions respectively).

Thus we found that high appraisal salience resulted in information organization according to persons in memory, greater recall of performance information, and, despite the greater recall, non-significant correlations between recall and ratings, indicating that raters were relying upon general impressions of ratees rather than specific performance information recalled – i.e., they were engaging in on-line processing. We also found that the introduction of a free recall task, prior to making ratings, seemed to equate the high and low appraisal purpose salience raters in terms of both recall and the accuracy of overall ratings. Note, though, that these results again point out the importance of understanding the processing mode most common in actual appraisal settings. High salience resulted in greater on-line processing of information, which led to greater recall, even if there were no differences in rating accuracy. But, as I noted earlier, appraisal purpose may *not* typically be salient to raters in the field, making on-line processing *less* likely to occur. Finally, to set the stage for a later discussion, the relationship between ratings and recall was not significant for low appraisal salience, as would be expected if on-line processing were occurring. But in field settings appraisals are usually used for *both* feedback and decision making. Even though raters engaging in on-line processing would be able to recall more performance information, they would not use it as the basis for their ratings. Thus, any feedback they could provide would probably be inconsistent with the ratings they provided, which might send confusing signals to the ratee.

In any event, these results indicated that raters were not very good at differentiating among different levels of performance exhibited by ratees in any condition, and this was problematic. It occurred to us that, although the recall task seemed to help the low salience raters, perhaps it took place too late to do them much good. That is, this intervention impacted on the recall stage only. Perhaps an intervention designed to influence the initial encoding of information might be more effective. Therefore, Study 2 was designed to examine the effects of introducing an organizing intervention earlier in the process. In this study, raters (sixty undergraduate students participating for partial course credit) followed the same procedures as in Study 1, except that, prior to observing the (unblocked) performance information, subjects were given instructions aimed at priming initial organization in memory. Raters in the *person-blocking* condition were told to mentally reorganize the information they observed so that the performance incidents for each ratee were grouped together; raters in the *task-blocking* condition were instructed to mentally reorganize the information such that all the information for each task was grouped together; while raters in the *unblocked* condition were given no instructions about mentally reorganizing information. This manipulation was followed by the purpose (appraisal salience) manipulation as before, and all procedures were otherwise identical to those from Study 1 *except* that all raters were given the recall task prior to the rating task.

The results for clustering of information in recall were quite a bit different from those of Study 1. This time, appraisal purpose salience was not an important factor for person clustering (although high salience resulted in somewhat greater person clustering as before, but the difference was not significant here). Instead, the encoding intervention was the critical determinant of clustering. More specifically, instructions to organize information by persons led to greater person clustering than did either task blocking instructions or no instructions (these instructions explained 21% of the variance in person clustering). While instructions to organize according to tasks led to greater task clustering than in the other two conditions, these differences were not significant. Also, high performance salience led to more performance incidents correctly recalled than low performance salience, and intervention instructions did not affect this recall. But it was the results for the ratings data that were the most interesting findings from Study 2.

Analysis of overall performance ratings indicated that, much the same as in Study 1, raters generally could differentiate the best performing ratee from the others, but were not very good at differentiating the 50% proficient ratees from the 25% proficient ratee, and there were no effects for salience or blocking instructions on these ratings. The results for the individual task ratings are provided in Table 4.3, and illustrate that higher appraisal salience led to higher mean ratings; mean task performance ratings were higher for the best performer than for the others; and that good task performance was rated higher than poor task performance. These results also reveal a significant three-way interaction (salience × task performance × ratee). Simple effects tests indicated that, when appraisal salience was high *and* when it was low, raters could differentiate incidents of good performance from incidents of low performance, but that when salience was low, all ratings of specific tasks were influenced by the overall level of performance exhibited by the ratee. That is, although these raters could still differentiate between good and poor performance incidents exhibited by the raters, they rated the good performance incidents significantly higher for overall good performers than for overall poor performers, and they rated the poor performance incidents significantly lower for the overall poor performers than for the overall good performers. The results of analyses involving blocking instructions indicated that raters who clustered information in memory according to persons were also more likely to rely

Table 4.3 Performance ratings for tasks performed correctly and incorrectly across all conditions

	Ratee 1 (25% correct)		Ratee 2 (50% correct)		Ratee 3 (50% correct)		Ratee 4 (75% correct)	
	Corr.	Inc.	Corr.	Inc.	Corr.	Inc.	Corr.	Inc.
High Salience								
Person blocking	5.40	3.07	4.55	3.45	5.60	3.00	5.87	3.40
Task blocking	5.60	3.30	5.00	2.50	5.15	3.15	5.33	4.00
No blocking	5.10	3.30	3.95	2.85	5.30	2.75	5.50	4.80
Low Salience								
Person blocking	4.10	3.27	3.75	3.10	5.25	2.65	5.73	2.70
Task blocking	3.90	3.30	4.55	2.65	5.05	3.05	5.10	2.80
No blocking	5.10	3.80	3.85	2.00	4.85	3.75	5.60	3.70

Note: Corr. = tasks performed correctly; Inc. = tasks performed incorrectly.
Source: Williams, Cafferty, and DeNisi (1990: Study 2)

upon overall impressions about the ratee (i.e., overall performance levels) in making specific task ratings, such that organization in memory according to task resulted in somewhat better ability to differentiate between different levels of performance exhibited by the same ratee, independent of the ratee's overall level of performance.

Thus, in both studies, appraisal salience appears to affect recall and ratings. High appraisal salience would seem to lead to on-line processing of information and organization in memory according to persons. In the present studies, this led to ratings that were not as effective in discriminating among different levels of performance exhibited by the same ratee. This is a condition that is commonly referred to as "halo error" (which we will discuss in more detail later), and more memory intrusions (where those who performed better overall were "remembered" as having performed well on tasks they actually performed poorly). It should be noted here that Murphy and Balzer (1989) found that on-line processing resulted in more accurate overall performance ratings, but we did not find any differences, and in fact we found that no raters were fully capable of differentiating among the three levels of overall performance exhibited by ratees.

Also, both papers indicated that reprocessing of information was a cognitively demanding task for raters. That is, it was relatively difficult for them to collect performance information for one purpose and then use it later for a different purpose. Yet in the field this is likely to be exactly what raters need to do. It is likely that raters obtain a great deal of relevant performance information when appraisal is not a salient purpose for them. They are likely to organize this information in ways that make it most accessible to them for the purpose that *was* salient when the information was being collected and they would have to reprocess it before they could use it effectively for making appraisal decisions. On-line processing also results in greater reliance upon person categories or general impressions. As noted, Murphy and Balzer (1986) argued that this resulted in *greater* accuracy for overall ratings of performance, but our results indicated that on-line processing, and reliance upon general impressions and person categories, may make it more difficult for raters to discriminate among different levels of performance exhibited by the same ratee. Further, on-line processing results in less correspondence between incidents recalled and ratings. An important implication of these findings is that on-line processing may interfere with a rater's ability to provide accurate and meaningful feedback to a ratee about her or his performance, even if it does result in more accurate overall ratings. We will return to this problem later when we discuss the topic of rating accuracy in more detail, but these results further suggest the importance of helping raters find how to organize performance information in ways that will enable them to access and use that information for making appraisal decisions. We turn, then, to a series of studies designed to investigate interventions that might meet those needs.

INTERVENTIONS TO AID IN THE ORGANIZATION OF INFORMATION

I The rating instrument

In the previous chapter I noted that the Cafferty, DeNisi, and Williams (1986) study was important, not only because it established a relationship between memory acquisition and ratings, but also because it made clear that a great deal of the information acquired by raters for appraisal decisions would not be organized in memory in a way that would make it easy to use it for appraisals. This led to the studies about the role for reprocessing objectives discussed earlier in this chapter, as well as to studies designed to investigate interventions that might help raters to organize performance information in a useful way. Three potential types of interventions came to mind, each aimed at a different point in the cognitive processing of information. The Williams, Cafferty, and DeNisi (1990) study found that having raters engage in a free recall task prior to making ratings, helped raters who collected information for a purpose other than appraisal. Earlier Williams (1984) had also noted that a structured recall task might help even more by imposing a specific order to that information, and that suggestion was echoed in the latter paper. We did not test the effectiveness of that possible intervention in a laboratory setting, although the results reported above would seem to suggest that it might be effective. We did test this possibility in a field setting, but that will be discussed in a later chapter. For now, suffice it to say that it seemed reasonable that a structured recall task might enable raters to impose structure on unorganized information (or on information organized in a way that was non-optimal for appraisal decisions) after it was acquired and initially encoded, but prior to its use for making appraisal decisions. But this was the end of the process. Could we identify interventions that might help raters organize information at earlier stages in the process?

One possibility was that we might be able to help raters organize information in specific categories as they acquired the information, by priming certain categories before the raters began acquiring information. Study 2 reported by Williams, Cafferty, and DeNisi (1990) seemed to suggest such a possibility, as did the results of another experiment conducted by Williams, Wickert, and Peters (1985). Ostroff and Ilgen (1986) also investigated the possibility of training raters to use certain categories to organize performance information they acquired, although they found little effect on rating accuracy. Our process model (DeNisi, Cafferty, & Meglino 1984) even suggested that the rating instrument itself might provide a rater with cues as to which categories were more important for appraisals, and might influence the priming of those categories. In addition, Ilgen and Feldman (1983) suggested that rating accuracy would be highest when information was organized in memory according to the same categories used on rating scales. Wherry (1952) made similar suggestions, and Johnson and Vidulich (1956) had actually examined the effectiveness of reorganizing rating scales, so that ratings were blocked by tasks instead of persons, in the reduction of halo error (although subsequently Johnson, 1963, suggested this had not been effective). Elsewhere, both Feldman (1986), and Peters and DeNisi (1990) suggested that rating scales needed to be constructed to make them more consistent with the information processing demands of performance appraisal. Thus it seemed that it might be possible to intervene in the process before raters actually began to acquire performance information, by providing them with categories they might use to organize the information as it was acquired. It also seemed reasonable to expect that the appraisal instrument itself might provide a means for providing these categories. Subsequent studies have provided further support for such a cognitive role for the appraisal instrument (e.g., McDonald, 1990; Murphy & Constans, 1987; Sulsky & Day, 1994).

We therefore designed a study (DeNisi & Summers, 1986) to test the effectiveness of the rating scale as a means of providing raters with the cognitive categories that would help them to organize unorganized information. We provided subjects (125 undergraduate students who participated for extra credit in their courses) with either a "trait-based" appraisal instrument, or a "task-based" appraisal instrument for evaluating the performance of three carpenters each performing four carpentry tasks (the same as in the previous studies), and subjects were provided standards with which to evaluate the performance of the ratees. The individual performance segments were presented in an unblocked format, and performance levels were manipulated so that one carpenter each was performing at a 75%, 50%, and

25% proficiency level. In all cases, subjects would observe the performance segments, engage in a free recall task, and then rate the carpenters. We manipulated the timing of the instrument such that raters received the instrument either prior to observation, after observation but prior to recall, or after observation and recall, but just prior to rating. We collected data on both recall (recall accuracy as well as clustering in recall) and rating accuracy. In this case, accuracy was computed as a function of the divergence of obtained ratings from "true ratings" (although accuracy is discussed below with the signs reversed to make the results more easily interpretable), so that accuracy here is *not* operationalized in terms of raters' ability to discriminate between incidents of good and poor performance exhibited by the same ratee.

The task instrument was essentially the same rating instrument that we had used in previous studies. Raters were asked to provide individual task ratings for each carpentry task on 5-point rating scales with appropriate anchors. The trait instrument was adapted from appraisal instruments we obtained from the technical school where the original videotapes were produced, and which were used to evaluate the students in the class. This instrument required ratings on motivation, attitude, initiative, and responsibility, and also used 5-point rating scales. As I described earlier, the videotapes were produced and pilot tested to ensure that they reflected different levels of performance on different tasks. Thus we could easily assess the accuracy of ratings made using the task instrument. We could not, however, easily assess the accuracy of ratings made using the trait instrument, since there were no known levels of "true" performance on these traits depicted in the videotapes. In order to obtain *some* measure of accuracy for the raters who used this scale, however, we did ask them, after completing the trait instrument, to also provide ratings using the task instrument.

We predicted that introducing the rating instrument prior to observation would have the greatest impact, since it would allow raters to organize the information as it was being acquired, and we predicted that the nature of the rating scale would dictate the nature of the categories used for organization, such that the trait instrument would result in greater person organization and the task instrument would result in greater task organization (we also completed performance level ARC scores for each subject to see if either instrument introduced at any time would result in greater organization according to performance level). Finally, we examined the role of the instrument, and the timing of its introduction on the evidence for on-line and memory-based processing. That is, in all cases we correlated the proportion of positive incidents recalled with the ratings provided.

The main results are presented in Table 4.4 and indicate that, as in many things, timing was everything. Introduction of the rating scale prior to observation resulted in the highest levels of information organization but, regardless of the type of rating scale used, organization according to persons was the most prevalent form of organization. Furthermore, levels of person organization were positively related to both recall accuracy ($r = .27$, $p < .05$) and rating accuracy ($r = .18$, $p < .05$). Thus these results indicate that the rating instrument *can* aid raters in organizing information as long as it is presented to them prior to observation, but, counter to prediction, the task instrument, not the trait instrument, resulted in the highest levels of organization by persons. It is interesting to note here that the levels of task organization were related to rating accuracy, but the results indicated that higher levels of task organization were related to lower levels of rating accuracy ($r = -.20$, $p < .05$).

Table 4.4 ARC person scores for rating instrument and timing conditions

	Task scale	Trait scale
Instrument distributed:		
Before observation	.46	.21
Before recall	.09	.18
Before rating	.26	.30

Source: DeNisi and Summers (1986)

The results relative to the processing modes were also quite instructive. The correlation between recall and ratings was non-significant for those who received the task rating prior to observation ($r = .05$, *ns*), while the correlation was high and significant for those who received the trait instrument prior to observation ($r = .73$, $p < .01$). On the other hand, correlations were significant (and reasonably large) for raters who received the instruments later, regardless of the type of instrument they received ($rs = .50$ and .54, both $p < .05$, for the task and trait instruments respectively). Thus it seemed that providing raters with the task instrument prior to observation increased the likelihood of on-line processing, while providing a trait instrument prior to observation might actually have increased memory-based processing. These results also provide clearer evidence for the notion that on-line processing results in greater ability of raters to distinguish among overall levels of performance exhibited by ratees, although these results cannot speak to the relationship between on-line processing and ratings that differentiate among different levels of performance exhibited by the same ratee. Finally, since Bernardin and Villanova (1986) suggest that raters in the field do not typically have access to the rating instrument during observation, these results also suggest the prevalence of memory-based processing in the field.

Thus, based on the results of this study, the rating instrument seemed to play a cognitive role in the appraisal process. The nature of the rating instrument does seem to be related to the categories used by a rater, and providing the rater with that instrument prior to the observation of performance seems to allow the rater to use those categories to organize the information encountered as it is encountered. Furthermore, since the trait rating scale may be viewed as inconsistent with the task performance observed in this case (as, perhaps, in other cases), these results also suggest that it is important to design rating instruments that invoke raters' use of categories that make information accessible and useful for the rating task at hand. But after raters have seen the rating instrument once, they may well already have those categories available to them, and so this intervention may lose its effectiveness over time. Furthermore, in this experiment it was easy for raters to have the rating instrument in front of them as they were observing performance. In the field, where observation takes place over a span of months rather than minutes, this might not be so easy. It was clear, therefore, that we needed to investigate other interventions that might aid raters in organizing information at other points in the process, and that might be more salient to them throughout the appraisal process. We turn now to the evaluation of such an intervention.

II Structured diary keeping

For years there had been recommendations that raters keep performance diaries or incident files, where they could record critical incidents of performance when they occurred. When appraisals were due the rater simply had to consult the diary to make an appraisal decision and, at the same time, the rater had ready access to specific incidents of performance to defend and/or explain the rating, as well as to provide the basis for performance feedback (Bernardin & Walter, 1977; Guion, 1965; Wherry, 1952: Theorem 10). As we discussed possible interventions to aid raters in organizing information, diaries seemed to offer some promise. The problem, though, was that we didn't know if all diary keeping was structured in the same way, that is, if there was more than one format which was favored by organizations where raters kept diaries, they might not offer the opportunity we had hoped for, since it would make no sense to compare diaries structured in different ways.

Although I was aware of organizations where raters were told to keep diaries, I knew little about the details of those diaries. After consulting several individuals involved in HR for large organizations, as well as several academic appraisal experts, it became clear that there was no single format in which performance diaries were organized in field settings. In fact, it became clear there were two formats for these diaries, which together accounted for all the cases I could identify. Specifically, organizations either had raters organize their diaries according to the persons being rated, or according to the performance dimensions being used. Since these two formats corresponded to the two major blocking patterns we had been studying, a comparative study of different diary keeping strategies appeared to make sense.

We designed a laboratory experiment to investigate the effectiveness of structured diaries for organizing unorganized information (DeNisi, Robbins, & Cafferty, 1989). Subjects (sixty-two undergraduate students who participated as a partial course requirement) viewed the videotaped performance of three carpenters (now named Bill, Michael, and John) each performing three carpentry tasks (sawing, sanding, and staining) twice apiece, for a total of eighteen performance segments, presented in an unblocked format. As in previous studies, we manipulated performance levels such that Bill performed two of six tasks correctly, Michael performed three of the six correctly, and John performed four of the six tasks correctly. All raters were provided identifying information so they could tell who they were observing and rating, as well as standards for performing the three tasks. While raters observed the performance (and kept their diaries as will be described below), they were also instructed to work on an in-basket task, adapted from Beatty and Schneier (1981). The in-basket consisted of ten items (messages or memos) that required some action on the part of the subject. Subjects were directed to work through as many of the items as they could, writing down their response to each item on the appropriate page and signing it. This was intended to better reflect the field situation where raters had other tasks competing for their attention. Although we stressed that *both* tasks were important, subjects apparently paid more attention to the rating task, although everyone completed at least one item from the in-basket. Twenty-four subjects actually completed all ten items, but the mean was six items, except in the no-diary condition described below, where the mean number of items completed was nine.

The raters were given small plastic boxes for holding index cards, and a supply of blank cards. All raters who kept diaries were instructed to write down one critical incident on each card. They were randomly assigned conditions which corresponded to the ways in which the diaries would be organized. In each box we included a set of colored tabs that were used to separate the cards. In the person-diary condition, the tab cards listed the names of the three ratees, and there were several blank cards behind each tab card. In the task-diary condition, the tab cards listed the tasks, and there were blank cards provided. There was also a no-diary condition, in which raters had no diaries to complete at all. Finally, there was a free-diary condition that requires some explanation, but involved providing blank tab cards and blank index cards, so that the raters could organize their diaries in any way they saw fit (and several possibilities were mentioned to them).

As I said, this free-diary condition requires some further discussion. In the studies we had conducted up to this point, raters really had little choice in how information was organized. We either blocked the information when it was presented, gave raters instructions to organize information one way or another, or introduced some other manipulation that we believed would induce organization in one pattern or another. Now we were providing diaries structured in either one of two ways, but we were concerned that raters might not prefer to organize the information in either pattern. Shortly before designing this study, we had conducted another study where raters were given a choice of how they wanted to acquire information (e.g., blocked by person, blocked by task, etc.), and then we presented them with the information in a pattern that was either consistent with their preferences or inconsistent with their preferences (Cafferty, Skedsvold, & DeNisi, 1988). Overall, we found that information blocked by persons was most easily recalled and resulted in more accurate ratings, but we found that this effect was diminished when subjects preferred to receive information organized in some other pattern. Furthermore, we found that raters were better able to access and use information blocked in other patterns when these were the patterns they preferred. Thus we realized that it was important to allow raters to acquire and organize information in the way they wanted. Furthermore, in the case of diary keeping, we knew from discussions with managers in the field that raters often resisted keeping diaries, and especially resisted keeping diaries organized according to company policy, when they actually preferred to keep them organized some other way. We were concerned, then, that if we found one diary structure that was most effective, *but* if this was not the way many raters preferred to organize their diaries, in the long run, any attempt to force raters to organize their diaries in the "optimal" manner would be futile. We therefore felt we needed a condition where raters could reveal their preferences for diary structure to us, and that was the purpose of the free-diary condition.

Raters viewed the videotape segments while making diary entries (except for those in the no-diary condition), and working on the in-basket task. When the videotape was completed (approximately 25 minutes later), subjects were instructed to stop work on the in-basket task, and to close the card box with the diary entries. They then engaged in a free recall task, where they were instructed to write down all the incidents they could remember, citing the ratee's name, the specific task, and the level of performance exhibited. This task was completed *without* access to the diaries. Finally, raters evaluated the performance of each carpenter on each individual task, as well as on overall performance, using 5-point rating scales. Raters who kept diaries were encouraged to use their diaries to make these ratings. We analyzed the diary entries simply by counting the number of correct and incorrect entries made. We analyzed the recall data by examining the number of incidents recalled, the percentage of errors recalled, and memory-improvement scores (Graesser, Woll, Kowalski, & Smith, 1980)

Table 4.5 Recall data for four diary keeping conditions

	Condition			
	Person diary	Task diary	Free diary	No diary
Person ARC score	.38	.12	.24	.10
Task ARC score	.05	.30	.13	.11
Incidents recalled	8.12	6.81	6.94	7.20
% Errors in recall	9%	39%	62%	76%
Memory improvement	.41	.25	.18	.14

Source: DeNisi, Robbins, and Cafferty (1989)

which indicated the level of recall corrected for the number of errors. We also computed person and task ARC scores based on the recall data.

The results for the recall data are presented in Table 4.5 but, before turning to those results, I need to say something about those raters in the free-diary condition. There were sixteen subjects in that condition, and eleven of them organized their diaries according to persons or ratees; two organized their diaries according to tasks; two organized their diaries chronologically, and the final subject did not use any organizing scheme we could discern. Thus, given a choice, there did seem to be a clear choice of how to organize a diary, and that choice was according to persons.

As can be seen in Table 4.5, raters tended to organize information in memory consistent with the way they organized their diaries, based on mean ARC scores, with the lowest levels of clustering occurring in the no-diary condition. Also, we can see that, although there were no significant differences in the mean number of incidents recalled, there were differences across conditions in the percentage of errors recalled (lowest for the raters in the person-diary condition) and the memory-improvement scores (highest for those in the person-diary condition). It is interesting to note that, although most of the raters in the free-diary condition organized their diaries according to persons, they did not perform, on average, nearly as well as those raters in the person-diary condition. Although some of the differences disappear when we consider only those raters who *did* organize their diaries according to persons, some differences remain. We can only speculate that the clear instructions made the organization of information in memory easier for the raters actually assigned to the person-diary condition.

Results for the ratings are presented in Table 4.6 (using the fictitious names we assigned to the ratees), and reveal a somewhat similar pattern. Overall performance ratings for the three ratees did not differ in the no-diary condition, indicating that these raters were unable to make even gross distinctions among ratees. The ratings did differ in the three diary keeping conditions, although in no case did post hoc tests reveal that all three ratings differed significantly from each other. Therefore, based on overall

Table 4.6 Mean task and overall performance ratings for each ratee across conditions

| | Condition | | | |
	Person diary	Task diary	Free diary	No diary
John				
Sawing (1)	3.08	3.13	2.83	2.83
Sanding (1)	2.94	3.12	2.63	2.87
Staining (2)	3.83	3.89	3.75	3.13
Overall	3.62	3.52	3.34	3.00
Michael				
Sawing (1)	3.13	2.99	3.06	2.90
Sanding (1)	2.94	2.88	3.19	2.90
Staining (1)	2.90	2.28	2.99	2.67
Overall	2.65	2.73	3.12	2.92
Bill				
Sawing (0)	1.85	1.77	1.81	2.60
Sanding (1)	2.66	2.77	2.50	2.67
Staining (1)	2.71	2.11	2.13	2.47
Overall	2.51	2.34	2.06	2.52

Note: John performed the sanding and sawing tasks *once* correctly and *once* incorrectly, and the staining task *twice* correctly. Michael performed each task *once* correctly and *once* incorrectly. Bill performed the sanding and staining tasks *once* correctly and *once* incorrectly, and performed the sawing task *twice* incorrectly. The numbers in parentheses in the table refer to the number of times the task was performed *correctly.*
Source:DeNisi, Robbins, and Cafferty (1989)

performance ratings, diary keeping allowed some, but not perfect, discrimination among ratees.

But remember that the differences in overall performance portrayed in the videotapes were fairly subtle. When we examine the results for individual task ratings, we find that only in the person-diary condition were raters consistently capable of discriminating between the good and poor performance incidents exhibited by a single carpenter. The fact that we should have found any such effects is really quite interesting, since the raters were able to refer to their diaries when making their evaluations, suggesting that the way in which diaries are organized has an effect even on fine distinctions made by raters. Therefore, the results of the study indicated that most raters, given a choice, would prefer to organize diaries according to persons or ratees, and that diaries kept in this way resulted in more accurate recall and better ability to discriminate across different levels of performance exhibited by the same ratee, when compared to diaries organized according to tasks. It is important to note, though, that these results also suggest that any attempt to use diaries to organize unorganized information is likely to result in a marked improvement over what raters will be able to do without the aid of a diary.

Thus, structured diary keeping appeared to be an effective way of aiding raters in organizing information so that they could access it and use it for making appraisal decisions. Of course, diary keeping could be a problem if the raters recorded incidents in a biased fashion. Although we did not find evidence of that here, there was also not much chance for the raters to develop expectations or other bases for bias in this study. It is noteworthy, though, that Balzer (1986) *did* report bias in diary keeping, consistent with expectations about performance, as had been suggested elsewhere (e.g., Darley & Gross, 1983). In addition, it has been suggested (e.g., Taylor, Parker, & Ford, 1959) that more experienced raters might develop their own organizing principles, and so might not need diaries to help them organize information. However, in Chapter 6 I will discuss the results of field studies which suggest that experienced raters *can* benefit from the use of structured diaries *and* that their diary entries do *not* seem to be biased. Finally, it occurred to us that raters probably saw diary keeping as an inconvenience, and might not keep at it over time. We conducted a study which will be described below to look at the effects of *not* keeping diaries over time after initial training, but the point is that, although diary keeping seemed to make sense as an intervention, there were probably limits to its usefulness. Before summing up what we learned about reprocessing and interventions aimed at helping raters organize information, it is worth taking a bit of time to discuss one follow-up diary keeping study that helped set the stage for our later field work.

A problem with interventions, especially those requiring continuing effort such as diary keeping, is that raters often see them as an intrusion on their time rather than as an aid to their decision making. In discussing diary keeping with managers in several organizations where diary keeping was supposedly required, those managers noted that most raters simply stopped keeping the diaries after a while. Given that this might well be the reality in the field, could an intervention such as structured diary keeping be effective even if raters did not persist in it? On the other hand, we were also interested in whether there was benefit derived from the actual diary keeping task, or if raters provided with someone else's diaries could do as well as if they had kept the diaries themselves. To try to answer this question we designed a study (DeNisi, Robbins, & Cafferty, 1988) involving evaluations at two different time periods. For the first rating period, subjects (120 undergraduates who participated for extra credit in their courses) observed three carpenters performing three carpentry tasks twice each, and the subjects were provided with standards to help them evaluate the performance. While they were observing these tapes, the subjects were also to be working on a ten-item in-basket exercise (from Beatty & Schneier, 1981). After viewing the tape and completing (or working on) the in-basket task, raters were dismissed and told to report back in one week.

At the second session, raters were first asked to recall and write down all the performance incidents they could from the first session, and then were asked to rate the performance of the three carpenters on each task, as well as provide a rating of Overall Performance (all using 5-point rating scales). Once the ratings had been completed and collected, the raters were shown a second videotape, portraying the same three carpenters performing the same tasks (but on different occasions with different specific incidents portrayed), and were told to view this tape while working on a second (modified) in-basket exercise. After a brief break while materials were collected and after instructions were provided, raters were asked to recall and write down all the performance incidents they could from this second tape, and then were asked to rate the three carpenters' performance from the second tape. Both videotapes presented the performance information in an unblocked format, and each carpenter performed the task correctly in half (three) of the segments.

Condition 1
Session 1: Raters are trained in diary keeping and critical incident techniques *but* they do *not* keep diaries. Training *does* emphasize that diaries should be kept organized according to persons.
Session 2: Raters receive critical incident training and are instructed to keep diaries but in any format they choose (all choose to organize according to persons).

Condition 2
Session 1: Raters trained as above, *but* they actually keep diaries organized according to persons.
Session 2: Raters received no special instructions and do not keep diaries.

Condition 3
Session 1: Raters receive no training or instructions and do *not* keep diaries. Prior to making ratings, though, they receive diary information supposedly collected by another rater. Diaries are organized according to persons and contain 12 incidents (the mean number for the study).
Session 2: Raters receive no special instructions and do not keep diaries.

Condition 4
Session 1: Raters receive no instructions and do not keep diaries.
Session 2: Raters receive instructions on critical incidents and are instructed to keep diaries in any format they choose (most choose to organize according to persons).

Condition 5
Session 1: Raters receive no instructions and do not keep diaries.
Session 2: Raters receive no instructions and do not keep diaries.

Figure 4.1. Experimental conditions for second diary keeping study
Source: DeNisi, Robbins, and Cafferty (1988)

Raters were randomly assigned to one of five experimental conditions, based on the diary keeping instructions they received. These conditions are outlined in Figure 4.1. As can be seen in the figure, there were several versions of a control condition for each session, but only in Condition 5 did raters not receive any training or keep any diaries for either session. There were fifteen subjects assigned to each condition.

The results for ratings of the first videotape largely replicated the findings we reported above, although differences among conditions were not as large after the one-week delay. Virtually every rater who was given a choice as to how diaries should be organized, organized diaries according to persons. The raters who were trained to keep diaries, but did not actually keep them for Session 1 (Condition 1) apparently still organized information about ratees in recall according to persons, but their ratings were not as accurate as those provided by raters who actually kept diaries. Raters who were provided with diaries kept by others apparently used that diary information, because their ratings were more accurate than those of raters who did not keep diaries. Their ratings were less accurate, though, than those provided by raters who kept their own diaries. The major focus of the study, though, was the ratings for the second videotape, and the associated recall data from that videotape, especially for the raters who had kept diaries for the first session but not the second (Condition 2), and these results are presented in Table 4.7. As can be seen, the raters in Condition 2, who had kept diaries organized by persons for the first session, continued to organize information according to persons even when they no longer kept their diaries, and those raters who received someone else's diary for Session 1 (Condition 3) also organized information according to persons for Session 2, even though they kept no diaries for either session. Raters in these two conditions exhibited levels of person organization for Session 2 that were comparable to those obtained for the raters who actually kept diaries for Session 2 (Conditions 1 and 4). Accuracy was defined here as the ability of a rater to discriminate between the incidents of good and poor performance exhibited by a ratee, since Overall Performance was designed to be the same for all three ratees. In fact, raters in all conditions exhibited no differences in overall ratings across the three ratees, but only raters who actually kept their own diaries for Session 2 were able to effectively discriminate between the two levels of performance displayed by the ratees.

The data for recall, based on Memory Improvement Scores (Graesser, Woll, Kowalski, & Smith, 1980), which indicate the extent to which recall is better than chance, indicate no differences in the accuracy of recall across the four conditions where diaries were kept for at least one session. Thus these results suggested that, although actually keeping diaries was the preferred outcome, raters could gain some of the benefits of diary keeping, especially relative to organization of information in memory and recall, as long as the person categories used to organize the information were

Table 4.7 Means for all dependent variables under five experimental conditions for Session 2

	Condition 1	Condition 2	Condition 3	Condition 4	Condition 5
Dependent Variables					
Person ARC score	.52	.63	.56	.50	.10
Task ARC score	.18	.08	.12	.10	.00
Memory					
improvement	.40	.38	.36	.40	.07
Ratings					
Correct incidents	4.20	3.29	3.31	4.34	3.18
Incorrect incidents	2.26	2.89	2.92	2.20	2.95
Overall					
performance	3.00	3.02	2.91	3.03	3.10

Source: DeNisi, Robbins, and Cafferty (1988)

somehow primed. Whether this happened because raters kept diaries for a while and then stopped, or because they were trained to keep diaries but didn't, or even because they were provided with someone else's diaries, didn't seem to matter. The major advantage of actually keeping the diary, though, came when we considered the ability of raters to discriminate between good and poor performance incidents performed by the same ratee.

With these two studies, then, we learned a couple of important things about diary keeping for our eventual trials in the field. First, when given a choice, raters preferred to keep diaries organized by persons or ratees. Since this was also the type of diary that seemed to produce the clearest effects, this meant that, if we tried to intervene by having raters keep diaries organized by persons, we should encounter less resistance than if we tried to introduce diaries organized in any other way. Second, we had learned that, if raters kept diaries for a while, even if they eventually stopped, some of the effects of that diary keeping would persist. Specifically, raters would continue to rely upon those categories in memory primed by the diaries, for organizing subsequent performance information, and this would help them in recall if not in ratings. Thus, structured diary keeping could be somewhat effective, even if raters did not keep up their diaries over time. Since this was likely to happen, this seemed quite an encouraging finding.

CONCLUSIONS

This chapter described a series of studies that followed from the results of the Cafferty, DeNisi, and Williams (1986) study. Those results had indicated to us that raters would be forced to rely upon a great deal of information for making appraisal decisions that was not initially obtained (and so organized) for the purpose of making appraisal decisions, and/or was not organized at all. Our studies of the role of reprocessing objectives revealed that, introducing the need for reprocessing was in fact, a problem for raters. Information initially obtained for one purpose was generally organized in a way that made it useful for that purpose, and this meant that it was probably not useful for appraisals. We did also find, however, that requiring raters to make deservedness-type decisions always required them to form impressions about all ratees, and this would make the reprocessing a bit easier.

In studying reprocessing objectives, we also began to look at the relative importance of on-line vs. memory-based processing in performance appraisal. We found, for example, that when appraisal salience was high (i.e., the rater acquired information for the purpose of making appraisal decisions) on-line processing was more likely to occur. In these cases, ratings tended to be a bit more accurate, but it was likely that, in the field, appraisal salience was more often low, which tended to result in more memory-based processing. Concerns about on-line vs. memory-based processing models continued to play a role in our research program, and we will return to this topic again later.

The earlier Cafferty *et al.* (1986) findings also suggested that raters would often have to use unorganized information for making appraisal decisions. Whether this was due to an unblocked acquisition strategy, or simply encountering performance information as it occurred (in no particular pattern), raters who did not organize performance information were found to have problems in recalling that information and making accurate ratings. We therefore investigated using the appraisal instrument and structured diaries as means of helping raters impose structure on unstructured information. In both cases, we found that organization according to persons resulted in the greatest recall of accurate information, and more accurate ratings, and we found that we could induce this type of organization either by ensuring that raters received task-based appraisal instruments prior to observing performance, or by having raters keep diaries structured by person. In fact, we even found that allowing raters to keep diaries organized in any way they liked would also probably lead to diaries organized by persons, and person clustering in memory with all its benefits. Finally, we found that some of these benefits of structured diary keeping would persist even if raters ceased to keep their diaries.

Thus we had further determined the importance of information organization in memory for allowing raters to provide accurate ratings, and had identified conditions which facilitated that organization, and others which hindered that organization. Clearly we had come a long way from trying to identify search strategies, but there was still another major hurdle we had to clear. Every one of the studies discussed thus far was conducted in a laboratory setting, using student raters who were rating fictitious ratees. Did these effects hold up in the "real world" as well? This was obviously a critical question, and in fact several scholars who have noted criticisms of cognitive approaches to appraisals (e.g., Banks & Murphy, 1985; Ilgen & Favero, 1985; Ilgen & Klein, 1988), have singled out the reliance upon laboratory settings as a major problem. Therefore we were forced to move to the field if we wanted to establish the legitimacy of this approach and, in any event, we were not content to study these effects in these artificial settings only. We will discuss those forays into the field in Chapter 6, along with some very special problems this research presented. But first, as the studies described in this chapter were being conducted, we were also conducting other studies that looked at other issues besides information acquisition and organization of information in memory. Therefore, before turning to our field research, I would like to take the next chapter to describe some of the other things we were doing while preparing to go into the field.

Other factors and other cognitive processes

Up until this point, I have been concentrating on studies dealing with information acquisition and organization in memory. But over the years we conducted a number of studies that focused on other processes as well. In addition, some studies were conducted which looked at external factors that might also influence cognitive processes. Specifically, in this chapter, I will describe studies dealing with the role of appraisal purpose, ratee gender, and rater affect towards ratees as potential factors impacting upon rater cognitive processes and ratings. These studies help fill in the picture of what goes on during the appraisal process, but a number of these studies were "one-shot" topics, where we did not plan or execute any follow-up studies. A noteworthy exception to this is the case of studies on rater affect. In this case there was a follow-up study in the field, and, although affect was not a big part of our original model or research propositions, I believe that factors such as affect and rater motivation (which *we* have not studied, but others have, e.g., Cleveland, Murphy, & Williams, 1989; Murphy & Cleveland, 1991) have already become "hot" topics for performance appraisal research, and will become more important in the future. In any event, the studies described in this chapter all have something to say about the appraisal process.

Appraisal purpose was originally specified as a critical factor in our 1984 model, so this was just one of the few aspects of that mode, other than information acquisition, that were actually tested. Ratee gender was always considered an important factor in the appraisal literature, and the study described here simply places gender issues into a cognitive framework. Rater affect, on the other hand, reflects a more recent acknowledgment that "cold" (i.e., non-emotional) cognitive models are probably deficient. Some of the studies described here were motivated by earlier findings, and represented a need on our part to understand what was going on, but others simply reflected changing interests and new areas for research. With these caveats, we turn to consider a set of studies designed to examine various aspects of the processing of information (i.e., the integration of information into a decision) in performance appraisal.

INFORMATION INTEGRATION AND PROCESSING

I. The role of appraisal purpose

In our model, as well as in any other cognitive model, after information is acquired and encoded, it is stored in memory. It is later recalled when appraisal decisions are due, and the pieces of information acquired are weighed and combined to form a judgment. In many ways, this stage in the process has received a great deal more attention traditionally than information acquisition or encoding, since more traditional approaches to studying appraisals have largely assumed that the information upon which to base a decision was a "given." Although we clearly did not make that same assumption, it was important to understand something of how raters used information to make a decision. Specifically, we examined the role of appraisal purpose on information utilization, and the importance of a schema about what constituted a "good worker," and what it took for a rater to abandon a set of expectations about a ratee. We also conducted a study to examine the role of ratee gender in the decision making process, and this led to a consideration of the role of rater affect, which we will consider separately.

Earlier, in Chapter 3, I discussed one part of a study we conducted to determine the role of appraisal purpose on cognitive processes (Williams, DeNisi, Blencoe, & Cafferty, 1985). Specifically, I discussed the results of Williams *et al.* (1985) Study 2, which was concerned with the role of purpose on information acquisition. We now need to discuss, briefly, the results of Williams *et al.* (1985) Study 1; which was concerned with the effects of purpose on information utilization. Recall that, in these studies, we operationalized appraisal purpose along two dimensions. The first considered purpose in the usual way, and here we examined appraisal decisions made for the purpose of salary increases, promotion recommendations, and remedial training referrals. We referred to the second dimension as the differences between designation decisions (where the rater had to choose one ratee for an outcome such as a salary increase) versus deservedness decisions (where the rater had to rate how deserving *each* ratee was of receiving a treatment such as a salary increase). Thus, our study used a 3 (purpose) × 2 (deservedness vs. designation) design, and the 120 subjects (undergraduate students who participated to fulfill partial course requirements) were randomly assigned to one of six experimental conditions.

In addition to examining the role of appraisal purpose, this study was also designed to determine if raters used performance information to make appraisal decisions, in a way consistent with the way in which subjects use covariance information to make attribution decisions (cf., McArthur, 1972; Major, 1980). Thus, we predicted that variation in the consistency and the distinctiveness of performance information should be more important than variations in consensus information in determining ratings, such that ratings would be highest when good performance is seen as consistent and non-distinctive, while ratings would be the lowest when *poor* performance is seen as consistent and non-distinctive. We were still using the administrative assistants, and we expanded the number of ratees to eight for this study, and all information was presented to raters in file folders. We needed to prepare two sets of vignettes, though. One set, used for promotion and pay increase decisions, began by describing the performance of all eight ratees on the budgeting task as "good". For the rest of the information presented, the eight ratees each represented a cell in a 2 (high vs. low consistency) × 2 (high vs. low distinctiveness) × 2 (high vs. low consensus) within-subjects covariance matrix. So, for example, high consistency information was represented by indicating that last month's budget was also done well; while low consistency indicated that last month's budget had not been done well. A second set of vignettes was prepared for the remedial training program, using the same basic idea except that it began by stating that all eight ratees had performed the budget preparation task poorly and proceeded from there. All subjects received the information in the same order (consistency–consensus–distinctiveness) because that made for the best flow, and because a pilot study indicated that there were no effects on ratings for differences in the order of information presented, although such effects had been reported elsewhere (e.g., Ruble & Feldman, 1976; Sherman & Titus, 1982). All subjects reviewed the materials for 20 minutes, and then were asked to rate the eight ratees on 7-point rating scales. Raters in designation conditions were asked to indicate how they felt about each ratee being the one to receive (for example) a promotion, using a scale anchored from "definitely not the one to be promoted" to "definitely the one to be promoted." Raters in the deservedness conditions were asked to rate how deserving was each ratee of (for example) a 6% pay increase.

The mean ratings in each purpose and outcome decision, for each level of consistency, distinctiveness, and consensus information, are presented in Table 5.1. The result of a series of ANOVAs indicated that raters in deservedness conditions gave significantly higher ratings than did those in designation conditions, and that ratings made relative to remedial training (reverse-scored) were higher than those made for either salary or promotion decisions, but the interaction between the two was not significant, and there were no other significant effects involving rating purpose. Furthermore, the two effects that were reported explained about 16% of the variance in ratings. Thus, there was not very strong evidence of differences in information utilization as a function of appraisal purpose. On the other hand, there were fairly large (and significant) effects for information consistency and distinctiveness, suggesting that, as predicted, raters gave higher ratings when there was low distinctiveness, and higher ratings when there was high consistency, while consensus information was not very important for ratings, nor were the interactions.

Table 5.1 Mean performance ratings as a function of covariance information, appraisal purpose, and outcome

Outcome	Purpose	Consensus	Low distinctiveness		High distinctiveness	
			Low consistency	High consistency	Low consistency	High consistency
Deservedness	Promotion	High	3.55	6.15	2.70	3.70
		Low	4.25	6.25	2.50	4.55
	Salary	High	4.00	5.80	2.60	4.50
		Low	4.80	5.85	3.00	5.00
	Training	High	4.55	5.95	3.70	4.30
		Low	4.70	5.70	3.70	4.55
	Mean		4.31	5.95	3.03	4.43
Designation	Promotion	High	3.80	5.00	2.80	3.80
		Low	3.75	5.25	2.60	4.30
	Salary	High	3.25	5.42	1.95	3.65
		Low	3.35	4.75	2.75	3.55
	Training	High	4.15	6.10	2.45	3.35
		Low	4.70	5.75	3.25	4.10
	Mean		3.83	5.37	2.63	3.79

Source: Williams, Wickert, and Peters (1985)

Thus, although the results of Study 1 provided support for our argument (from the DeNisi, Cafferty, & Meglino, 1984 model) that raters utilized performance information in a way similar to how judges used covariance information to make attributions, it did not provide support for our predictions about the reliance upon different types of information for making appraisal decisions for different purposes. In fact, the only effects we found indicated, consistent with earlier studies (e.g., Sharon & Bartlett, 1969), that raters tended to be more lenient when making decisions that focused on negative consequences for ratees. Unlike our results for information acquisition, we found that appraisal purpose did not really affect information utilization, although I must sound a note of caution about interpreting these results. We *did* find effects for appraisal purpose on information acquisition, but finding effects for utilization in a laboratory study is surely even more difficult. Although these results are instructive, we cannot expect to fully capture all the factors that a rater considers when making decisions with consequences for ratees. Although we tried to capture some dimensions of those consequences, surely this is an area where field studies are more appropriate.

II. The effects of schemata

As noted earlier, most of the cognitive models of the appraisal process suggest some role for information processing based on pre-existing categories or schemata. This is a more important feature of the Ilgen and Feldman (1983) model than of ours, but our model does suggest that raters will use schemata as a way of organizing and thus processing incoming performance information. These suggestions have recently led Borman (1987, 1991) to begin to describe performance models held by raters, and to explore how these models might influence the way raters processed information (I will discuss this research a bit more in Chapter 7). Some time earlier, Allyn Blencoe's dissertation (Blencoe, 1984) investigated similar processes in a laboratory setting. In that study, Blencoe drew upon some work in social psychology used to develop and identify stereotypes (McCauley & Stitt, 1978), to develop a schema or prototype of a "good worker" and one for a "poor worker." The prototypes were largely dependent upon traits (which is also consistent with Borman's later work), and they were formed on the basis of Bayesian probability estimates concerning the extent to which workers possessed a trait, the likelihood that someone possessing the trait would be considered a good (or poor) worker, and the likelihood that someone who was considered a good (or poor) worker would possess the given trait. Subjects (graduate students) provided the information to create the prototypes, and a second group of graduate students (from the same program) later served as raters. Raters were presented with information about levels of performance, but were also provided with information to suggest that a given rater was either a good or poor match for either the good or poor worker schema. Although actual performance information was found to be a more important determinant of ratings than the match with either schema, Blencoe did find that once subjects believed there was a "match" they then proceeded to use the schema to provide their ratings, in much the same as we usually think of halo error operating.

Thus Blencoe's dissertation suggested that, once rater's identify a ratee as fitting a prototype, they often relied upon the prototype rather than actual performance information when making ratings. But, once raters categorize a ratee, can they never change their minds? Feldman (1981) and Ilgen and Feldman (1983) had argued that raters engage in automatic processing (Schneider & Shiffrin, 1977; Shiffrin & Schneider, 1977) once they can categorize a ratee but, when raters encounter information inconsistent with that category, they switch to controlled processing as they can no longer rely upon the category or schema for processing information. But what would it take for a rater to change categories or schemata? For example, if a rater decided after a short interaction that a ratee was a "good worker" or was "reliable", how much contradictory information would the rater have to encounter before she or he would reclassify the ratee? This was an intriguing question, and we conducted two laboratory experiments to try to understand how raters came to abandon one schema and adopt a different one.

III. Schema abandonment

The first of these experiments was rather simple. DeNisi, Cafferty, Williams, Meglino, and Blencoe (1982) had raters (120 undergraduate students, participating for extra course credit) evaluate a group of administrative assistants. Prior to receiving present performance information (provided in file folders), the raters were given information about prior performance and previous performance evaluations. This information triggered a schema-based expectation that the ratee would perform at either a high, average, or low performance, and we checked to be sure that these expectations were in fact triggered. Raters were then given performance information that was either high, average, or low, such that we crossed all levels of prior performance with all levels of present performance. The results suggest that our subjects, for the most part, rather than simply abandoning expectations and schemata, simply used the new information in an averaging model. That is, when there was an expectation that the ratee would perform at a high level, the ultimate ratings were highest when actual performance was high, lower when actual performance was average, and lower yet when actual performance was low. Ratings made when performance expectations were low converged towards the center from the opposite direction (surely raising the possibility, by the way, that we were only observing regression towards the mean), but the ratings provided when expectations were high were never lower than the ratings provided when expectations were low, regardless of the levels of actual performance information presented. Thus, these raters modified their schemata based on subsequent performance information, but they did not appear to abandon the schemata completely. Raters who began with expectations that performance would be average, on the other hand, hardly modified their schemata at all. That is, regardless of the level of actual performance information presented, ratings remained as roughly "average," and never overlapped with the ratings in either of the other two conditions.

We could only speculate why this particular pattern of results occurred. Perhaps an "average worker" schema is more resilient and more resistant to change than either a good or poor worker schema. Perhaps a rater can more easily accommodate incidents of good or poor performance into a schema of "average" than he or she can accommodate incidents of good performance into a schema of poor worker, or vice versa. This speculation led to some interesting ideas about what it meant to be considered "average." If we believe someone is good at something, we probably believe that they usually perform a task well; and if we believe someone is poor at something, we probably believe they usually perform the task poorly. But perhaps when we believe someone is average, we don't necessarily expect them to perform the task at an "average" level, but instead expect them to be inconsistent or variable. If this were the case, it would very difficult for a rater to encounter information that was truly inconsistent with that expectation, since incidents of both good and poor performance would occasionally be expected. Perhaps, then, the greatest "curse" for anyone who is evaluated, is to be considered "average," since once this happens there is almost no way to change the classification.

In any event, the DeNisi et al. (1982) study only examined pre-performance expectations and final ratings. We did not examine any of the processes that might drive the change in schemata or the abandonment of one schema for another. In order to examine such processes, it would be necessary to establish expectations and then provide pieces of information one at a time, and see how the rater used each piece of information to change or maintain expectations and schemata. In fact, Kevin Williams's M.S. Thesis (Williams, 1982) conducted that same year, was designed to do exactly that.

Williams (1982) argued that schemata were useful to raters to help interpret and organize incoming information, and that raters would naturally try to interpret any novel information in a way that was consistent with the schema, so that the schema could be maintained (see Markus, 1977; Neisser, 1976). He also argued (consistent with the early orientation of our research program) that raters might use differential causal attributions in an attempt to explain information that was inconsistent with a schema, while maintaining the schema. Specifically, he noted that a number of studies had found that judges were able to maintain existing schemata by attributing schema-inconsistent information to unstable causes, such as luck and effort, and attributing schema-consistent information to stable causes such as ability and task difficulty (e.g., Deaux, 1976; Deaux & Emswiller, 1974; Frieze & Weiner, 1971; Lau & Russell, 1980; Zuckerman, 1978).

But, despite the ability of judges to maintain schemata in the face of inconsistent information (also see Lord, Ross, & Lepper, 1979; Ross, Lepper, Strack, & Steinmetz, 1977), eventually the inconsistency becomes so overwhelming that the initial schema, and any predictions based upon that schema, become untenable (e.g., Hemsley & Marmurek, 1982). Still, the exact process through which this abandonment occurs was not clear. Rothbart (1980) suggested that there were two feasible models to describe this change. In the first case, consistent with Anderson's (1974) weighted average model of impression formation, disconfirming information would be accepted and averaged in with previous information and the prevailing schema. Eventually, the disconfirming information would simply gain the upper hand, and the scale would begin to tip in favor of a different schema. The process would be gradual, and change in schemata incremental. But Rothbart (1980) personally favored a more catastrophic model, where the judge would suddenly be "converted" to a new view of the ratee. Here, the disconfirming information would be somehow discounted (probably through the attributional mechanisms described above) until the rater reached a saturation point. The rater would then immediately switch to a different schema, so that there was no gradual change in schemata – the rater either held one strongly, or switched to another one that was also held strongly. Williams's thesis would allow a comparison of these two explanations, by asking raters to make judgments and provide attributions as each new piece of information was introduced.

Specifically, he had eighty-nine undergraduates (participating in the study for fulfillment of partial course requirements) rate the performance of "John," who had just been transferred from one department to another. Subjects were provided with performance evaluations from John's previous assignment indicating that, across several dimensions, John's average performance rating had +3.5 on an 11-point scale (ranging from −5.00 to +5.00, with a zero point), or that his prior average performance was −3.5, depending on the schema-based expectation condition. Subjects were then asked to rate how well they expected John to perform on his new job, using the same scale. They were presented with nine separate performance incidents for the new job, all of them inconsistent with expectations. These were presented to the raters one at a time and, after each one was presented, the raters were asked to rate John's performance and to indicate the extent to which they attributed that performance (using 5-point scales) to ability, effort, task difficulty, and luck. Half the raters provided ratings before attributions in each case, and half provided attributions before ratings.

The results indicated that, for those subjects with the positive performance expectations, the initial performance rating (expectations) was 9.87, but the final rating was 3.44; while for the subjects with negative expectations, the initial rating was 3.28, while the final rating was 8.50. Thus, performance expectations were manipulated as intended, and raters did seem to abandon their expectations, or at least dramatically revise those expectations, in the face of inconsistent information. The results, presented graphically in Figure 5.1, also indicate that schemata were abandoned rather quickly by these raters. After only the second piece of inconsistent information the plots for the ratings provided in the two expectation conditions cross, and the data support a linear trend in the ratings, suggesting a gradual shift, but only after a fairly dramatic one. These results also indicated that causal attributions changed over time as well, especially ability attributions, which started off low and then significantly increased over time, and effort attributions, which started off high and decreased over time. These effects

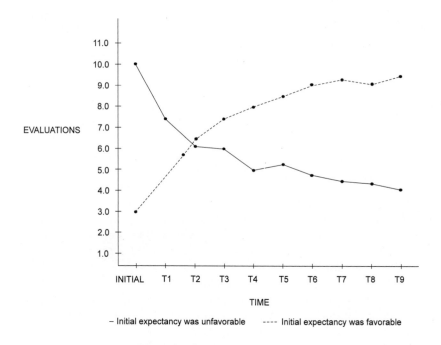

Figure 5.1 Changes in evaluations over time as a function of the number of incongruent performance incidents
Source: Williams (1982)

were relatively weak, but become clearer when we consider some individual differences in reactions to the disconfirming information.

Thus the results provided some evidence for both catastrophic and gradual change, but a closer look at how individuals reacted to the inconsistent information is useful. "Jumpers" were defined as raters who changed their ratings at least 3 scale points from one incident to the next. The results indicated that thirty-two subjects jumped immediately after seeing one piece of disconfirming information. For these subjects, the schemata triggered by the prior performance information was obviously not very resilient, either because the initial schema wasn't strong to begin with, or because the subjects placed much more weight on performance information they observed personally as compared to ratings from a prior rater. Twelve more subjects jumped at time 2, and six more at time 3, suggesting an only slightly more resilient schema. But the remaining subjects never "jumped." That is, their ratings were gradual throughout the nine trials. As above, patterns of attributions changed accordingly; jumpers moved from making strong external attributions to making strong internal attributions for the inconsistent performance, while non-jumpers continued to make external attributions throughout the study.

Thus, although many raters abandoned their expectations rather quickly, others persisted. Williams did not collect any data on individual differences (other than rater gender which was not a factor), so we cannot say what might be behind these differences, but the results clearly suggest that attributions mediate the move from one schema to another. Surely raters in the field, who have more time to develop schema-based expectations, would be less likely to abandon those expectations so quickly, but even in the laboratory some raters hung on and only gradually gave up their expectations. In any event, these results suggest that raters can abandon initial schemata in favor of new ones, and that this process is probably mediated by differential attributions to stable and unstable causes. We never pursued this any further, but the suggestion that different people abandon schemata at differential rates remains an intriguing idea.

These studies, then, examined information processing activities in a fairly broad sense. The results indicated that appraisal purpose had some (but slight) effect on how information was processed, and that the presence of a "good worker" and "poor worker" schema might also affect how information is processed. Finally, we tried to trace the process by which schemata and expectations are abandoned or modified over time, in the face of inconsistent information. The remaining studies I discuss in this chapter deal with specific sources of rating "bias," and try to assess how these factors reintegrate into appraisal decisions. I place "bias" in quotes because, although one might agree that considering ratee gender is a source of bias, the situation is not nearly so clear when we consider the role of affect towards a ratee. But I am getting ahead of myself; first we will turn to a study examining the role of ratee gender on some of the processing of information.

A COGNITIVE VIEW OF GENDER BIAS IN APPRAISALS

Throughout the various studies over the years described in this book, we never examined possible gender or race bias except in one study. As noted in the review by Landy and Farr (1980) ratee gender (as well as rater gender) has long been considered an important factor in performance evaluations, and it was even planned, at one point, to develop another set of videotapes depicting women performing the carpentry tasks, so that we could fully integrate ratee gender into our studies. In fact, in many of the studies described thus far (and that will be described) it occurred to us that either gender or race might play a role in some of the cognitive processes, and so we worked hard to make sure we kept these factors *out* of the studies we conducted. The plan was always to examine the issue without considering factors such as gender or race, since they might confound the results. Once a phenomenon was established, though, we could then replicate the study incorporating race and/or gender. Despite these good intentions, and a genuine interest in examining how gender and/or race might affect cognitive processes, the one study I am about to describe is the only one where ratee gender was explicitly made part of the design. I will discuss some ways in which these variables might be better integrated into cognitive appraisal research in Chapter 7, but for now let me turn to the one study where it was considered.

Robbins and DeNisi (1993) designed a laboratory experiment designed to determine where in the cognitive processes underlying appraisal decisions ratee gender might make a difference, and what role contextual factors might play in the importance of ratee gender. We noted that the results of studies examining the extent of bias against women in performance appraisal had produced rather mixed results, with some researchers finding no differences in mean ratings (e.g., Gupta, Beehr, & Jenkins, 1980; London & Stumpf, 1983; Stumpf & London, 1981), and still others finding bias *in favor* of women (Pulakos & Wexley, 1983; Peters, O'Connor & Weekley, 1984; Tsui & Gutek, 1984), while the compelling body of evidence makes it clear that bias *against* women is operating in real world evaluations (Blau & Ferber, 1987; U.S. Dept. of Labor, 1991). This inconsistency suggested to us, not that women might not be facing discrimination in appraisals, but that there were clearly situational determinants of the amount and nature of that discrimination (see Heilman, 1980; also see reviews by Dipboye, 1985; Nieva & Gutek, 1980). From a cognitive perspective, this led us to question the process by which gender bias might influence ratings.

For example, bias might play a role at the outset in determining what raters looked for or attended to. If raters only looked for poor performance in women, or attended to incidents of poor performance in women, they could continue through and process, recall and integrate performance information only to find that, indeed, women were performing more poorly. Even an on-line processing proponent could argue that this initial bias influenced the general impression formed about women, again resulting in poorer evaluations. Alternatively, raters might encode performance information for women differently than they did for men. Different categories might be activated for women resulting in information being interpreted in a less favorable way for women (see Beauvais & Spence, 1987; and Hastie, 1981, for more specifics about such categories and their impact). Different expectations or different schemata might also result in differential recall of performance information for women (although Taylor and Falcone, 1982, reported that recall errors and categorization based on gender were uncorrelated).

Note that, in all these cases, a biased rater might believe that he or she was evaluating women in an unbiased way. Surely it was not the rater's "fault" that he or she only observed poor performance for women, or only recalled incidents of poor performance for women. Of course, ratee gender might also enter the process in the final stages where gender would be just another piece of information to be considered and weighed in forming a final evaluation. Here, we would suspect, bias would be more conscious. But it also seemed possible that ratee gender could influence ratings by influencing ratee affect. That is, a rater might not "like" a female ratee as much as a male ratee and it would be this difference in affect that would ultimately account for any differences in ratings – and these effects tend to become important in latter stages of processing (Robbins & DeNisi, 1991). The Robbins and DeNisi (1993) study, then, tried to identify the subprocess at which bias entered the decision, but focusing on recall and integration; it also examined the role of situational factors in determining bias against women in appraisal.

The evidence for situational or contextual factors was clearer, but the exact nature of any such factors was not clear. For example, several studies have found that bias against women is greater for managerial jobs than for non-managerial jobs (e.g., Baron & Abrahamsen, 1981; Mobley, 1982; Stevens & DeNisi, 1980); others have found that women fare worse on jobs that are traditionally "male" jobs such as police officer (Morash & Greene, 1986); or that women fare best when they are evaluated by same-gender raters (Cline, Holmes, & Werner, 1977); while others have argued that contrasting gender among a group of ratees to be evaluated is important (e.g., Heilman, 1980; Tudor, 1980; Wexley, Yukl, Kovacks, & Sanders, 1972), especially when women have "solo status" in a group of ratees (Taylor, Fiske, Close, Anderson, & Ruderman, 1977).

In order to examine these issues we conducted a laboratory study using seventy upper-class undergraduates (who participated for extra credit in their courses), thirty-four of whom were women. Subjects were provided with performance information about three administrative assistants performing the same four tasks as in earlier studies, *or* about three carpenters performing the same four woodworking tasks as we used in earlier studies. Statistics indicate that women are over-represented in clerical jobs, accounting for nearly 90% of workers in administrative support jobs (Fisher, 1987; U.S. Dept. of Labor, 1991), while women account for less than 1% of the employees in construction trades (U.S. Dept. of Labor, 1991). Therefore we believed that these two jobs represented "gender-appropriate" and "gender-inappropriate" jobs respectively.

In all cases, performance information was presented in an unblocked format, and each ratee was presented as performing two tasks correctly and two tasks incorrectly. The independent variables for context involved the mix of genders on each type of job. Specifically, there were four conditions. In two conditions there was more than one gender-inappropriate ratee (either two female carpenters or two male administrative assistants), and in two conditions there was only one gender-inappropriate ratee (i.e., the inappropriate ratee had "solo status"; so there was either one female carpenter or one male administrative assistant). Raters were presented with the performance information, and were asked later to recall as many incidents as they could, and were finally asked to rate the four ratees. We considered total recall, recall corrected for errors, and the nature of any recall errors. Specifically, we considered whether the rater recalled a ratee performing a task correctly when it has been performed incorrectly (positive error) or the rater recalled a ratee performing a task incorrectly when it had actually been performed correctly (negative error).

Table 5.2 presents the mean recall indices and ratings provided for the ratee in each condition. As can be seen, there were no differences in any recall index according to ratee gender, or any gender × condition interactions. No effects were found for rater gender, nor were there any interactions involving rater gender. Yet overall ratings did differ, but only when a woman was performing a gender-inappropriate job and she did *not* have solo status on that job. In fact, the same result was found for men performing the (for them) gender-inappropriate job, and there were two men on the job. Upon closer inspection, we found that, in these cases, only *one* person was given lowered ratings, the other was rated about the same as the gender-appropriate worker. Thus, raters may find it easier to discriminate against one member of a group when there is another member present who is not discriminated against. Relative to where in the process this bias enters, these results would suggest that they occur only at the final stage, since there was no evidence of biased recall, which would also suggest no bias at acquisition or encoding. As we shall see a bit later, there is evidence for the operation of affect at these later stages only as well.

Table 5.2 Recall indices and ratings across conditions and by ratee gender

	Total recall	Corrected recall	Overall ratings
Condition 1			
Females	3.38	2.85	2.69
Males	3.54	3.00	3.31
Condition 2			
Females	3.33	3.11	3.28
Males	2.83	2.33	3.00
Condition 3			
Females	3.50	3.20	3.30
Males	2.86	2.68	2.90
Condition 4			
Females	2.71	2.53	3.03
Males	2.58	2.53	3.32

Note: *Condition 1*–Male-typical job with two female and one male ratees; *Condition 2* – Male-typical job with one female and two male ratees; *Condition 3* – Female-typical job with two male and one female ratees; *Condition 4* – Female-typical job with one male and two female ratees.
Source: Robbins and DeNisi (1993)

Thus, the results of our only attempt at seriously integrating ratee gender into the research program indicated stronger effects for context than cognitive processes as a source of bias. Unfortunately, these results also provide evidence of more blatant gender bias, in that it seems to occur independent of biased recall. On the other hand, this might be good news since bias in information acquisition, encoding, or recall may be too subtle to deal with effectively, especially if a rater could still maintain the image of being unbiased. But, as noted above, we had argued in that paper that some of these effects could be due to differences in affect, and we cited an earlier paper by Robbins and DeNisi (1991). Eventually, we designed a more elaborate experiment in the area of affect, which I will discuss shortly. Although gender bias in appraisals is a serious issue, I believe that studying affect may provide insight into a more pervasive type of bias that may well influence ratings of women as well. We turn, then, to a study based on Tina Robbins's dissertation (Robbins, 1991), and published in the *Journal of Applied Psychology* (Robbins & DeNisi, 1994). In the next chapter, I will discuss another study that attempted to move this same perspective on the role of affect to a field setting.

THE ROLE OF INTERPERSONAL AFFECT

With the Robbins and DeNisi (1993) paper we had begun to move beyond more basic cognitive processes in our research program. This study marked the beginning of an attempt to bring some convergence between our research program, based primarily upon cognitive processes, and other process-oriented appraisal research programs. One construct that seemed a good candidate for this potential integration was rater affect. As you may recall, when I discussed the various other rater process models that had been proposed, there was one proposed by DeCotiis and Petit (1978) that explicitly included a role for the affect a rater had towards a ratee. Our own model had also included some recognition of the role of affect, but this was really tangential to the more central cognitive processes we focused upon.

But others had established a role for affect as a determinant of rating accuracy (Cardy & Dobbins, 1986) and rating errors (Tsui & Barry, 1986), indicating that the way a rater felt about a ratee influenced ratings as well as the kinds of errors that might occur. These studies, though, tended to involve a rater's reactions to the manipulation of affective traits concerning an unknown ratee (i.e., Cardy & Dobbins, 1986; Nisbett & Wilson, 1977; Park & Sims, 1989), and Dipboye (1985) among others, has criticized them, noting that they are passive studies where no real relationships develop between rater and ratees. Nonetheless, research in social cognition has suggested that affect influences cognitive processes in evaluative settings, and it is important to understand exactly where this influence might occur (e.g., Forgas, 1981; Isen, Johnson, Mertz, & Robinson, 1985; Zajonc, 1980).

We designed a study (Robbins & DeNisi, 1994) in an attempt to understand how affect might influence cognitive processes, but we also had another goal in mind. As I mentioned above, most of the studies of affect involved manipulation of affective traits, so that raters would be moved to "like" some ratees better than some others. These manipulations were always carried out independent of actual performance because, from a design perspective, this would be the only way to independently assess the effects of affect. But we weren't sure that, in the field, affect really developed independent of performance. Fiedler (1967) had operationalized a "low-LPC" leader as someone who could not separate personal feelings from past performance, and, when past performance has been studied independent of affect, it seems to have much the same influence on ratings as has been suggested for affect (cf., Murphy, Balzer, Lockhart, & Eisenman, 1985). Finally, from a purely logical perspective, one might expect raters to generally like ratees who perform well and don't give them problems, although there are surely cases where raters can and do separate performance from affect. Thus we were also interested in investigating the possibility that, in the field, there might be little utility in considering a construct called "affect" as being independent from one called "past performance." And, if this were the case, it would seem preferable to rely upon past performance since this would be easier to document and defend.

As noted, though, there had been some research linking affect to ratings and to cognitive processes in evaluations. For example, Dipboye's (1985) model of evaluations suggests a role for affect that occurs after all information has been acquired and processed, portraying affect as a source of bias with a direct effect upon ratings themselves. This is consistent with the work of Kingstrom & Mainstone (1985), who suggest that this bias is derived from a need to maintain past relationships with ratees, as well as with the work of Katz and Glass (1979) who suggest that ratings of both effective and ineffective behaviors are inflated when raters "like" ratees.

But rater–ratee affect might play a role by influencing individual cognitive processes as well, in much the same way as we had discussed the possible role of sex bias in appraisals. Our model had suggested that preconceived notions about ratees could influence information acquisition, with raters seeking information consistent with their affect towards a ratee. We also suggested that these preconceived notions might influence encoding, and others have also suggested that familiarity with a ratee, possible consequences, and affect might all influence how information was interpreted and stored (e.g., Pryor & Ostrom, 1981; Pryor, Ostrom, Dukerich, Mitchell, & Hernstein, 1983). Forgas (1981), and others (Isen, Shalker, Clark, & Karp, 1978; Minsky, 1980), have suggested that affect can also influence the recall of information, with the rater more likely to recall information that is consistent with his or her affect towards the ratee, and Murphy, Gannett, Herr, & Chen (1986) have also suggested that raters are more likely to recall information consistent with prior impressions.

Thus, there was reason to believe that affect might influence ratings either directly or through its influence on cognitive processes. If affect influences rating indirectly through cognitive processes, there was the question of at what stage the bias entered. Finally, there was the question of whether any biasing effect of affect was independent or cumulative. That is, if affect biased the processing at one stage, its influence would be likely to carry over to subsequent stages as well. If affect continued to influence these subsequent processing stages, there would be a cumulative effect of affect on the ratings that would likely be rather strong. It is really at the final stages in the process (recall and integration) that this distinction becomes important since bias introduced at earlier stages would still show up here, even if there was no bias in recall or integration. Quite simply, the information recalled and integrated would already be tainted by the affect.

We had eighty-three undergraduate management students serve as raters in our study. They participated for extra course credit, and were told that the project was designed to explore alternative forms of teacher evaluations. The ratees in the studies were three professors in the management department who were named in the study. Every rater was enrolled in the classes of all three professors for the semester during which the study was conducted.

Rater affect towards the three ratees was assessed prior to the beginning of the study, but about 10 weeks into the semester, by asking the students to complete a measure of interpersonal affect based on feelings of respect, admiration, and liking, using a scale developed by Tsui and her associates (Tsui, 1983; Tsui & Barry, 1986; Tsui & Gutek, 1984), and based on the work of Kahn, Wolfe, Quinn, Snoek, and Rosenthal (1964). The total affect scores for the eighty-three raters were divided into thirds, indicating the top, middle, and bottom thirds of rater–ratee affect, and an ANOVA indicated that there were significant differences across the three groups, suggesting that there was sufficient variance on affect in this study.

Several weeks later, near the end of the semester, the raters were presented with nine behavioral incidents, supposedly observed the previous semester, for each ratee. In fact, these incidents were derived from a Behaviorally Anchored Rating Scale (BARS) developed for evaluating professors (Hom, DeNisi, Kinicki, & Bannister, 1982), and each ratee was described as exhibiting three behaviors each that had been rated as "below average," "average," and "above average" in the original BARS study. There were two conditions for the study. One was concerned with assessing the independent potential effects of affect on each stage in the process, as raters were presented with different pieces of information and asked to follow procedures described below at each stage. In the cumulative condition, raters were given one set of performance information and went through all the individual stages described below with the same information. In both cases, the cross-classification of affect and performance information allowed us to consider information as affect consistent (any time the level of performance matched the level of affect) and affect inconsistent (all the others).

In the cumulative effect condition, raters began with information acquisition, and were able to choose whichever and how many of the twenty-seven incidents of performance that were available. All choices were made via personal computer, much the same as we had done in many of our earlier studies. These raters then indicated which of the incidents they had selected were considered "meaningful," as a means of assessing which incidents would be encoded. This procedure had been described as a means of assessing encoding earlier, by Cronshaw and Lord (1987). Next, all materials were removed from these raters and they were asked to recall as many of the incidents as they could. To be considered a "recalled" incident, the rater had to correctly pair a ratee with a level of performance on an incident observed. This was expressed as a ratio of incidents recalled to incidents observed. These raters were then asked to assign weights to each of the behavioral incidents recalled, indicating how important it would be in determining the overall evaluation. These ranks were adjusted so that ranking an incident as first of only two items recalled was not considered as important as ranking an item first out of nine items recalled. Finally, these raters were asked to rate the overall performance of the three professors, using the performance information supplied *only*, using the BARS originally designed by Hom *et al.* (1982). Thus, for these raters, any bias introduced at early stages in the process, was carried over into subsequent stages, and any subsequent bias that was introduced was accumulated. A total of forty-four raters participated in this condition.

In the independent stage condition, the raters began by receiving all twenty-seven performance incidents, presented to them using an overhead projector. They did not acquire information in the same sense as the other raters, and so there was no possibility of bias entering here. These raters were then asked to rate the meaningfulness (i.e., encode) of all twenty-seven performance incidents as well, using the same scales and procedures as the raters in the other condition, but again without being able to deal with only a subset of the performance incidents. This is the same information these raters were asked to weight and subsequently use in their ratings. Thus, at each stage, they had *all* the information, not just the information they had decided to consider at earlier stages, possibly because of the effects of affect.

Before beginning these procedures, all raters were also asked to rate the past performance of the three professors, using the same BARS scales as above, but basing their ratings on the first part of the semester. Remember, no raters had as yet seen any of the experimental materials. Raters were also asked to rate the three ratees on what we called "social affect" which was based on perceived similarity of interests and non-work activities, specifically unrelated to anything that happened in the classroom.

The means for both conditions on all process-related dependent variables are presented in Table 5.3. Furthermore, within each condition, data are presented for neutral information, affect-consistent information, and affect-inconsistent information. In all cases, the mean for acquisition was based on the proportion of total incidents available actually acquired by the rater, and so was related to the proportion of incidents that were actually observed, while the means for recall reflect the proportion of items recalled in each category. The means for meaningfulness reflect the average ratings for the items in each category, while the mean weight is the average weight produced by the ranking procedure, and the mean ratings are the average scale responses.

The results indicated that there was no significant effect for affect consistency on information acquisition, although the ratee who had the highest average affect score also had the fewest incidents acquired. There was also a

Table 5.3 Means for process variables under two conditions for neutral, affect-consistent and affect-inconsistent information

	Cumulative processing			Single-stage processing		
	Neutral	Consistent	Inconsistent	Neutral	Consistent	Inconsistent
Acquisition	.79	.70	.70	NA	NA	NA
Encoding	3.90	4.11	4.08	3.65	3.78	3.66
Recall	.33	.27	.31	.23	.18	.16
Weighting	7.05	6.24	5.97	5.73	5.02	5.57

Source: Robbins and DeNisi (1994)

marginally significant effect for affect consistency of encoding ($F = 3.02$, $p < .06$) suggesting that affect consistency had an independent influence of encoding and that raters found affect-consistent incidents to be the most meaningful. The results also make it clear that this was not due to any carry-over effect from the acquisition stage. Affect consistency did not have a significant effect on recall, and so there was no concern about carry-over at this point. Affect consistency *did* have an effect on weighting however, with raters assigning higher ranks to affect-consistent incidents (since these are ranks, the means should be interpreted as reverse-scored) and, again, these results indicated that this effect was independent of any carry-over from the earlier stages.

A discussion of the ratings data requires another set of means, and these are presented in Table 5.4. An inspection of the data here indicates that there was a significant effect for affect, but the effect was asymmetrical. Low affect *did* result in lower ratings overall, but positive affect did not result in rating inflation. The results also indicate significant effects for both true score ($R^2 = .23$, $p < .01$) and condition ($R^2 = .23$, $p < .01$), indicating that, although there were effects of bias based on affect, raters did pay attention to the relevant performance information, and also suggesting that raters in the cumulative condition gave higher average ratings than those in the single stage condition.

Table 5.4 Mean ratings for two conditions and across levels of affect and true score

	Cumulative processing	Single-stage processing
Affect		
Low	4.34	3.69
Average	4.98	3.89
High	5.15	3.53
True score		
Low	4.60	2.94
Average	4.81	3.37
High	4.98	4.80

Source: Robbins and DeNisi (1994)

We also re-ran the analyses, computing affect consistency on the basis of social affect. The results were almost identical to those reported above, although there was some evidence for an influence of social affect consistency bias in information acquisition as well (but, since these results indicated a bias *in favor of* affect-neutral incidents, this seemed less critical). Finally, analyses of actual ratings using past performance (we could not use past performance consistency to study the process variables because there were five levels of ratings of past performance, but only three levels of affect), indicated identical results to those reported above. Consistent with these results, we also found a significant correlation between past performance and both job-related affect ($r = .42, p < .01$) and social affect ($r = .35$, $p < .01$); the two types of affect were correlated ($r = .62, p < .01$) and past performance, job-related affect, and social affect were all related to overall performance ratings ($rs = .17, .07$, and $.11$, respectively, all $p < .01$).

Thus these results indicate that affect does play a role in both cognitive processes and ratings related to performance appraisal. Specifically, raters consider information that is either affect consistent or affect inconsistent as more important than information that is affect neutral but, when it comes to ratings, negative affect may be more important than positive affect. But these ratings also raise the distinct possibility that affect, in a field setting, cannot be considered independent of past performance. That is, rather than viewing performance ratings as being only the result of affect, our data suggest the strong possibility that performance determines affect as well as subsequent ratings. Thus, if there is a causal relationship here, performance may well be determining affect. In fact, it may well be the case that, in the field, interpersonal affect does not need to be studied in its own right, but that everything we need to know about its effects, we can learn by looking at information about past performance

CONCLUSIONS

With the studies described here, we attempted to move beyond the consideration of rater acquisition activities, and the role of information organization in memory and reprocessing objectives, which had represented the major focus of our efforts. These studies were mostly concerned with information integration for decision making, and considered factors that might influence integration activities, other than the cognitive processes described in the rest of our model. The notion of matching information with a schema of what constitutes a "good worker" (Blencoe, 1984) is consistent with Borman's later work on "folk theories of performance" (Borman, 1987), as well as with work in other areas (see Lord & Maher, 1991) suggesting that information is processed, in part, by comparing incoming information with well-established (at least for the rater) views of what constitutes successful performance on the task at hand. As I will discuss in Chapter 7, I believe this is one of the major directions for cognitive appraisal research to take in the future, and that it has the potential for drastically altering our views of how raters view performance on the job.

Williams's thesis (1982) follows up on those ideas by taking the next step. That is, several cognitive models suggest that raters depend upon schemata as a major organizing force in processing performance information. The studies I have described in this chapter try to identify what some of those schemata might be but, once we can determine what schemata raters rely upon, we also need to examine what forces result in their abandoning one schema in favor of another. If raters do *not* abandon schemata in some way, it would mean that, once a set of expectations is established for a ratee, there would be nothing he or she could do to change the rater's impressions of them. Williams's thesis provides some preliminary information about the process by which a schema is abandoned and replaced by a different one.

But it is really with the last two studies described that we see a departure from our earlier work. With the consideration of ratee gender and ratee affect, as factors that influence cognitive processing in appraisal decisions, we begin to move from "colder" processing models to "hotter" models, where emotional aspects of the rater are recognized as playing a role in how information is acquired and processed for decision making. As I noted above, these two studies begin to examine models of bias that are much more subtle than those usually described, since the biasing factor insinuates itself into the more basic cognitive processes until its role is not readily apparent – even to the rater. The affect study (Robbins & DeNisi, 1994) is intriguing on yet another level, since there we presented data to suggest that rater affect may not be a source of bias at all. Instead, it may simply reflect information about past performance that led to a rater evaluating the dependability of a ratee (see also Borman, 1991, for a discussion about how "dependability" may well play an important role in performance models, in the military at least). It is also worth noting that recent work in the area of leadership, utilizing Graen's Leader–Member Exchange Model (LMX; e.g., Liden, Wayne, & Stilwell, 1993; Wayne & Ferris, 1990; Wayne & Green, 1993), also raises the possibility that rated performance is not simply a result of more positive leader–member exchange, but that perceived performance may actually be an input in determining the quality of that exchange (see Ferris, Judge, Rowland, & Fitzgibbons, 1993).

Therefore, with these studies, we begin to move beyond the conceptual description of rater processing models, and begin to move closer to demonstrating how those models can help explain other phenomena of interest in performance appraisal. We also begin to integrate other variables of interest to appraisal researchers, such as gender and affect, with the cognitive process variables that were our original focus. This is, as I will discuss later, another important direction for cognitive research to take in the future, as we consider yet other variables of interest, such as rater goals and motives, and work to integrate them into cognitive models as well. Thus, these studies demonstrate that cognitive research can be focused on problems and issues that are important to organizations, and also that non-cognitive factors that might influence appraisal decisions can be considered within a cognitive framework as well.

These studies also marked the end (for the time anyway) of work in the laboratory, and the move into field settings. Those field studies will be described and discussed in the next chapter, but they represent more of an attempt to demonstrate that our results generalized to the field than an attempt to test new theory (although there was some new testing as well). At this point, we had conducted twenty-eight laboratory experiments, involving over 400 subjects. Some of those experiments simply involved trying alternative methods for information presentation, but most of them involved testing hypotheses that were either derived directly from our model, were derived from the results of earlier studies, or reflected the general maturation of cognitive appraisal research. What had we learned?

We had learned that raters do engage in systematic searches for information. We had also learned that this was by no means the *only* way in which raters acquired performance information, but specific strategies could be identified and categorized. Specifically, raters appeared to search for performance information in ways similar to the ways in which we acquire covariation information for making attributions. Person-blocked search (similar to acquiring consistency and distinctiveness information) dominated, followed by task-blocked search (similar to acquiring consensus information), although there was also a great deal of unblocked search (where a rater shifted both ratee and task across search episodes). More critically, we learned that the manner in which raters acquired information *did* affect ratings, although this process seemed to be moderated by the way in which information was stored in memory.

We also learned that, as we had predicted in our model, the purpose for appraisal, preconceived notions held by raters about ratees, and the nature of the rating scale, all affected the ways in which raters acquired and/or processed information. These relationships were not exactly as we had predicted, but these factors were found to be important for cognitive processes. In fact, the purpose of the appraisal appeared to have a greater impact on information acquisition than on how it was used. Furthermore, preconceived notions about ratees, operationalized as ratee schemata, did influence information acquisition and use, but, when a rater was faced with information that conflicted with expectations and schemata, the rater did not hang onto those expectations for very long, and a new schema replaced the old. Also, the rating scale did influence how information was stored in memory, but only when it was introduced prior to the observation of performance information, and, even then, both of the scales we investigated resulted in organization by persons. But we also learned some things that were not part of our original model.

For example, we learned that the way information was stored in memory, rather than the way it was acquired, was probably the most important determinant of successful processing of information for appraisal decisions. This led us to suggest that interventions, such as structured diary keeping, would prove to be an effective aid to raters, since it would enable them to organize otherwise unorganized information in memory. We also learned that contextual factors, such as ratee gender (especially when this interacted with the sex-appropriateness of a job) and rater affect for the ratee, could also influence cognitive processes. Furthermore, our results suggested that, at least in the case of affect, this factor may not develop independent of ratee performance. In fact, we might speculate that, from a cognitive perspective, even ratee gender operates through its influence on ratee affect. Thus we came to see ratee affect as an important part of any cognitive model.

Finally, we learned that, in some cases, rater memory processes may not be as critical because raters engaged in on-line processing which did not require retrieval of specific information from long-term memory. It seemed, however, that if raters knew that, when they were acquiring performance information it would be used for appraisal decisions, and if they had competing demands upon their time (as would usually be the case), memory-based processing was more likely to dominate and, with it, a reliance upon longer-term memory processes.

Thus, by the time we moved to the field, we were working with a model that looked a bit different from the one we began with. Although there was never an attempt to explicitly revise and update the appraisal model, what

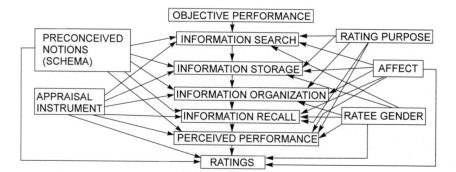

1 IF DECISION IS MEMORY-BASED

2 IF DECISION IS MADE ON-LINE

Figure 5.2 A "revised" cognitive model of the appraisal process

we learned in the lab *did* affect how we viewed the appraisal process. Figure 5.2 is a close approximation of what that new model looked like. As can be seen we clearly recognized by now that we needed to consider memory-based and on-line decisions separately. More complex memory processes, and the organization of information in memory, were only important in memory-based decisions. In on-line decisions, updated impressions were all that mattered. Also, although our models were now quite a bit simpler, information organization *was* important in memory-based decisions, and so it was critical to determine if interventions which enabled raters to organize information in the lab could also be effective in the field. Finally, our revised models placed ratee affect in a critical role, and so it became important to examine the role of affect in field settings as well.

Thus, with these studies and this "revised" cognitive model, we ventured into the field. It was vital that we could show that the processes we described in the lab really mattered in the field, but it meant giving up the control we enjoyed in the lab, as well as the ability to directly measure some process variables. Also, field research brings with it its own set of problems and considerations, and so I will begin the next chapter with a discussion of some of those issues, as I describe our efforts to move our research project into the "real world."

Chapter 6

Cognitive research moves to the field

The most frequently repeated criticisms of cognitive research on performance appraisal is that the research has restricted itself to laboratory settings with no major attempt to determine if any findings generalize to the field. As early as 1985, Ilgen and Favero (1985) noted that cognitive research considered psychological phenomena that might not operate in the same ways in the field, and suggested that this research would have only limited applications to field problems. This criticism seemed a bit premature since, by 1985, only a few of the empirical studies described here were published, and there was no reason to believe that cognitive research would *not* move to the field – only that it had not as yet. But these criticisms continued (e.g., Banks & Murphy, 1985; Ilgen & Klein, 1988; Murphy & Cleveland, 1991). Criticizing research for not moving to the field is an interesting process, since surely everyone who does laboratory research *knows* that the research must eventually move to the field. This is the *only* way to determine if the lab results could be generalized, but it is not always easy to get organizations to allow us to try out those ideas. Of course, cognitive studies pose a special problem for the field since they require some detailed data collection from raters, but it was always our intention to move our research into the field.

Furthermore, if one is interested in the kinds of processes such as we were, it seems necessary to begin in the lab. For example, in laboratory settings levels of actual performance can be controlled. So, when, based on field data, someone reports that men are rated higher than women (e.g., Mobley, 1982), we can never be sure if these differences reflect true differences in performance or bias against women. Also, in the last chapter I discussed one study dealing with the role of affect, and several others that had investigated how affect might influence cognitive processes. If we had begun our research in the field, where rater affect will naturally develop, we could never be sure how much of the processing we observed was tainted by affect. Only after the processes have been clearly identified is it okay to include other contextual variables that might muddy the water. In fact, if I were to describe an ideal program of research, it would begin by studying the phenomenon of interest in very tightly controlled settings with little concern about external validity. Over time, studies still conducted in the lab would begin to add one, then another, contextual variable, which would allow us to have some insight into what might actually be going on in the field. Only then would it make sense to move into the field. At that point, we would be fairly confident that the phenomenon existed, and we would even have some ideas of what contextual factors mattered, so we wouldn't waste an organization's time. We didn't follow this script to the letter, but this was the idea behind the progression from simple to more complex lab studies, and eventually to the field. By the late 1980s, the time had come.

In 1989, Larry Peters and I wrote a grant proposal which we submitted to the National Science Foundation to do cognitive research in the field. Much of the proposal was based on conversations we had with Vicki Vandaveer who was working for Southwestern Bell at the time. Vicki has been one of the few practitioners that has consistently seen a practical side to cognitive research on performance appraisal (I will discuss some aspects of this in the next chapter), and was willing to work with us on a project that would have raters keeping structured diaries, and would also involve some data that the organization had collected on perceived performance models as part of a recent change in appraisal systems.

We received the grant from NSF, but Vicki had since left Southwestern Bell, and no one else there had the will or the vision to get the project approved by top management. We were therefore in the uncomfortable position of having some money from NSF, but no clear way to spend it as was intended. Fortunately, Larry's Dean at Texas Christian University, Kirk Downey, had been putting together an advisory board for the College of Business, and thought he might be able to convince two of his supporters to give us access to their organizations. As I write this, it occurs to me that neither organization ever agreed to have their names associated with this project, so we'll need to create pseudonyms. "Texas Manufacturing" is the manufacturing division of a large multinational company that builds computer-related products and sells them directly to the public. "Texas Transportation" is a large multinational firm that is involved in all aspects of transportation in markets all around the world. These two organizations allowed us to conduct large-scale field experiments, the results of which are reported in the three papers discussed below. Our biggest problem had been solved – we had field samples. We had also decided, by this point, to focus on three aspects of cognitive processes in performance appraisal for this project. These were (1) the role of affect in appraisal decisions; (2) the efficacy of structured recall as a means of organizing information; and (3) the efficacy of structured diary keeping as a means of organizing information. Nonetheless we realized that, even with field samples and ideas about research questions, we still had some formidable problems to overcome. Since I believe these same problems face any researcher who is interested in doing appraisal research in the field in the 1990s and beyond, I feel it is important to discuss those problems here, and to report on our solutions.

SPECIAL PROBLEMS ASSOCIATED WITH COGNITIVE RESEARCH IN THE FIELD

Some of the problems we faced *were* particular to the kind of research we were interested in conducting. The input for most appraisal studies conducted in the field is simply the set of actual appraisals. That is, we would be most typically interested in some aspect of those ratings given by a group of raters, but data on ratings could usually be obtained from company records without much problem. In fact, with complete access to company records (assuming all parties were agreeable), we could get longitudinal data as well as cross-sectional data. For example, Klaas and DeNisi (1989) examined whether the fact that an employee filed a grievance against his or her supervisor, and whether that grievance was upheld, would have any influence on performance evaluations. We were able to examine ratings before and after successful and unsuccessful grievances were filed, and found that there was some evidence of retribution on the part of the supervisors. But these data required *no* real cooperation from the raters themselves, nor from their subordinates.

But to assess cognitive processes in the field we would be required to collect fairly detailed data from the raters themselves. A frequent solution to this problem, of course, is to find a setting where the raters are particularly accessible. Did you ever notice how many BARS and BOS rating instruments have been developed for teacher evaluation in university settings? In the previous chapter, I described a study (Robbins & DeNisi, 1994) where we did get data from raters and, again, it involved teacher evaluations. These classroom settings are fine for many aspects of performance appraisal research, and I truly believed it allowed us to look at affect that developed over time in the study I described. But these settings are still unique. These are the only settings where, on a regular basis, the raters are also evaluated by their ratees, and the grades students receive from their instructors often have more impact than do the teacher evaluations received by the instructor. Furthermore, it has long since been suspected that teacher evaluations can be largely dependent upon such factors as expected grade in a course (DeNisi, Hom, Bannister, & Kinicki, 1980). This is not to say that appraisals in the field are *not* subject to biases themselves, but the nature of those biases are different.

Thus, to move our research into the field we would have to have access to raters for extended periods of time, so that we could collect the kinds of data (such as recall data) that would allow us to make some inferences about the cognitive processes underlying appraisal decisions. Even if we could convince the management of an organization that our research had some applied pay-off, we would also have to convince the much tougher audience consisting of the raters themselves. Some of us are less concerned about the applied value of our research, with some suggesting that they study the phenomena they do *only* because they find them interesting, and that they haven't the least concern whether their research has any "bottom line" applications. But, when you are asking a group of supervisors or middle managers to devote their time to providing you with data about the structure of their recall, you must first convince them that there is some practical reason for doing so.

It is interesting to note at this point that there *has* been another approach that has been used to access data on cognitive processes. Researchers who work in the area broadly known as "managerial cognition" have often been concerned about the beliefs, values, and attitudes of top management personnel in organizations (e.g., Walsh, 1988). These scholars have focused on managerial cognitions and values and beliefs as they might pertain to a variety of organizational issues other than performance appraisal. For example, there have been studies investigating the relationship between homogeneity (or heterogeneity) of values and attitudes among the board members of a corporation, and various strategic decisions made, as well as firm performance (e.g., Hambrick & Mason, 1984; Michel & Hambrick, 1992). But, in very few of these studies are the researchers actually able to collect data from busy executives about their beliefs, attitudes, or cognitions, and there is very little data about actual interactions among board members which is the process through which these cognitive variables are supposed to operate. Instead, most have measured other variables, for which data are available, and used these as proxies of managerial cognitions. The proxies typically used, however, include such things as the functional area from which the director came (e.g., marketing vs. finance), whether the director was an inside director or an outside director, and even the ages of the directors and the kinds of schools they attended (e.g., Murray, 1989; also, see review by Pfeffer, 1983). The links between these proxies and actual cognitive processes do not always seem clear, but I am hard pressed to suggest a way in which one might actually collect detailed cognitive process data from these executives. As a result, the managerial cognition scholars have relied upon proxies while, for the most part, the cognitive appraisal researchers have simply not ventured into the field. Clearly, the kinds of data one needs to study cognitive processes in the field are extremely difficult to come by, and we will probably never be able to get the detailed data that it is possible to collect in a laboratory setting (recall, especially, the discussion of detail reported by Banks & Roberson, 1983). Nonetheless, we must follow the lead of our colleagues in other areas, figure out how to collect the best data we can, and use it to test important questions in field settings. The remainder of this chapter deals, for the most part, with the specific issues facing cognitive appraisal research in the field, and a discussion of how we attempted to deal with these issues.

THE CRITERION PROBLEM IN FIELD RESEARCH

The biggest problem facing any researcher interested in studying performance appraisal in the field, though, relates to the decision of what is the proper criterion variable. In our brief review of the research on performance appraisal we cite many field studies from the early days of appraisal research. Whether these studies deal with issues of rater training (e.g., Bernardin, 1978; Brown, 1968; Latham, Wexley, & Pursell, 1975) or the best way to construct a graphic rating scale (Bernardin, Alvares, & Cranny, 1976), the criterion for evaluating these efforts was typically expressed in terms of rating errors. We made some reference to this at the very beginning of this book, but now it is time to address the problem in earnest, because it represents a serious challenge to any researchers interested in performance appraisals conducted in the field.

Whether implicitly or explicitly, the researchers cited above (among others) assumed that rater errors were related to rating accuracy. Some of these studies talked about accuracy, but actually measured the presence or absence of rating errors, while others simply used rating error and interrater reliability as criterion measures without explanation. Thus, any conclusions about the best rating scale format, or the best anchors for a graphic rating scale, or the best type of training program, are all based on studies where the criteria involved rating errors.

There were other studies, though, where a different, but still (it seems) misguided criterion measure has been used. For example, in a number of studies (e.g., Barrett, 1966; Bernardin, 1977; DeCotiis, 1977; Friedman & Cornelius, 1976), ratings that were lower, or were less extreme in either direction, were assumed to be more accurate. In these studies, which usually compared ratings from different sources, it was assumed that raters had an incentive to inflate ratings, but no incentive to deflate them. Thus, the lower ratings were assumed to be closer to "true." Although this logic seems more defensible, it does ignore the fact that raters may have any number of motives in giving specific ratings, and so mean levels alone may not be a good indication of accuracy.

But what of the relationship between rating errors and rating accuracy? We will turn to the larger question of whether rating accuracy should be considered at all a bit later, but for now we will be content with discussing the relationship between errors and accuracy. The problem actually begins with disagreements over the operational definitions of different rating errors. This would seem to be the easy part, but, when Saal, Downey, and Lahey (1980) reviewed the literature on rating errors, they noted that there was no consensus agreement on the operational definition of rating errors such as halo and leniency, and not even consensus on the conceptual definitions of these errors.

Halo error is an excellent example of this problem. What exactly *is* halo error? It has been defined as a rater's *attending to* global impressions of performance, while ignoring differences in performance levels across specific aspects of the job (Borman, 1975); as well as, an *unwillingness* on the part of raters to distinguish among different levels of performance exhibited by a ratee (DeCotiis, 1977); or even, a *tendency* to place ratees at the same level on different dimensions (Bernardin, 1977). Is halo a problem of cognitive processing, a rater motivational issue, or a form of response bias? Is it the result of increased attentional demands on raters (Murphy & Balzer, 1989), conceptual similarity among rating categories (Cooper, 1981a; Kozlowski & Kirsch, 1987; Kozlowski, Kirsch, & Chao, 1986), or the result of rater categorization of ratee into prototypes (Mount & Thompson, 1987; Nathan & Lord, 1983)? As a result, should halo error be operationalized in terms of the average intercorrelation among ratings, the standard deviation of ratings within a ratee, or in terms of a comparison between observed and true halo among ratings?

At this point, the answer to none of these questions is clear, although Lance and his associates (Fisicaro & Lance, 1990; Lance, LaPointe, & Fisicaro, 1994; Lance, LaPointe, & Stewart, 1994) presented data to suggest that halo is always the result of a general impression held by a rater about a ratee that permeates all ratings. But, even here, the authors of one of those studies (Lance, LaPointe, & Stewart, 1994) admitted that they, like others, operationalized halo at the group level of analysis rather than at the individual level of analysis, even though halo is defined at the individual level. But it is not my intention here to critique those studies, or to propose that I have the answer to the problem. Instead, all I want to make clear is that we have been arguing (in the literature) about the relationship between errors, especially halo error, and accuracy, and we cannot even agree upon one clear conceptual and operational definition of halo.

Even if we cannot agree on the definition of such errors as halo, we can at least agree on the definition of rating accuracy. Or so it would seem. Unfortunately, this is not the case. As I noted several times throughout the book, the issue of how to define and measure accuracy has always been problematic, and there is really little agreement concerning the correct way to operationalize rating accuracy. Much of this work has focused on the different operational definitions posed by Cronbach (1955) which include elevation accuracy, stereotype accuracy, and differential accuracy, as well as several combinations of the above. Here, a number of scholars have demonstrated that we obtain different relationships with independent variables, depending upon the definition of accuracy we use (Day & Sulsky, 1995), and these differences even extend to relationships with rating errors (Murphy & Balzer, 1989). Therefore, we have a situation where a variety of operational definitions of rating errors are being related to a variety of operational definitions of rating accuracy, making it impossible to arrive at any clear statements about the relationships involved (see Balzer & Sulsky, 1992). And since halo error is a particularly popular error to investigate, these definitional problems have resulted in several authors arguing that halo error is positively related to rating accuracy (e.g., Bernardin & Pence, 1980; Cooper, 1981a; Murphy & Balzer, 1989; Nathan, 1986; Nathan & Tippins, 1990), while another group argues that, when variables are operationalized "correctly" (remember the problem with this), and raters have time to familiarize themselves with ratees, the relationship between halo and accuracy is negative (e.g., Fisicaro, 1988; Kozlowski & Kirsch, 1987; Kozlowski, Kirsch, & Chao, 1986).

So what is a field researcher to do? Rating errors have been the traditional criterion measure, but there is considerable evidence that the relationship between the presence of these errors and rating accuracy is not what we have assumed. Rating accuracy might be an alternative but there really is no consensus on how to operationalize accuracy and, in addition, although Balzer and Sulsky (1992) suggest that it might be possible to assess rating accuracy in the field, many of their suggestions are impractical in most cases (e.g., random assignment of ratees to raters and multiple raters for each ratee, where all raters are at the same level in the organization). Before discussing an alternative view though, there is one final point I want to make about definitions and discussions of accuracy.

The most useful distinction I have seen has been presented most clearly by Murphy (1991). He suggests that, before we argue about the right measure of accuracy we should think about the goals or purpose of the performance appraisal. At the simplest level, appraisals are done to aid in decision making (i.e., merit-pay increases) and to provide developmental feedback. Although we typically use the same appraisal to satisfy both purposes (despite the warnings *not* to do so from some thirty years ago; Meyer, Kay, & French, 1965), we usually are more interested in one set of outcomes than the other. If we are interested in decision making, then the only type of accuracy that concerns us is the type that suggests that the "best" performer receives the highest ratings, and so on, suggesting a positive correlation between true scores and ratings of overall performance. This he terms "classification accuracy." He contrasts this with "behavioral accuracy" which involves a concern that the specific behaviors correctly performed by a ratee are identified as such, and are differentiated from those which are performed incorrectly. This type of accuracy should concern us most when feedback and developmental purposes are more important. There are trade-offs between the two, and I will return to this distinction in the final chapter's discussion of directions for future research but, for me, of all the arguments about different types of rating accuracy, this distinction makes the most sense.

But, to return to the problem at hand, if errors have a questionable relationship with accuracy, and assessing accuracy in the field is difficult if not impossible, we still don't have much to offer to the field researcher. Or do we? Much of the dilemma I've just described is tied up with the assumption that rating accuracy *is* the right place to begin. The major criticisms of using rating errors is that they are considered as "errors" and so, sources of inaccuracy, when perhaps they are not. In fact, as suggested by Murphy and Cleveland (1992), we cannot really determine if a rating "error" is an error unless we know the true, underlying distribution of ratings. We can, of course, determine true scores and true levels of covariance in a lab setting, where ratings can be constructed to reflect specific relationships, but we cannot do this in the field. The absence of any "true score" frustrates any such attempt. So, why fixate on accuracy?

In a recent book, Ilgen (1993) suggests that this concern grows out of a background in psychometrics, which leads us to want to design perfect appraisal systems which are free of measurement error, and the fact that much of the appraisal research is conducted in the lab, where we can assess accuracy, only reinforces this desire. But perhaps in the field, rating accuracy is *not* a meaningful goal for its own sake. I would surely agree that, all other things being equal, ratings that were psychometrically accurate would be preferable to ratings that were not but, since measures of accuracy (whether classification or behavioral) require some objective measures of true performance which are difficult to come by in the field, perhaps we should turn our attention elsewhere. Perhaps, instead of measuring accuracy we can assess other outcomes that are directly relevant to organizations, and which are assumed to be associated with more accurate ratings in any case.

In order to make this point clear, we need to go back and reconsider the reasons for organizations conducting appraisals in the first place. One reason is to help in decision making. Here we might want accurate ratings because we hope that merit-pay increases and the like will motivate employees to work harder on their jobs. If the ultimate goal were performance improvement (and I believe this is the ultimate goal for all appraisals), then we should be able to relate ratings to some outcome measures indicating that performance has improved following an "accurate" appraisal. But notice that, even here, accuracy is only important because we assume that, at some level, everyone knows who is the best performer, and when that person gets rewarded, it motivates everyone else to try harder to perform at the same level. What's really important, then, is that the ratees perceive the decision as being fair. Accurate ratings *may* help ensure that, but we don't really know. What we do believe we know, however, is that employees will be more motivated working under systems that they perceive as fair. This simple suggestion, contained in Wherry's (1952) model, was included in work by Bernardin on the role of perceived trust in the organization (Bernardin, Orban, & Carlyle, 1981) which led to studies of the determinants of perceived fairness by Landy and his colleagues (e.g., Landy, Barnes, & Murphy, 1978; Landy, Barnes-Farrell, & Cleveland, 1980), and underlies a review of the research on the importance of ratee attitudes towards appraisals presented by Dickinson (1993).

Thus, in the field, rater and ratee attitudes towards the process and the outcomes (i.e., perceptions of distributive and procedural justice; see Folger, Konovksy, & Cropanzano, 1992) of appraisal may be more important to the ultimate effectiveness of any appraisal system. Ilgen (1993) also suggests that mastery of one's job might be another outcome that is more important to the organization. One might imagine, in other organizations, such goals as improved team performance, reduced costs, or even higher levels of job satisfaction. An effective appraisal system, then, would be one that max-imized these goals rather than the goal of rating accuracy. Note again, it is not that these goals would be operating counter to the goal of trying to make ratings more accurate (whether we are interested in classification or behavioral accuracy), they would simply make that goal somewhat irrelevant.

Could the more traditional criterion of rating errors also play a role in this view of appraisal effectiveness? Perhaps. First, of course, we must stop considering them as errors, since they can only be errors in the sense that they deviate from the "truth." If we don't know the truth, how can we have errors? Halo indices, as they are usually measured, provide some information about the variance across rating dimensions, but within ratees. Elsewhere, we have suggested that these indices be termed "within-ratee discriminability indices" (DeNisi & Peters, 1992, in press) because they tell us if the rater is distinguishing among different dimen-sions of the ratee's performance. Notice, I am not saying that the rater is either right or wrong in discriminating in this way. That is, if a ratee performs well on *all* aspects of the job, an accurate appraisal would give him or her high marks in all areas, producing little within-ratee discriminability. But, since we don't know the true levels of performance, we can say that an appraisal that discriminates more has better potential for providing feedback than one that discriminates less. It may also be true that a ratee is more likely to believe high ratings when there is some variance rather than when the ratings *may* be influenced by an overall impression.

Furthermore, if we considered "leniency error" to simply be an elevation index, this too might provide useful information. For example, Hauenstein (1992) suggested that ratings are *erroneously* elevated when raters lack clear standards but, even without concern for error, elevated ratings might sug-gest a problem with standards. Furthermore, it has been suggested that less elevated ratings are more useful to organizations because they allow the organization to discriminate among ratees at the more critical end of the ratings distribution (i.e., it allows the organization to recognize those that are truly outstanding; Bernardin & Buckley, 1981; Buckley & Bernardin, 1980). Finally, Kane, Bernardin, Villanova and Peyrefitte (1995) argue that elevated ratings can undermine incentive pay systems (similar to the arguments cited above), and also present legal problems for organizations when they attempt to terminate poor performers. Thus elevation indices may provide organizations with important information about their appraisal systems and how they are working.

Finally, if within-ratee discriminability provides information about the potential for providing useful feedback (which would seem to be related to a concern for behavioral accuracy), it would also make sense to consider an index of between-ratee discriminability. Such an index is not really reflective of any single rating "error" but, if a rater consistently fails to discriminate across ratees on performance dimension, it would be difficult to imagine that the rater would have very high classification accuracy, and decision making would be difficult. Also, it would be difficult to imagine ratees seeing everyone getting the same ratings and perceiving such a system as fair or even "accurate."

I have devoted a considerable amount of space to the criterion problem in the field, because I think it must be solved if we are going to do theoretically meaningful research in field settings where we don't have access to huge databases. I will have more to say about this in the chapter discussing directions for the future, but I believe it is critical that we loosen our ties to rating accuracy and its potential proxies in the field. Organizations carry out appraisals for reasons, and they expect certain things to happen. For some of those things to happen, raters and ratees must trust the system and believe in the ratings being given. As a result, intermediate goals relating to rater and ratee attitudes and perceptions of trust and fairness would appear to present reasonable and useful alternatives to rating errors or rating accuracy. Other intermediate outcomes that provide information about the distributions of ratings, both within and between ratees, would also seem to provide some potential as criterion measures. But of course these are just intermediate goals and outcomes. From an organization's perspective, if an appraisal system is working, there should be learning, continuous improvement, and increased productivity as well as increased satisfaction. Tapping these criterion measures will require moving to a more macro-level of analysis, and represents a different set of challenges and concerns that will be discussed later. For now, it seems clear that we should move away from accuracy-related criterion measures, and begin moving more towards effectiveness-related criterion measures. With this discussion behind us, we can turn now to those field studies we ultimately designed and executed as cognitive appraisal research made its first real venture into the field.

STRUCTURED DIARY KEEPING IN THE FIELD

As noted several times, a criticism of cognitive approaches to performance appraisal has been their limited focus of laboratory studies. We finally turn to two field studies designed to determine if some of the major findings from our lab research generalized to field settings (DeNisi & Peters, 1991, 1992, in press). Specifically, we were interested in whether interventions designed to improve rater organization of information in memory would be effective in the field as well, where raters had long-standing relationships with the ratees. The first field study was concerned with the effectiveness of structured diary keeping. Recall that, in an earlier lab study (DeNisi, Robbins, & Cafferty 1989) we had found that, not only did diary keeping help raters to recall information and provide more accurate ratings, but that having raters structure their diaries according to ratees (i.e., person-blocked) resulted in information being organized in memory according to persons, and produced the highest levels of recall and rating accuracy. Would such a structured diary keeping intervention work in the field as well?

Our sample for this study was 112 first-line supervisors (mostly Caucasian males, average age 41, and average tenure of 2.5 years) from various manufacturing plants of the "Texas Manufacturing Company." The supervisors in our study were randomly selected from the roll of all first line supervisors by an HR executive in the firm, and they were randomly assigned to the various experimental conditions I will describe below. Although supervisors identified for participation in the study could choose not to participate, such a decision was counter to the organization's norms – even though the study was carried out on personal time (e.g., weekends). The supervisors were contacted by the management of the company, and were told that they had an opportunity to gain some skills and information that would make it easier for them to evaluate their subordinates, and that they would be participating in a study to evaluate a possible appraisal system that could be used across the organization. Until that time, each plant was free to design and implement its own appraisal system, and there was no standard approach used in all facilities. We can only take the management's word that participation was truly "voluntary," although we had a fair number of "no-shows" and, as I will describe later, a number of supervisors did not return for a second, follow-up session, suggesting that those who *did* participate, really did so because they wanted to.

All supervisors reported to a corporate training facility in large groups for a half-day of training to improve appraisal skills. We tried to keep the supervisors in the different conditions in separate sessions, and we succeeded for the most part, although not entirely, and different attendance rates at different sessions also resulted in unequal numbers of supervisors assigned to each condition. We *did* manage to keep all raters assigned to the "no-diary" condition separate, however, and that was the crucial group to keep away from the others. The training for all raters included a discussion of the importance of critical incidents of performance, the establishment and communication of clear rating standards, and the role of performance coaching, but, for the "no-diary" raters, these were the only topics discussed. For the other supervisors, training also included a discussion of the role of memory in performance appraisal decisions, and stressed how diaries could be used to record critical incidents to make appraisal decisions easier. The training program emphasized that it was important to record descriptive rather than evaluative incidents, and to focus on correct as well as incorrect incidents in their diaries. Training sessions also included the opportunity to practice identifying and noting critical incidents using videotaped performance, and feedback and group discussion reinforced the major points. At no time was there any discussion of rating accuracy or rating errors. The emphasis, instead, was on accurate observation of performance on the job, and the keeping of a diary or incident file.

Near the end of the training session, raters were given three-ring binders to be used for diary keeping. They were also given instructions (consistent with the condition to which they were assigned) regarding how those diaries were to be organized. Finally, a date was set (3 months later) when the supervisors would return to the training center, with their diaries, and would be asked to rate their subordinates using an instrument that would be provided. Since supervisors had a varying number of direct-reports whose performance they rated, everyone was told to focus on no more than eight ratees for the diary keeping task. We decided to use eight ratees, because there were eight rating dimensions on the form used and, as I will explain below, this ensured that everyone was keeping diaries for the same number of categories. Raters were asked to select the ratees they would concentrate on at the first session, and everyone wrote down the names of those ratees. Raters who had responsibility for fewer than eight subordinates would simply focus on all their subordinates for the task. All supervisors were given a copy of the evaluation form they would be asked to use in the second session.

Approximately 3 months later, we began the follow-up sessions. Only eighty-five of the supervisors returned at that time. All those who did return, and who had been asked to keep diaries, brought completed diaries with them, and we assumed that those who did not return had not carried out the diary keeping task, or had not found it useful, although some may just have had schedule conflicts. When the supervisors returned, we collected the diaries from them (for those in any of the diary keeping conditions), and provided "blue books" to be used to recall all the specific performance incidents they could from the last 3 months, for the ratees whose names they had provided to us at the earlier session. The supervisors were given 30 minutes in which to complete this recall task, and the booklets were then collected from them. We then distributed the appraisal instrument. We explained that this was a form being considered by the organization for use with all ratees, and that the ratings they provided *would* be retained in the subordinates' personnel files, although we did not know the extent to which they would be used later. When we gave them the rating forms, we also returned the diaries to the supervisors. They were told that they could refer to them however they wanted in completing the ratings. When they had completed the rating forms for all the subordinates in question, we distributed a questionnaire asking for their reactions to the training, the diary keeping, and the ratings they had made. We collected the rating forms (copies were provided to the organization), the diaries, and the measure of their reactions, answered all questions, thanked the raters for their time, and sent them home. We followed all the same procedures for the "no-diary" supervisors, except, of course, there were no diaries to collect before the recall task, and no diaries to refer to during the completion of the rating forms.

There were a total of four experimental conditions, paralleling the conditions from the DeNisi, Robbins and Cafferty (1989) study. The "no-diary" condition served as a control, the raters were not told about the importance of memory processes, were not given diaries to keep, and, as described above, completed the rating forms without diaries. A total of twenty-two raters in this condition returned for the second session. Supervisors assigned to the "person-diary" condition (26 supervisors in this condition returned for the second session) were told to write down the name of each one of the eight ratees whose names they had provided on a "tab" or divider sheet, and were told to write down the incidents they observed for each ratee in the section with that ratee's name. Supervisors assigned to the "performance dimension-diary" condition (24 supervisors in this condition returned for the second session) were given binders with the tab sheets already completed. On each sheet was written the name of a performance dimension, and they were told to write the incidents they observed, for any ratee, relevant to that performance dimension, in the appropriate section.

There were eight performance dimensions that would be used on the rating form, and having the supervisors in the "person-diary" condition select eight ratees assured that everyone would be using the same number of dimensions for organizing their diaries. Supervisors assigned to the "free-diary" condition (16 supervisors returned for the second session) were given binders with eight tabs, but were told that they should organize these diaries in any way they saw fit. We discussed a number of possibilities with them for organizing principles, but they were told to consider no more than eight subordinates (they wrote down the names as well) and, of course, they had copies of the rating instrument with its eight dimensions. They were told they did not need to use all eight separators if they did not want to, and could organize information according to the month during which observation occurred, or the level of performance observed, or any other scheme they wanted. Once they decided upon a scheme, however, we asked them to label the tabs accordingly.

As described above, upon returning for the second session, all raters were asked to complete a recall task. Supervisors who had kept diaries were not able to refer to their diaries during this task, and the recall information was independently coded by two Ph.D. students who were not informed about the purpose of the study. The coders were trained and experienced, so that we obtained just under 90% agreement for the number of positive, negative, descriptive, and evaluative items recalled (there was perfect agreement for the number of incidents recalled). From these data we created five recall indices: (1) total number of incidents recalled; (2) percentage of positive incidents recalled; (3) percentage of negative incidents recalled; (4) percentage of descriptive (non-evaluative) incidents recalled; and (5) percentage of evaluative incidents recalled. Note that the percentage of descriptive and evaluative incidents recalled summed to 100%, and the percentage of positive and negative incidents recalled referred only to the evaluative incidents recalled. In addition, we computed Adjusted Ratio of Clustering (ARC) scores for all ratees, for clustering according to both persons and performance dimensions, as we had in the earlier lab studies.

All ratings were made on 5-point rating scales (1 = poor performance, 5 = exceptional performance), for each of eight performance dimensions: Reactions to Pressure, Communications Skills, Job Knowledge, Interpersonal Skills, Timeliness, Problem Solving, Adaptability, and Initiative. There was also a rating for Overall Performance. These performance dimensions were chosen after consultation and discussion with members of the corporate HR staff. They believed that these dimensions were critical for all manufacturing supervisors, and would allow a common form to be used in all locations. Raters were also asked to rate subordinates on twelve additional rating dimensions, but these were not planned to be used in the standard rating instrument (raters were not told this), and data for these ratings were not analyzed for this study. The ratings data were used to create three rating indices: rating elevation (simply the mean rating, across all ratees, given by a rater, on each performance dimension, as well as for Overall Performance), within-ratee discriminability (the average within-ratee standard deviation considering all rating dimensions, standardized within each dimension following the recommendation of Pulakos, Schmitt, & Ostroff, 1986), and between-ratee discriminability (the average standard deviation of the ratings given by a rater for all ratees, on each separate dimension as well as for Overall Performance). Thus, for each rater, there were nine indices of rating elevation, one index of within-ratee discriminability, and 9 indices of between-ratee discriminability. The data contained in the diaries were also coded by a Ph.D. student who was also blind to the purpose of the study, and me (who was only blind to the condition to which the rater was assigned). There was over 90% agreement on the scoring, and these data were used to compute indices identical to those described above for the recall data, except that we didn't compute any ARC indices for the diaries.

Finally, all raters completed a 13-item reactions questionnaire, assessing their reactions to the rating process and the ratings themselves. The items were based on available measures of reactions to ratings (especially the instrument developed by Landy, Barnes, & Murphy, 1978), and all employed 5-point rating scales, where higher scores indicated more positive reactions. In addition, the supervisors assigned to one of the diary keeping conditions completed an additional 5-item measure asking for their reactions to the diary keeping. We did a principal component analysis of the reactions data, and found four factors underlying the 13-item measure,

Table 6.1 Reaction items and their resulting dimensions

Dimension 1: "Clear understanding of what to attend to" (alpha = .77)
I know what performance indicators to attend to when making these ratings.
I know where my subordinates stand on all relevant performance indicators.
I have a well-organized picture of how my subordinates contribute to the company.
My subordinates and I agree upon the duties and responsibilities for evaluations.

Dimension 2: "Fair appraisal program" (alpha = .71)
Performance appraisal policies and responsibilities are adequately explained.
My subordinates know what they are being evaluated on.
Performance appraisal here at——is a fair process.
My subordinates would regard these evaluations as fair.

Dimension 3: "Accurate and defensible ratings" (alpha = .58)
These performance ratings are accurate evaluations of my subordinates' performance.
I can easily recall specific examples from work upon which to base my evaluations.
I could easily defend these evaluations to a subordinate who might disagree with them.

Dimension 4: "Ratings would not be surprising to ratees" (alpha = .59)
My subordinates would not be surprised to receive these ratings.
I know enough about my subordinates' behaviour to rate their performance accurately today.

Dimension 5: "Keeping a diary helped me in the appraisal process" (alpha = .81)
I tended to notice critical noteworthy behaviors.
I wrote down critical noteworthy behaviors in an incident diary.
I am better able to remember critical noteworthy behaviors.
I found it helpful to have an incident diary.
I will continue to keep an incident diary.

which we labeled: (1) "Clear understanding of what to attend to"; (2) "Fair appraisal program"; (3) "Accurate and defensible ratings"; and (4) "Ratings would not be surprising to ratees." The additional five items completed by the raters who kept diaries, all loaded on a fifth factor which we labeled (5) "Keeping a diary helped me in the appraisal process." The actual items loading on each dimension are provided in Table 6.1.

The hypotheses we tested with these data were mostly derived from the earlier lab study. We predicted that diary keeping would be superior to no diary in terms of recall, the ratings indices, and reactions to the process. We also predicted that organizing diaries in a specific pattern would result in organization in recall according to that same pattern. Finally, still following from the lab study, we predicted that organizing diaries according to persons, or ratees, would be superior to any other type of diary keeping in terms of all these measures, as well as relative to the data in the diaries, and reactions to the diary keeping (the separate 5-item measure).

The results are presented in Tables 6.2 through 6.5 for the various outcome measures. Before discussing the specific results, though, I should point out that *every* supervisor in the "free-diary" condition chose to organize their diary according to ratees. This was consistent with the results from the lab study and further suggested that diaries organized by persons or ratees is the preferred style. As a result, when I discuss the major results, whenever I refer to supervisors keeping diaries organized by persons, I will be referring to *both* those supervisors assigned to the "person-diary" condition *and* those assigned to the "free-diary" condition. Turning to the results themselves, Table 6.2 shows that, as predicted, the type of diary kept was related to the way information was organized in memory. There were significant differences across conditions for both ARC person scores ($F = 10.76$, $p < .001$) and ARC performance dimension scores ($F = 3.24$, $p < .05$). In fact, the diary keeping condition explained 12% of the variance in ARC person scores, and 5% of the variance in ARC performance dimension scores. Post hoc tests indicated significantly greater organization by ratees for those raters keeping diaries organized by persons as compared to those keeping diaries organized by performance dimensions or raters keeping no diaries. Supervisors in the "performance dimension" condition also had significantly higher ARC person scores than those not keeping diaries at all. Also, there was greater organization according to performance dimensions for raters keeping diaries organized that way, but the difference between the "person" and "no-diary" raters was not significant. Thus the results suggest that, even in the field, keeping structured diaries influences how information is organized in memory, especially when those diaries are organized according to persons.

Table 6.2 also presents the data for recall, while Table 6.3 presents the results for the elevation indices, and Table 6.4 presents the results for the between-ratee and within-ratee discriminability indices. Beginning with the

Table 6.2 Means for recall indices in experimental conditions

		Experimental condition: diaries organized by:		
Index	Person (N = 26)	Performance dimension (N = 24)	Free (N = 16)	No diary (N = 22)
Total recall	27.8	16.1	26.8	9.3
Per cent positive	17.0	41.2	21.5	62.3
Per cent negative	20.5	25.4	27.2	22.8
Per cent descriptive	62.7	33.0	51.2	14.7
ARC person	.91	.29	.99	.75
ARC task dimension	.08	.45	.06	.07

Source: DeNisi and Peters (in press)

recall data, we can see that raters keeping diaries, in general, recalled a smaller percentage of positive incidents, a greater percentage of descriptive incidents, and a greater total number of incidents. In addition, those supervisors keeping diaries organized by persons recalled a greater number of total incidents, a greater number of descriptive incidents and a smaller percentage of positive incidents than those supervisors keeping diaries organized by performance dimensions. These results suggest that recall is enhanced by diary keeping, especially when diaries are organized by persons. It is puzzling, though, that we found the effect for the number of positive incidents recalled that we did, since the training emphasized the importance of recording positive as well as negative incidents.

In terms of the elevation indices, the results of a MANOVA suggested lower ratings for raters keeping diaries as compared to those not keeping diaries, and subsequent univariate tests indicated that this pattern held for

Table 6.3 Mean elevation indices in experimental conditions

		Conditions: diaries organized by:		
	Person	Performance dimension	Free	No diary
Rating dimension				
1 Reaction to pressure	3.56	3.63	3.67	3.87
2 Communication skills	3.77	3.81	3.53	4.04
3 Job knowledge	3.84	4.01	4.00	4.31
4 Interpersonal skills	3.48	3.56	3.58	4.08
5 Timeliness	3.60	3.69	3.70	3.96
6 Problem solving	3.41	3.50	3.59	3.71
7 Adaptability	3.43	3.39	3.50	3.67
8 Initiative	3.57	3.46	3.53	3.89
Overall performance	3.31	3.42	3.43	3.67

Notes: Rating elevation was computed as the mean rating given by a rater for the dimension across ratees. Sample sizes are as follows: Person (26), Performance dimension (24), Free (16), and No diary (22).
Source: DeNisi and Peters (in press)

Table 6.4 Mean discriminability indices in experimental conditions

		Conditions: diaries organized by:		
	Person	Performance dimension	Free	No diary
Between-ratee discriminability[a]				
1 Reaction to pressure	.96	.80	.87	.57
2 Communication skills	.97	.73	.92	.69
3 Job knowledge	.73	.75	.68	.46
4 Interpersonal skills	.99	.70	.90	.46
5 Timeliness	.84	.70	.76	.76
6 Problem solving	.92	.74	.90	.61
7 Adaptability	.68	.76	.90	.50
8 Initiative	.85	.75	.89	.90
Overall performance	.65	.66	.67	.45
Within-ratee discriminability				
Average	.81	.71	.86	.60

Note: [a] Computed as the standard deviation of the ratings for that rater on that dimension.
Source: DeNisi and Peters (in press)

all eight performance dimensions as well as for Overall Performance. We found no differences in elevation, though, between those raters keeping diaries organized by persons and those keeping diaries organized by performance dimension. The results for the within-ratee discriminability indices indicated that raters keeping diaries discriminate more within ratees than those not keeping diaries, and that raters organizing diaries according to persons discriminated better than those organizing dairies according to performance dimensions. These results indicate that diary keeping provides a clear advantage for ratings relative to these distributional indices, but that organizing diaries according to ratees helps only in terms of within-ratee discriminability. Since this is the index that would seem to be most closely related to behavioral accuracy (Murphy, 1991), and feedback, this still suggests an advantage for diaries organized according to persons, but these results were not as clear as those from the lab study.

Finally, the results for the reactions measures are presented in Table 6.5. As can be seen, there are differences in reactions between raters keeping diaries and those not keeping diaries (a MANOVA considering all four general dimensions simultaneously was significant), but univariate tests revealed that these differences were attributable to differences on only one dimension – "Accurate and defensible ratings." The results of post hoc comparisons also indicated that supervisors organizing diaries according to persons scored higher on this dimension than those organizing diaries according to performance dimensions. In addition, supervisors organizing diaries according to persons scored higher on "Keeping a diary helped me in the appraisal process" than did those organizing diaries according to performance dimensions.

Table 6.5 Means scores for reactions dimensions in experimental conditions

| | Conditions: diaries organized by: | | | |
	Person	Performance dimension	Free	No diary
Reactions dimension				
1 "Clear understanding of what to attend to"	23.28	22.13	22.69	23.12
2 "Fair appraisal program"	26.16	26.17	25.67	25.89
3 "Accurate and defensible ratings"	18.08	16.68	18.48	16.69
4 "Ratings would not be surprising to ratees"	11.60	11.52	12.07	12.04
5 "Keeping a diary helped me in the appraisal process"	16.75	13.36	18.01	N.A.

Source: DeNisi and Peters (in press)

Thus, in general, the results of this field study paralleled the results of our earlier lab study, with a few exceptions. Structured diary keeping *did* affect the organization of information in recall much as it did in the lab. Furthermore, the type of diary kept (i.e., the structure) was related to the nature of the information recalled, and was related to actual ratings, *even though* the raters all had access to their diaries when making their ratings. Therefore, we can conclude that cognitive processes involving the organization of information in memory are important for the recall of performance information and for ratings, and that structured diary keeping is an intervention that might influence these processes. And we can conclude that these statements are true for the "real world" as well as for lab studies.

The results were not identical to those we found in the lab, however. The effects of person-organized diaries were not as strong, relative to ratings, as they had been in the lab. Specifically, some of the advantages of person-organized diaries (and organization of information in memory according to persons) that we had found in the lab, did not seem to generalize to the field. This suggests that, perhaps, the type of structure is less critical in the field, as long as there is some structure, although we cannot totally discount the advantages to person-organized diaries that we *did* find. There were elevation differences and differences in within-ratee discriminability, but not in between-ratee discriminability. The lab results supplied evidence for effects on both of these discriminability indices, but the fact that person-organized diaries might be related to better within-ratee discriminability would still mean that this intervention would facilitate developmental feedback where a person's strengths and weaknesses needed to be discussed. Since these diaries surely produce no *worse* between-ratee discriminability, these results would still seem to argue for person-organized diaries.

Earlier in the chapter, I spent a considerable amount of time discussing reasons why criteria other than those related to ratings themselves should be considered, and, in this case, that refers to the reactions data. Of the four dimensions of reactions that we identified, ᵛ   nces for only one. This one, relating to perceptions that the ratings were fair and defensible, is surely a critical one, but there were no differences on the remaining three dimensions. Would reactions on one dimension such as this be enough to sway raters to favor ratings made using diaries? We cannot tell from these data. It is worth noting, though, that for the one dimension where we found differences, it was also true that there was an advantage for person-organized diaries over performance dimension-organized diaries and, of course, the data here clearly point to person-organized diaries as the preferred route from the raters' point of view. We should also note that, recalling the information about who showed up for the second session, we may have a behavioral index of reactions to the process. Approximately 85% of the supervisors who were assigned to the "no-diary" condition returned, as compared with 65% for the "person-diary" condition, and 61% for the "Performance dimension-diary" condition. These figures might suggest that diary keeping is an onerous enough task that a reasonable number of supervisors simply will *not* do it (recall, though, that I described the results of the DeNisi, Robbins, & Cafferty, 1988, study which suggested that even if raters didn't persist in keeping diaries, there was some benefit associated with training them to do so). But, the return rate for the supervisors in the "free-diary" condition was perfect. They all returned, with completed diaries, suggesting that giving raters a choice in how to organize their diaries makes the task more acceptable. Since, based on these results anyway, raters will choose to organize their diaries according to persons when given a choice, this might be the best route to take when trying to implement a diary keeping intervention.

So, it would seem that structured diary keeping can work in the field as well as the lab, but there is a problem with convincing raters that they really need to keep diaries. We had a meaningful drop-out rate in this study, and the raters only had to keep the diaries for 3 months. What would happen over longer periods of time? Again, our lab data from an earlier study (DeNisi, Robbins, & Cafferty, 1988) would suggest that some benefits accrue even if raters don't keep up with their diaries, but we still needed to investigate interventions that might be less intrusive. One such intervention, that enjoyed some success in the lab (Williams *et al.*, 1986, 1990) was a structured recall task prior to completing evaluations. This would require a relatively short period of time, just before ratings, and would not require raters to keep diaries. It worked in the lab, but would it work in the field? This was the question our second field study set out to answer.

STRUCTURED RECALL IN THE FIELD

The second field study was conducted at "Texas Transportation," and involved 118 middle-level managers from various departments in the organization. Each of these managers evaluated someone who was at least at the level of supervisor, and the sample was, again, mostly Caucasian males, with an average age of 40, average tenure with the company of 16 years, and with an average of 6 years at their present jobs. Thus this sample was somewhat more experienced in management (and in the firm) than the manufacturing sample had been, and these individuals also tended to be working at higher levels in the organization. The managers were, again, randomly chosen by representatives from the corporate HR staff, and randomly assigned to conditions. This time, the sessions took place on company time, and there was only a single session to attend. Nonetheless, the focus of the session was again on training the managers to do a better job of performance appraisal.

Training took place at a corporate training facility, and managers reported in large numbers to each session. Again, we were largely successful in keeping raters assigned to different conditions separate, but there was no need to treat the control group any differently in this study. All managers were provided with a 3-hour workshop that focused on the importance of memory issues in performance appraisal, and the role of critical incidents. We again discussed some important issues with critical incidents (trying to get them to focus on positive as well as negative incidents, and to record descriptive rather than evaluative incidents), and allowed them to practise identifying critical incidents with some videotaped performance segments. Also, we did not mention anything about psychometric errors or rating accuracy during the training.

There were four experimental conditions for the study. After the training (including the practice and discussion of issues and questions), managers in all three of the recall conditions were instructed to take 30 minutes to write down all the performance incidents they could recall for their subordinates over the past three months. The managers had between 2 and 12 direct reports and we asked them to identify and focus on no more than 8 of these (or all of them if they had 8 or fewer direct reports). Managers in the "person-organized condition were instructed to write the incidents for one subordinate, and then do the same for the next, and so on. Managers in the "performance dimension-organized" condition were asked to write down the incidents relative to one performance dimension (to be described later) for all subordinates, then turn to the second performance dimension and so on. Managers in the "free-organization" condition were told to organize their recall data in any manner they chose. Managers in the "no-recall" condition did not complete a recall task, but simply completed the ratings.

We first conducted a pilot session which we conducted as a "person-organized" session. The pilot went very smoothly and we scheduled the remaining sessions. We decided to retain the data from the pilot session, though, since no changes had been made following that session, and no one had been told it was a pilot session. Therefore, the sample sizes for conditions were quite different with 48 participants in the "person" condition, 21 in the "performance dimension" condition, 28 in the "free" condition, and 21 in the "no-recall" condition.

After completing the recall task, *all* managers were asked to rate their target subordinates on the standard appraisal instrument used by the organization. This instrument actually uses eighteen performance dimensions, and all raters rated all subordinates on all eighteen of them. However, since we had raters focus on only eight ratees in the "person" condition, we instructed raters in the "performance dimension" condition to focus on only eight performance dimensions. These were randomly selected, and were provided to the raters before they began the recall task, and all of our analyses focused on only those eight performance dimensions. The managers were told that copies of their ratings would be retained in the subordinates' files, but would not be shared with the subordinates, which was actually the usual practice in this organization. After completing the ratings, all managers completed an 11-item "reactions" questionnaire similar to the one we used in the first field study, but not including the additional five items used in that study to assess reactions to training.

We again analyzed their recall data as we had in the first field study. We computed indices reflecting the total number of incidents recalled, the percentage positive, the percentage negative, the percentage descriptive, and the percentage evaluative, as well as ARC person and ARC performance dimension scores, using the same judges as in the first study. Ratings were made using the organization's standard eighteen dimensions, and 5-point rating scales, but data were only used from eight randomly selected dimensions, namely: Leadership Skills, Reactions to Pressure, Developing People Skills, Written Communication Skills, Interpersonal Skills, Decisiveness, Adaptability, and Initiative, as well as Overall Performance. The ratings data were used to compute elevation, within-ratee discriminability, and between-ratee discriminability indices as in the first study. The measure of reactions was the same basic measure as that used in the first study, and a principal component analysis of the data from this study yielded the same four factors as in the first study (with only slight differences in the magnitude of the actual loadings of items on factors).

The hypotheses we were testing here were, again, basically replications from the lab data. We predicted that a structured recall task would result in better ratings, as well as more positive reactions, as compared to ratings made without benefit of the recall task, and we predicted that recall structured according to persons would result in superior recall, superior ratings, and more positive reactions than recall structured in any other way. Once again, there was a very strong tendency for managers in the "free" condition to organize their recall according to persons, with only one participant in the "free" condition failing to do so. Therefore, in this case, I will present the data for the "person" and "free" conditions together, and, when I discuss the results for raters keeping diaries organized by persons, I am referring to the raters for both the "person" and "free" conditions. By the way, we *did* analyze the data with and without the one person in the "free" condition who did *not* organize recall according to persons, and it changed nothing, so we just kept him in.

The means for the recall data are presented in Table 6.6. As expected, differences in ARC-person scores were obtained across conditions, with the mean for the "person" and "free" conditions not differing from each other, but differing significantly from the "performance dimension" condition. The same pattern of results was obtained for the ARC performance dimension scores, except that the scores were highest for the "performance dimension" condition.

Table 6.6 Means for recall indices in experimental conditions

| | Experimental condition: recall organized by: | | |
	Person	Free	Performance dimension
Index			
Total recall	38.5	39.2	41.5
Per cent positive	30.6	31.3	38.5
Per cent negative	26.0	25.8	23.2
Per cent descriptive	43.4	42.9	36.6
ARC person	.99	.95	.24
ARC task dimension	.10	.06	.93

Source: DeNisi and Peters (in press)

The data for the elevation indices, for the eight performance dimensions and Overall Performance, are presented in Table 6.7. Also presented there are the average within-ratee discriminability indices for each condition (only one was computed for each condition), and the between-ratee discriminability index for Overall Performance. The between-ratee discriminability indices for each performance dimension are not included because in no case were the means significantly different across the conditions. As can be seen in Table 6.7, the conditions differed significantly on elevation indices. A MANOVA indicated that the pattern of elevation indices differed between the recall and no-recall managers. Subsequent univariate tests confirmed these differences for all eight performance dimensions, as well as for Overall Performance, and post hoc tests indicated that, in every case, ratings were less elevated when raters participated in a structured recall task. In addition, the ratings were the least elevated for 6 of the 8 performance dimensions, as well as for Overall Performance, when the recall was structured according to persons. Although, as I noted above, there were no differences in between-ratee discriminability for any of the individual performance dimensions (and so no data are presented for them in

Table 6.7 Means for ratings indices in experimental conditions

		Recall condition	
	Person + Free	Performance dimension	Control
Elevation			
1 Leadership	2.93	3.29	3.34
2 Reaction to pressure	3.30	3.73	3.90
3 Developing people skills	3.14	3.33	3.90
4 Written communication skills	3.12	3.20	3.52
5 Interpersonal skills	3.18	3.45	3.50
6 Decisiveness	3.11	3.36	3.40
7 Adaptability	3.40	3.41	3.89
8 Initiative	3.46	3.72	3.90
Overall performance	3.25	3.64	3.89
Between-ratee discriminability			
Overall performance	1.02	0.85	0.59
Within-ratee discriminability			
Average	1.00	0.77	0.50

Source: DeNisi and Peters (1991)

Table 6.7), there was a significant difference across conditions for this index relative to Overall Performance ($F = 16.22$, $p < .01$), and further analyses indicated that between-ratee discriminability was greatest when recall was structured according to persons. Finally, the conditions differed in terms of within-ratee discriminability ($F = 11.52$, $p < .01$), with raters in the structured recall conditions exhibiting more discriminability than the "no-recall" condition, and raters in the "person-recall" condition exhibiting greater discriminability than raters in the "performance dimension" condition.

The data for the four reactions dimensions derived from the 11 items used are presented in Table 6.8. We found that the conditions differed on two of these dimensions, "Fair and accurate appraisal program" and "Ratings would not be surprising to ratees." In both cases, post hoc tests indicated that raters in the structured recall conditions had more positive

Table 6.8 Means for reactions dimensions across recall conditions

Dimension		Recall condition		
	Person	Free	Performance dimension	Control
1 "Clear understanding of what to attend to"	11.35	7.79	11.17	10.21
2 "Fair and accurate appraisal program"	15.34_a	15.61_a	15.50_a	11.24_b
3 "Defensible ratings"	16.37	16.43	15.89	16.18
4 "Ratings would not be surprising to ratees"	11.21_a	11.40_a	10.21_b	9.56_c

Source: DeNisi and Peters (in press)
Notes: Means for the same reactions factor with different subscripts differ from each other, $p < .05$ or less. Maximum sample sizes are as follows: Person (48); Free (28); Performance dimension (21); and Control (21). Sample sizes for specific analyses may differ because of missing data.

reactions than those in the "no-recall" condition. Finally, raters in the "person" conditions also exhibited more positive reactions to "Ratings would not be surprising to ratees" than did those in the "performance dimension" condition, but there was no significant difference on the other reactions dimension.

Once again, the results generally confirmed the efficacy of the lab-based intervention in a field setting. Structured recall appeared to be related to differences in rating and reactions, and the total time needed for this intervention was only 30 minutes per rater. As before, though, the advantage for structuring recall according to persons was not as clear in the field as it had been in the lab. In fact, it is worth noting that the pattern of results for the two interventions was virtually the same. In both cases, the person-organized intervention was associated with better recall and less elevated ratings, as well as greater within-ratee discriminability, but in neither case was there much of a difference in between-ratee discriminability. Structured recall seemed to have a somewhat greater effect on reactions than did structured diary keeping, but here too the advantage for person-organized recall was a bit weak. As in the first experiment, though, raters given a choice, seemed to strongly prefer to organize recall according to persons or ratees. Thus, again, it would seem reasonable to suggest that organizations introduce these interventions, but allow raters to organize information however they choose, since, in most cases, this will still yield whatever advantages accrue to person-organization.

The results of both these studies also mark an important step for cognitive-based performance appraisal research. The results obtained in the lab *do* generalize to the field, for the most part. Recall is enhanced, ratings are less elevated, there is more within-ratee discriminability, and raters indicate somewhat more positive reactions. Furthermore, structured diary keeping *does* seem to be associated with organization of information in memory as was found in the lab. We cannot be sure from the results of these two studies that all the processes that we identified in the lab generalize to the field, and this should surely be the target of future research, but we do have evidence that at least some of what we learned in the lab about the role of cognitive processes applies in the field as well. We need to move this research into the field in earnest, but these results suggest that laboratory research *does* play an important role in helping us to understand what happens in performance appraisal (see also an excellent description of this role in Cardy & Dobbins, 1994).

Thus our ventures into the field were largely successful, but both of these studies focused on generalizing results from the lab to the field. In addition, we used some of these data in one additional study that tried to extend what we know about the role of affect on ratings. As I noted in the previous chapter, most of that research had been conducted in the lab, and the Robbins and DeNisi (1994) study represented an attempt to move that beyond simple lab settings. Robbins and DeNisi (1994) were also interested in identifying which processes affect might influence and, as such, tried to tie research on affect to research on cognitive processes. I will now turn to a field study of affect with somewhat more modest goals, but interesting results nonetheless.

THE ROLE OF INTERPERSONAL AFFECT IN THE FIELD

As I noted in the previous chapter, there have been a number of studies that have examined the role of interpersonal affect on performance ratings (e.g., Cardy & Dobbins, 1986; Tsui & Barry, 1986; Williams & Keating, 1987), as well as other studies that have dealt with undifferentiated affect or "mood" and its effect on appraisals (e.g., Nisbett & Wilson, 1977; Trost, Kinicki, & Prussia, 1989; Williams & Alliger, 1989). But, as I also noted, most of these studies have been lab studies where interpersonal affect was purposefully manipulated to be independent of performance. In our earlier study (Robbins & DeNisi, 1994) we presented evidence to suggest that affect and performance may not be unrelated and that, in fact, affect may be the result of past performance. In the study I now want to discuss (Varma, DeNisi, & Peters, 1993; 1996) we still were interested in examining if affect precedes or follows from performance evaluations, but we also had a different goal in designing the study.

Although interpersonal affect has surely been found to influence ratings, its effect on all ratings may not be the same. For example, Alexander and Wilkins (1982) reported that *subjective* measures of performance were more prone to the effects of interpersonal affect than were more objective measures. Also, Park and Sims (1989) found that, although positive affect towards a ratee influenced all ratings, these effects are stronger for trait-like ratings as opposed to task-related ratings. The results of both these studies suggest that, when raters are asked to evaluate ratees on more subjective aspects of work, or aspects that require inferences, or that lack clear standards, we are more likely to see an effect for interpersonal affect. Thus we attempted to study this possibility in the field. We examined the relationship between interpersonal affect and ratings on a series of trait-like ratings and a series of task-related and outcome-related ratings. Based on the previous research, we predicted that the relationship between affect and ratings would be greatest for the trait-like ratings.

But we also tried to include another aspect of cognitive processing in this study. As I reported earlier, we had found that, in both the lab and the field, structured diary keeping resulted in better recall and better ratings, and that diaries organized by persons or ratees were associated with better recall in both settings as well. We argued that, if affect had its greatest effect in situations where ratings were more ambiguous (e.g., required inferences or lacked clear standards), diary keeping, by aiding the recall of specific incidents of performance, might be able to reduce the influence of affect on ratings.

We used the same supervisors from "Texas Manufacturing" as we did in the diary keeping study described above. You may recall that I mentioned the fact that the raters in this study were also asked to rate their subordinates on twelve additional scales that were not planned to be used as part of a standard instrument, and we didn't analyze the data for those ratings in the study described earlier. Instead, those ratings were part of the data for this study. We realized that the eight dimensions chosen by the organization included both trait-like and task-related or outcome-related dimensions, and added an additional set of ratings so that we would have ten trait-like ratings, and ten outcome or task-related ratings. We submitted these rating dimensions to a group of Subject Matter Experts (sixteen faculty or advanced Ph.D. students in HR from Rutgers) and asked them to classify each dimension as either "trait" or "task/outcome." All trait ratings were correctly classified by at least 80% of the experts, but only six of the task/outcome ratings were reliably classified. We used these sixteen items to construct two rating instruments, a trait instrument (ten items, alpha = .89) and a task/outcome instrument (six items, alpha = .81). These instruments were the primary focus of our analyses.

Affect was measured using five items adapted from the scale developed by Tsui and Barry (1986), and the scale had adequate reliability (alpha = .75). In addition, as described above, we had randomly assigned these raters to diary keeping conditions. In the present study, we combined those raters in the "person" and "free" conditions and considered them as keeping person-organized diaries (41 supervisors). We also used the raters in the "performance dimension" condition (21 supervisors), and those in the "no-diary" condition (23 supervisors).

We analyzed the data for the average trait ratings and the average task/outcome ratings, as well as for Overall Performance, and the primary data are presented in Table 6.9. As can be seen, interpersonal affect was significantly related to ratings for the task/outcome ratings ($r = .50, p < .01$), the trait ratings ($r = .59, p < .01$) and Overall Performance ($r = .52, p < .01$). All data were analyzed at the level of the ratee, so that our sample size was 404 ratees rather than 85 raters. A comparison of the correlations for the two major sets of ratings indicated that affect explained significantly more variance in trait ratings than in task/outcome ratings ($z = 3.17, p < .01$), as predicted. When we compared the influence of affect for the diary keeping and non-diary keeping raters, though, our results were opposite to what we predicted. Affect-rating correlations were *higher* for the diary keeping raters for both task/outcome ratings and trait ratings (both differences $p < .01$), and the difference between the two sets of raters on Overall Performance was not significant. Thus, diary keeping was associated with a greater effect for interpersonal affect, and in fact these effects were even stronger for those raters keeping diaries organized by persons.

Table 6.9 Correlations between ratings and affect across conditions

	All raters	Diary keeping	Non-diary keeping
Average trait	.59	.65	.31
Average task	.50	.55	.42
Overall	.52	.55	.48

Note: The ratings refer to the average of all ratings on the Trait Scale; the average of all ratings on the Task/Outcome Scale; and the ratings of Overall Performance.
Source: Varma, DeNisi, and Peters (1993)

At first blush, the results for the two rating instruments would seem to support the well-known recommendation that performance appraisals should focus more upon task-related indicators than upon traits (cf., Bernardin & Beatty, 1984). But the results for diary keeping complicate that simple conclusion. We have shown in both the lab and the field that diary keeping is associated with better recall and ratings, and yet here, diary keeping was associated with stronger rather than weaker effects for interpersonal affect. Why?

There are at least two possible explanations for this finding. The first is consistent with a study by Balzer (1986) where he reported that entries in diaries were biased to begin with, and so ratings based on diaries would also be biased. In this case, it might be that the diaries were already biased by interpersonal affect and reliance upon these diaries only strengthened the effects of the bias. We examined the actual content of the diaries and the free recall to see if there was any evidence for this bias occurring. We found that correlation between the number of positive incidents recorded in the diaries and the rating of Overall Performance was slightly lower ($r = .47$) than the correlation between the number of positive items from free recall and the rating of Overall Performance ($r = .54$). Furthermore, these correlations were significantly higher (both $p < .01$) than the correlations between these indices and affect ($rs = .27$ and $.28$ for the diaries and free recall respectively). Thus, neither measure seems to be especially biased by affect, and there is agreement between the two suggesting that the diaries did *not* contain overly biased entries.

The second explanation is quite different. In the previous chapter, and again earlier in this chapter, I suggested that interpersonal affect might be the result rather than a cause of performance ratings. Positive affect, then, might result from a superior realizing that a given subordinate is performing his or her job well, and in that case diary keeping, which facilitates recall, might make the effect stronger. That is, a rater who keeps a diary, especially one organized according to persons, might have better access to performance information about ratees, and so might be able to form stronger affective ties with those ratees. Such a position is consistent with the results of the classic study by Lowin and Craig (1968) and, as I mentioned in the last chapter, is also consistent with a view that is taking hold in the study of leader–member exchange (e.g., Heneman, Greenberger, & Annonyuo, 1989; Liden, Wayne, & Stilwell, 1993; Wayne & Ferris, 1990). This view is also consistent, of course, with the conclusions we reached in the Robbins and DeNisi (1994) study.

But this position also requires a re-thinking of the idea that ratings should, in general, be made using task-related rating dimensions. *If* correlations with affect reflect valid variance and influence, then the fact that trait ratings are more highly correlated with affect would argue *for* their use instead of against it. In fact, in our study, the Overall Performance rating was more highly correlated with the average trait rating than with the average task/outcome rating. All of this might argue that trait ratings are the more desirable ratings, and that, in fact, most managers' implicit performance models are built around traits rather than tasks or outcomes (cf., Borman, 1987, 1991). Finally, these results also seem consistent with results reported by Borman *et al.* (1995), which suggest that rater evaluation models place relatively more importance upon interpersonal factors than upon ratee skills and abilities.

CONCLUSIONS

This seems a good note upon which to end the chapter. When our cognitive appraisal research moved into the field we found that many of the findings from the lab did generalize to the field, and we also began to gain more insight into complex issues of what is valid variance in ratings and what is bias in ratings. The results of our two large field experiments would seem to suggest that the organization of information in memory is as important in the field as we had found it to be in the laboratory. Furthermore, interventions designed to help raters organize information in memory, such as structured diary keeping and structured recall, also seem to be effective in the field. Effects were not as clear in the field as they were in the lab, and the relative advantage of organizing information according to person categories was reduced a bit, although this pattern of organization still seemed to aid raters in recall of information. Furthermore, our field study on the role of affect further suggested that affect may be a result of ratee performance rather than a source of bias influencing the rating of that performance. If one accepts this possibility, our results also suggest that trait-based ratings may be superior to task- or outcome-based ratings *because* the trait ratings capture more of the affective reactions to ratees.

Moving to the field has also forced us, and other researchers, to confront the issues relating to criterion measures discussed at the beginning of the chapter. Cognitive researchers helped move the focus of research from rating errors to accuracy, and eventually led to a more serious consideration of the relationship between those errors and accuracy. But, as this research moves to the field, we find ourselves in a dilemma. We have argued that accuracy, not rating errors, is the proper criterion, and that errors and accuracy may well be positively related. But then we move to the field and we can no longer assess accuracy. This leads some scholars to start questioning whether or not accuracy *should* be the criterion measure, and we eventually begin examining other measures such as reactions to ratings and changes in performance. All of these developments I view as positive, as they all move us to think more about what we want to measure and predict. Thus, even if moving cognitive research to the field did not demonstrate the generalizability of our lab results, it would have still made a contribution simply by forcing us to re-examine assumptions about criterion measures. That, and other contributions, will be discussed more fully in the next chapter.

Chapter 7

Implications for theory and practice

The previous chapters have presented discussions of numerous lab and field studies that I've conducted over the years with my various colleagues. There is a lot of information here as I attempted to describe, sometimes in considerable detail, the design and results of these various studies. But, although the results of any one study may make a contribution, it is time to step back a bit and look at the bigger picture. What contributions can be cited that follow, not from an individual study, but from this whole program of research? As background to this, it is important to remember that the entire cognitive approach to performance appraisal began as a reaction to years of studies that, for the most part, considered the rater as simply a messenger in the process. Certainly there were studies of rater training which tried to make raters "better raters," but these mostly concentrated on elimination of rating errors and, as Bernardin and his associates (Bernardin, 1978, 1979; Bernardin & Buckley, 1981) have noted, most of them simply substituted one response set for another, but nobody really noticed. With Landy and Farr's (1980) paper, and the subsequent models of the appraisal process, including ours, scholars were saying that we had ignored the role of the rater in the appraisal process. Raters were not just messengers, they were active gatherers and processors of information, who imposed their own feelings and schemata upon the performance information available to them. Thus, from a theoretical perspective, the cognitive approach and the research I have described here have helped to change the way we considered the rater in the process. As I will discuss below, it has resulted in a new recognition of the importance of thinking about raters as active decision makers, a new view of rater training, and new ideas about accuracy and rating errors. Furthermore, with the intersection of research on cognitive processes, and research on rater affective and political processes, we have come to appreciate more fully the complexity of the decision making process in performance appraisal.

In addition, I think this approach *has* provided a number of important ideas for practice. At first, managers who I tell about my research in performance appraisal, tell me that it all sounds interesting, but what does it have to do with performance appraisal? But it does not take a lot of persuading to show how rater memory is an important part of the process when ratings are done so infrequently. When you tell managers about assessing rating accuracy, some of them react very positively, although they wonder how one really measures the accuracy of any set of ratings. But when you talk about the recall of information to allow raters to provide better and more concrete feedback, they react very positively. This positive regard increases even further when the topic turns to the importance of documentation for legal cases. As I will discuss below, I think the cognitive approach has also made a contribution to practice in what it has told us is *not* as important as we thought. Rating scales of one type or another, rating errors, and even rating accuracy may not be very important, but rating acceptability, the meaningfulness of feedback, and the commitment of raters is important, and this recognition marks another important contribution.

Therefore, I turn now to a discussion of some implications and contributions from our research program, as well as from studies conducted by others on related topics. Although there are implications for both research and practice, as a scholar, rather than a practitioner, I am surely more attuned to the contributions to theory and research. Nonetheless, the implications for practice may actually be more sweeping than those for research and theory. Furthermore, many important contributions of this research to theory are probably yet to come. That is, since, as I noted, cognitive appraisal research was really founded as a reaction to previous approaches to studying appraisals, I believe it is still evolving and will continue to evolve. The cognitive models that have been behind most of the appraisal research for the past 10 to 15 years or so, have brought us a long way from where we were when Landy and Farr first published their paper, but I do not believe that these models will be enough to carry us to the next phase in this research process. That will require more integrative models and new directions for research, and I will try to discuss those in the next chapter. For now, I will review some of what we have learned thus far, from both theoretical and practical perspectives, and I will begin with the implications of this work for theory and research.

IMPLICATIONS FOR THEORY AND RESEARCH

As I noted above, we must remember that this approach to studying performance was largely reactive. After years of studying rating scale formats and rater training programs designed to eliminate halo, we realized that we had not made much progress, and we had not really learned much that was new about the process. Cognitive appraisal research focused our attention on the process, and on the role of the rater. I don't know if the rater accounts for the most variance in appraisals or not. I realize that, in these days of Total Quality Management and Statistical Process Control, we are being told to be more aware of system factors as determinants of individual performance (e.g., Cardy, Caranikas-Walker, Sutton, & Wade, 1991; Dobbins, Cardy, & Carson, 1991), but this approach is more concerned about making us aware of who or what is responsible for variance in performance. This clearly has implications for how we should go about evaluating the performance of employees, but I believe the primary focus of that work is to tell us when individual appraisals make more or less sense, rather than to help us understand rater decision making processes. That is, in situations where situational factors and/or constraints clearly drive individual performance, it makes little sense to try to evaluate anyone's performance, since system performance will dominate. Furthermore, in situations where work is designed and/or incentives are designed to favor group efforts, it makes no sense to evaluate, and so draw attention to, individual performance, when it is group performance we are trying to improve.

Perhaps true levels of performance are the most important determinant of performance ratings, or perhaps it's all politics, but I am sure that we would not even have discussions of the role of rater interpersonal affect, mood, and politics in the literature if we hadn't focused our attention on the rater. Thus, even if the rater does not turn out to be the critical player in the process, or if we need to consider far more about the rater than our present models suggest, I still believe we learned a lot by spending so much energy trying to understand how raters make appraisal decisions. But there are more specific areas where this line of research has made contributions as well, and I will turn to these next. Before doing so, however, it is worth recapping our process model as it would look after the results of the various lab and field studies.

At this point, memory-based processing models seem to make the most sense for most appraisal decisions made in the field, although surely some decisions are made on-line. Therefore we will primarily concern ourselves with memory-based decisions and simply refer to cases where on-line processing may dominate. Also, although many of the same factors we considered from the outset would still be seen as important, it is now clearer that these factors (e.g., appraisal purpose and the nature of the rating scale) influence any number of parts of the decision making process. I would also suggest, at this point, that most of our cognitive models have been concerned with predicting performance judgments, and that issues such as appraisal purpose and affect, as well as political considerations and organizational culture and norms, will jointly (with the appraisal judgment) determine the actual rating a rater provides. Performance schemata and expectations should also be reconfigured to represent more complex performance models that raters have, and use in the appraisal process. Finally, it seems quite clear that affect towards the ratee (whether determined by factors such as race and gender, or by actual levels of performance) pervades the various cognitive processes we have described. This

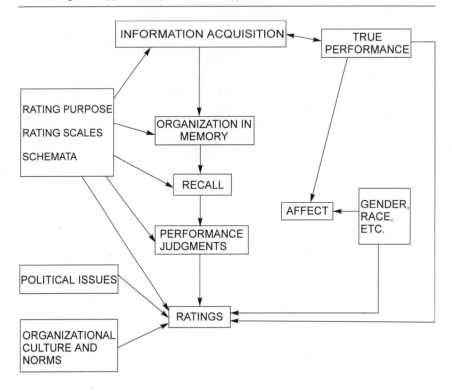

Figure 7.1 My latest thinking about a cognitive model of the appraisal process

further revised model is presented in Figure 7.1, and the remaining discussion will assume this more current model of the appraisal process.

Observation and memory issues

Focusing on raters has also allowed us to realize that processes associated with observation (or acquisition of information) and memory processes are important for appraisal decisions. In most organizations, formal appraisals are infrequent events, with more than two annual appraisals almost unheard of. Traditional models of appraisal seemed to suggest that the performance behavior exhibited by the ratee was always available to the rater. That is, the rater would be aware of (at some level) all the behavior, or all the related outcomes of that behavior for the entire evaluation period. Surely Wherry's model of the appraisal process recognized that this was not the case, but, more typically, the input for appraisal decisions was always assumed to be the actual behavior of the ratee. But formal appraisals, as I noted several times, occur infrequently and so raters may well forget something they saw by the time they get around to making an appraisal decision. Furthermore, since raters typically have multiple ratees and other duties to carry out, raters will usually not even be able to see a reasonable sample of all the behaviors and outcomes exhibited by a ratee. Although this may make sense, what difference does it make for research on performance appraisal?

Simply put, it makes no practical sense, and even less theoretical sense to consider the actual behavior exhibited by the rater as the standard against which all appraisal decisions are judged. Only if a behavior is observed by a rater can he or she be expected to evaluate that behavior. Thus, if we want to construct true scores in a meaningful way, we need to focus on only those behaviors observed by the rater. Any behaviors not observed, cannot be considered in trying to construct a standard against which a rater's evaluation will be compared. Instead, we should only judge a rater's evaluations against a standard of those behaviors which he or she has actually observed. This has been the approach used in the leadership area, as well as in the area of appraisal research by Bob Lord and his colleagues (Cronshaw & Lord, 1987; Lord, 1985a). They present raters with a variety of information about ratees, but have them note (usually via a computer) those behaviors they notice or observe. Robbins and DeNisi (1994) used a similar approach in their affect paper, to determine what behaviors raters encoded, and Kinicki and Lockwood (1985) used a similar approach to ask raters how they perceived chunks of information from a running film of a ratee performing a job. Furthermore, Kinicki and Lockwood (1985) based their work on earlier work of the same kind by Newtson and colleagues (e.g., Newtson, 1973; Newtson, Engquist, & Bois, 1977). Thus there are methods and examples available for other researchers to get a handle on what is actually observed or attended to, rather than simply what is presented.

It is worth noting, however, that I am using the term "observed" rather broadly here. For the most part, I literally mean behaviors that are physically observed by a rater – but a rater can acquire similar information in other ways as well. For example, raters can observe the products of a ratee's behavior, and infer the behaviors or even infer traits such as initiative. Furthermore, raters can learn about ratees' performance by asking a co-worker or a supervisor, or by checking some other records. Therefore, when I say that a rater must observe a ratee's behavior, I simply mean that he or she must have access to some information about that behavior, even if it is not first-hand. Performance-related behavior that is not observed or that has not been accessed through some other means, cannot possibly be considered as part of the appraisal decision.

The correctness of any decisions or judgments is then based on how well the rater uses the information he or she observes or attends to, and behavior not observed is not part of the standards for evaluation. You may recall that it was the failure to recognize this simple fact that caused us so many problems when we were trying to relate information acquisition activities to ratings. The important point for research, though, is that, regardless of the methods used to do so, we must identify those behaviors that are actually observed or noticed, and consider *only* these behaviors in any assessment of a rater's judgments or feedback provided.

But, of course, appraisals are infrequent behaviors. So even if a rater observes or notices a behavior (and even if it is encoded), the rater must actually recall the information at the time of the appraisal for it to make a difference. Surely we would want to consider information that is forgotten (or recalled incorrectly) as a type of error, but there are still implications for how we evaluate the accuracy of any ratings made. Although forgetting is not good, a rater cannot be expected to consider any information for a rating unless he or she can remember it. This is, of course, the basis for interventions such as diary keeping, but ratings cannot be any more accurate than the information recalled by a rater. Thus, examining rater memory processes should demonstrate to us that, although we need to be concerned about memory loss, any such information should not be considered when constructing measures of rating "accuracy."

Thus, a better appreciation of the importance of information observation and memory issues has allowed us to develop better models of rating accuracy. The work of Lord and others has already begun embracing this new knowledge, although I think we need to push this even a bit further and consider recalled information as yet another alternative basis for determining accuracy. In the past, by ignoring the information loss due to non-observation and forgetting, we were more likely to over-estimate the amount of inaccuracy in ratings. Again, I am not suggesting that failure to observe behavior or remember it is not a problem, but, if we are concerned about rating accuracy, it makes no sense to "penalize" a rater for information he or she either didn't see or cannot remember. Instead, we should be more concerned about helping raters to be better observers and help them to recall better what they have observed.

Learning from social cognition

The move to cognitive appraisal research has also allowed us to tap into a large body of theory from the field of social cognition. Scholars trained in areas such as industrial/organizational psychology, human resource management, and organizational behavior rarely take courses in cognitive psychology. I can recall, as a Ph.D. student, wondering why I would ever need to know anything about cognitive psychology for my research. I was clearly misguided then, but the truth of the matter is that many of us don't have much exposure to cognitive psychology. But while I am not suggesting that cognitive psychology is unimportant (obviously I've changed my mind on that), it is true that scholars in social cognition have already "translated" some of that research for us, and have applied it in areas where we feel more comfortable. Although social cognition scholars may not be contributing directly to the straight cognitive literature, when we began to adopt a cognitive view of performance appraisal we were able to access the social cognition literature and at least integrate this "second-hand" cognitive psychology into our own work. I'm not sure what that says about any of us as cognitive psychologists, or even as social cognition researchers, but it does seem to have worked.

Concepts and constructs from social cognition have, in fact, become well integrated into the performance appraisal literature. As we shall see later in this chapter, information acquisition, integration, and recall now play an important role in everything from scale development to rater training programs. Most appraisal scholars are also cognizant of the distinction between on-line and memory-based processing, and most discussions of the role of affect in appraisals now consider how affect influences decision making processes underlying appraisals. Regardless of whether an appraisal researcher considers herself or himself a "cognitive" researcher or not, all appraisal scholars are now aware of and give consideration to the role of the rater and memory processes, and all now discuss issues of rating accuracy in a much more informed manner. All of this is a direct effect of the integration of social cognition into the appraisal literature.

It should also be obvious by now that the integration of work from social cognition was extremely important for our own research program, since many of our ideas about organization of information in memory came from social psychology. In terms of further implications for research though, I would look to Feldman as the person who has shown us, more than anyone, what social cognition can bring to our appraisal research (especially his chapter, Feldman, 1994). But in more casual discussions and remarks at conferences, Feldman has also had an impact. For example, although I'm not sure this is published, Feldman has long warned of the problems in comparing cognitive processes of novice and expert raters. Kozlowski and his associates, for example, have heeded this warning and have found that more knowledgeable raters relied less upon halo-influenced general impressions about ratees than did less knowledgeable raters, and, in fact, engaged in somewhat different cognitive processes as part of appraisals (Ganzach, 1994; Kozlowski & Ford, 1991; Kozlowski & Kirsch, 1987; Kozlowski, Kirsch, & Chao, 1986; Kozlowski & Mongillo, 1992).

Ilgen & Favero (1985) warned us about the limits to which we can adopt models and processes from social cognition, but I believe that the field of performance appraisal research has become much richer for that borrowing, and the introduction of social cognition research has also led scholars in other areas to demonstrate how these theories and models can be applied (e.g., Northcraft et al., 1988). We now are concerned with processes, cognitions, and motives in performance appraisal research as well as in research in other areas. I maintain that these interests are derived mainly from social

cognition and that research such as ours and that of other cognitive appraisal scholars has been responsible, in part, for the large scale introduction of
social cognition to I/O, HR, and OB (Industrial Organization, Human
Resources, and Organizational Behaviour). Finally, as I will mention again
in the next chapter, a much broader area of management research, referred
to as "managerial cognition", has also learned to borrow from social cognition to better understand some unique aspects of executive decision making
in organizations. Here again I believe that our success in applying social
cognition to appraisal decisions was partly responsible for making researchers aware of the richness of those models and how they could be applied to
a larger set of decisions.

But for now we need to recognize how big a change this has been. These
fields, and especially I/O psychology, have been driven largely by psychometric and measurement considerations. Performance appraisal systems, for
example, were designed with an eye to problems of levels of analysis and
reliability of measurement. As such, they were fairly atheoretical. Cognitive
research in performance appraisal, and the associated cognitive approaches
in other areas, have made these fields, such as performance appraisal, much
more theoretical. It has allowed us to consider developing a scale not based
on measurement principles alone, but on consideration of how it will help
or hinder a rater trying to make a decision. This represents a veritable
revolution in how we think about these problems. In short, by establishing
clear links between I/O or HR problems and social cognition, we have
opened the door for other applications of that work, and we have moved
our research more in line with some more mainstream theoretical models
from social psychology.

Contributing to social cognition

Although we have clearly learned from social cognition researchers, and we
have acknowledged that, I also think that some of our research can contribute to the field of social cognition as well, although this has not really
been acknowledged. Let me cite three specific examples where research
conducted by myself and colleagues, as well as by others, has made a
contribution beyond where the social cognition researchers were going.
One of these is concerned with the use of individuated versus non-individuated information. As I have noted repeatedly, the research in social cognition has largely suggested that organization of information in memory
according to persons is the most popular organizing scheme and the most
effective. We found this to be the case as well, but there is a critical
difference. In most of the social cognition research, the information presented to raters is individuated (I discussed some of these ideas back in
Chapter 3). That is, raters are told that Billy Crystal is a comic and Barbra
Streisand is a singer. Since the information on each target person is unique

to that person, what reasonable organizing scheme would there be for raters other than to organize according to persons? Of course, in the arena of evaluation, information is *never* individuated, but instead we have information about similar aspects of the person for all ratees. In such situations, there are alternative organizing principles available to raters.

As I noted, our research has generally found a preference for organization according to persons even with non-individuated performance information (the original Cafferty, DeNisi, & Williams, 1986, comes closest to an exception to this), but then again, we are asking raters to evaluate *people* in a performance appraisal, and the very nature of the task could be determining the one best organizing principle. In fact, in several studies where we asked observers to evaluate task difficulty (as a foil when we were going to ask them to provide appraisals later), we found that they preferred organizing information according to tasks. Furthermore, in the Cafferty *et al.* (1986) study, information organized by tasks resulted in the best ratings. Thus I believe our research has shown that person-organization is not *always* the best way to organize information, even if it is best most of the time. By including non-individuated performance information we have at least allowed raters to use some alternative organizing scheme so, when we find that they still prefer to organize information by persons, this is probably a fairer test than we usually see in social cognition research.

I believe another area where our work has something to say to the social cognition researchers is in the area of the influence of interpersonal affect. Social cognition researchers have been considering the role of affect longer, and have been more proactive in integrating affect with cognitive processes. But those scholars are still considering interpersonal affect as a source of bias. They are still studying the role of affect in lab settings, and they are systematically manipulating affect independent of other information. I think several of the studies we have conducted (Robbins & DeNisi, 1994; Varma, DeNisi, & Peters, 1996) have at least raised the possibility that interpersonal affect is *not* a source of bias, but is simply the result of an evaluation made about a ratee. As I noted, similar arguments have been made by others as well, but these are all scholars interested in performance appraisal, not social cognition. Recognition of the possibility of this "reverse" causality, would seem to have the potential to make a real contribution to those social cognition researchers as well.

Finally, there is the issue of rater motives. When social cognition scholars began to consider interpersonal affect they began to talk about "hot" processing models, because they were considering emotions. Our research program has not moved in the direction of considering rater motives, but the proposals of Murphy and Cleveland (1992) and Cardy and Dobbins (1994) see rater motives as being critical. Here we are talking about rater motives in appraisal other than trying to identify who is the best performer. These motives are based on goals of the raters other than those imposed on them by organizations or researchers (e.g., goals of evaluation vs. observation in social cognition). I think this represents much "hotter" processing models than the social cognition researchers have considered, and that they could benefit from recognizing that, in the final analysis, the motives of the rater or decision maker will have the greatest impact on the judgments made.

Other decision making tasks

I have discussed some of the broad implications of cognitive appraisal research for other appraisal research, and I will discuss some more specific implications below. It is important to realize though, that cognitive appraisal research has implications for areas of research other than performance appraisal as well. For example, research on Assessment Centers seems to be less popular lately than it was a few years ago, but the most direct application of cognitive appraisal research, outside of performance appraisal, is to decisions made in Assessment Centers. For years, scholars have studied decision making processes within these centers, but Assessment Centers may provide a real-world research site that comes closest to the artificial situations we have created in the lab. Here, observation is over a limited period of time, and assessors have, as their primary responsibility, the observation of assessees. This is more like the lab setting, where raters sit and observe videotapes, than any other setting I can think of. Applying cognitive research methods to Assessment Center decisions may prove to be the most useful application outside of performance appraisal for this work, and Zedeck (1986) has, in fact, proposed an approach to studying Assessment Centers that relies heavily upon cognitive processes such as those described in our model.

Scholars in other areas have already begun including the same cognitive process variables as we consider in performance appraisal. I have referred to the work of Lord in the leadership area several times, but it would be unfair to suggest that he took his ideas from appraisal research. Instead, his work has contributed as much to our own as almost anyone actually studying appraisals. But job analysis research has begun including cognitive variables, especially stereotypes about jobs. Several studies have examined how such stereotypes might influence job descriptions, independent of what actually takes place on the job (e.g., Smith & Hakel, 1979; Cornelius , DeNisi, & Blencoe, 1984; DeNisi, Cornelius, & Blencoe, 1987; also, see review in Harvey, 1991). Surely this work can be expanded as we consider how and why stereotypes develop about jobs, and how schemata about jobs, and self-schemata, influence the way people behave at work and describe their jobs. There have even been studies of the selection process that have taken a cognitive perspective and examined how decision makers relied upon schemata and decision heuristics in making selection decisions (e.g., Huber, Neale, & Northcraft, 1987; also see review by Motowidlo, 1986), and relative to the interview process (e.g., Eder & Buckley, 1988). In each of these areas, as well as others, cognitive research from areas such as performance appraisal has changed the way many scholars study problems, and will continue to have implications for research in those areas in the future.

Rating scale research

Most of this discussion, relative to appraisal research, has been fairly broad and sweeping, but the impact of cognitive research on performance appraisal has also been focused on specific issues. As I noted above, the development of rating scales has been traditionally driven by measurement considerations. Scales were developed to eliminate rating errors, or to provide more reliable measures. Cognitive research on performance appraisal has not necessarily suggested that that approach is useless. It has instead, suggested that there are other considerations as well. Feldman (1986, 1994) proposed models for the development of rating scales based on processing models, not measurement models, and we have also proposed an approach based on cognitive processes (Peters & DeNisi, 1990). These approaches suggest that the scale used should match the performance model underlying the job in question, and that it should be designed to reflect the number of categories accessible to and usable by a rater, rather than simply reflecting a set of rules about how to design rating scales.

Our study of specific rating scales (DeNisi & Summers, 1986) is an example of another way in which this research has implications for research on rating scales. Recall that, in that study, we were interested in whether different scales were more or less prone to the effect of interpersonal affect, and whether or not different types of rating scales trigger different processing models. One can imagine a small-scale wave of replications of various comparative studies of rating scale formats where the dependent variable is neither accuracy nor rating errors, but refers to different cognitive processing models. In any case, I think this research has suggested that, if rating scales do play a role in the appraisal process it is only through their influence on category accessibility and cognitive processes. In fact, in one sense, the greatest impact of the cognitive approach on rating scale research is to make it clear that differences in rating scale formats are not a major factor in determining appraisal effectiveness, regardless of the criterion for effectiveness used.

Diary keeping research

As I noted earlier in the book, critical incident diaries (or something closely related them) have been suggested as far back as Wherry's work (1952), and have been the focus of research ever since (e.g., Bernardin & Walter, 1977). But those studies were, for the most part, designed to test whether keeping a diary made a difference. With our research on diary keeping we shifted the focus to a consideration of what kinds of diaries work best. More critically, we moved research to recognize that diaries represented more than just a place to take notes, but could actually influence cognitive processes. Potentially, the most interesting of these studies (DeNisi, Robbins, & Cafferty, 1988) even suggests that diaries can exert an effect on the organization of information in memory (and so on its subsequent recall and use) when raters are trained to keep diaries and keep them initially, but do not continue to use their diaries.

Of course, our field study of the role of interpersonal affect (Varma, DeNisi, & Peters 1996) also suggests that, by focusing raters' attention on ratee performance, diaries might actually increase the effects of interpersonal affect on ratings. The question is whether or not that is bad, but the point remains that this represents a different view of what one can study relative to diaries. Finally, in a related vein, Balzer's (1986) paper on diaries also represents a more cognitive approach to studying their use, as he proposed that diary entries are, in fact, biased, and so reliance upon diaries can result in biased decisions. All of these ideas, though, point to the possibility of studying diaries and diary keeping in their own right, and not just as a means of taking notes.

One point that has frustrated us in our study of diary keeping has been the relative inability to relate diary entries to ratings. It is true that, in our field studies, we have been generally capable of relating diary information collected at the level of the rater with ratings tendencies (i.e., distributional indices) measured at the level of the rater, but we have had problems in relating diary entries themselves to ratings, except in tightly controlled settings. We tried to establish a relationship between diary entries and individual affect and ratings, but this can only be done when diaries are kept organized according to persons *and* the rater is conscientious about including the name of each ratee. As I have noted, Balzer (1986) discussed biased diary keeping, but, again, he could do so only with data collected under more controlled settings. I also noted earlier that, in one study involving diaries and the role of affect in appraisal decisions (Varma *et al.*, 1996), we reported data to suggest that diaries were *not* biased, even though person-organized diaries were associated with stronger relationships between affect and ratings. In any case, our work on diaries as organizing forces in appraisals, and Balzer's work on bias, as well as our own work on diaries and bias, would suggest even more interesting directions for research on the diaries themselves in the future.

Rater training research

My own research has really not focused on issues of rater training (other than a quick consideration in my dissertation), but cognitive approaches to performance appraisal have clearly resulted in a shift in the way rater training programs are viewed. We are past the time when research is devoted to whether training can reduce psychometric errors. Frame of Reference Training and other proposed techniques (see Feldman, 1986) have focused, instead, on enabling raters to make better decisions and on improving their processing of information. Several studies (Sulsky & Day, 1992, 1994; Woehr, 1994) have begun to investigate *how* Frame of Reference Training works, instead of being content to know that it does work, and their research has focused on the effects of this training on various cognitive processes similar to those proposed in our model.

As we begin discussing areas such as rating scales, diary keeping, and rater training, we edge closer to the realm of practice. Although I believe that our research, and the research of others in this area, has clear implications for research on these issues, I also think it has clear implications for practice, and I would like to discuss some of those implications next. But before moving to practice, I want to state again my central point in this discussion, that is, that cognitive appraisal research has had a major impact on appraisal research because only after cognitive models identified the importance of rater information acquisition, storage, recall, and integration, did we begin to focus our attention upon the rater as the key player in the process. That focus has yielded the most interesting findings in terms of the relationships between accuracy and errors, between recall and ratings, and between affect and ratings. As I will discuss in the next chapter, this impact will become even more profound in the future.

IMPLICATIONS FOR PRACTICE

The criticism of the cognitive approach has always included the notion that there were no real implications for practice. Banks and Murphy (1985), in fact, saw the move to more cognitively oriented research in performance appraisal as having the effect of widening the gap between theory and practice. I have always disagreed with this view. I am an I/O psychologist, and I believe that I do applied research. As such, I have always thought about how the results of my research could be applied in practice, and I think there are a number of important implications of this research for practice.

Focus on the rater as a decision maker

Of course, I would return to this theme when discussing implications for practice as well. Typical appraisal systems do *not* consider the importance of this role. Rater training, similar to Frame of Reference Training is advocated in the literature, but not in practice. Raters are involved in the development and design of rating scales only if they are based upon goals (and then they get involved in the goal setting process), and organizations still impose forced distributions to influence raters to provide ratings that follow certain distributions. I see these efforts as misguided. Not only do they not help, but they hinder the organization's ability to manage performance effectively. New rating scales and new appraisal systems are *not* the answer to effective performance management. That can only be accomplished by working through the rater. Research has indicated that rater affect, rater motives, and even rater mood can affect appraisals. The message here is clear – the rater and the rater alone will determine how effective any appraisal system will be.

Raters must acquire and process information to make decisions. What can organizations do to aid in this? Rater training can certainly help. Whether it is Frame of Reference Training (which also provides help in identifying standards), or just a simple training effort designed to help raters identify and look for critical incidents, it would be likely to help the raters in information acquisition. Clearly, diary keeping interventions would help in the processing of information, since they would enable raters to better recall specific performance incidents (which would help in feedback as well as decision making). But our research suggests that a short recall task, conducted before ratings are due, should also be effective. This is an intervention that would require no more than 30 minutes or so, on the occasions once or twice a year when formal appraisals are due, and yet we would expect it to aid substantially in the recall of performance information.

Rater motives and rater affect are important determinants of ratings. Traditionally, organizations seem to have recognized this and reacted by trying to make it difficult for raters to act upon their feelings or motives. This seems misplaced as well. I am convinced that raters will do whatever they need to do to give the evaluations they believe they should give. Designing rating scales that trick raters will only mean that they will spend more time trying to figure out how to give the evaluations they want to give. Forced distributions or penalties for ratings that are too lenient or too severe will simply result in raters working to find ways to avoid penalties, or "beat the system" and still give the ratings they want to give. Organizations must, instead, recognize the potency of rater goals and affect and try, instead, to work *with* raters. Organizations should work to convince raters that their best interests are served when the rater also carries out the ratings the way the organization wants. Now this is dependent, in part, upon what the organization wants to accomplish but it shouldn't be that complicated.

Assume the organization wants to ensure that the persons performing the best are actually rated the highest and rewarded accordingly. This is vaguely an "accuracy" goal, and a rater can be convinced that this is consistent with his or her own goals. It becomes difficult to motivate workers if they don't see a connection between their efforts and some outcomes. If raters, in fact, rated subordinates "accurately" they should be easier to motivate, as they would more readily perceive that their efforts would be rewarded. Providing ratings that were too lenient would not serve a rater's purposes either. This would not result in *no* employees complaining about ratings. Instead, the poorer performers would be happier because they were being rated higher than they should be, but the better employees would be unhappy since their efforts would be wasted. And since these employees would have the most mobility, the supervisor would be faced with higher turnover among the best employees. Surely this would not be consistent with the goals of most supervisors. I could go on with examples, but the idea here is that the goals of the organization may well be consistent with the goals of the rater, but the organization needs to explain this to the rater. By ignoring, or trying to thwart the raters' goals, the organization is ensuring that the appraisal system will fail. Thus it seems to me that the central notion that the rater is key to the appraisal process represents one of the major implications of this approach for *both* theory and practice.

Before leaving this area for practice, there is one additional point I would like to stress. As scholars we assume that performance appraisal is important to an organization. We have been taught, and we teach others, that performance appraisal information informs organizations in a number of critical areas, and so is used for making decisions about pay increases and promotions, among other things. Whenever I have asked a manager, especially an HR manager, about whether performance appraisal is important, they also argue that it is critical. But if everyone agrees that performance appraisal is so important, why are raters *not* motivated to do a better job? Perhaps they simply don't understand why it is important for them, as well as for the organization, that performance appraisals are done well, or perhaps the organization inadvertently *tells* them that performance appraisal is not important.

In a sales job, everyone knows that sales are important. The organization tells the employee that, and the organization backs it up by basing pay, promotions, and even a job, on a person's sales figures. In the case of a supervisor, everyone says that performance appraisal is important, But where are the rewards and punishments associated with good (or poor) performance on this task? I have heard of organizations where ratees are asked to evaluate the rater in terms of timeliness of appraisal and meaningfulness of feedback, but even then the information is used for feedback and not decision making. If an organization really wanted to reinforce a position that performance appraisal is crucial, and effective performance on appraising employees was valued, it would develop ways to measure appraisal behavior (such as asking subordinates) and would tie rewards (or sanctions) to the successful (or unsuccessful) demonstration of those behaviors. Perhaps rater motivation would be less of a problem if organizations just worked harder to convince them that good appraisals really *were* valued.

Role of rating instruments

Somewhat related to the points about the central importance of the rater is the relative unimportance of the rating instrument. Although many organizations are moving away from more traditional performance appraisal systems, they still look to changes in instruments as a way to improve appraisals. Perhaps we are seeing more goal-oriented appraisals, and surely appraisals from multiple sources (e.g., "360° feedback") are becoming increasingly popular, but even these approaches reveal a belief that there is "salvation" in an improved appraisal instrument. It seems that one of the clearer messages from the cognitive approach to performance appraisal is that the type of rating instrument used probably doesn't matter very much.

What does matter, though, is ease of use and acceptability by raters. Thus, whether or not organizations are willing to go through all the steps of developing a Behaviorally Anchored Rating Scale or not, obtaining input from raters would seem to be important. Rater acceptance and "buy in" is much greater for an instrument they help design, and raters are more likely to develop an instrument that meets their needs as raters. Tying this back to the discussion of the implications of our work for research on rating scales, turning to the raters for input might produce rating instruments that look very different. To use an example that is probably salient to most readers, if a group of raters can only distinguish between two ratings categories – "tenureable" and "not tenureable" – then there should only be two points on the rating scale, and that is more likely to happen if the raters have a hand in developing the rating instrument.

This also suggests that the development of a total performance management system, in which raters can trust, is more important than worrying about what dimensions should appear on a rating scale. Recent work on perceptions of justice in performance appraisal (Folger, Konovsky, & Cropanzano, 1992) suggests that the process of performance appraisal is at least as important as the outcome, and we need processes and systems that raters and ratees perceive as fair. Ratings must translate into real outcomes, and everyone must take the appraisal process seriously.

The importance of memory processes

If raters were convinced that performance appraisals were important, they might also be more willing to accept organizational interventions designed to help them. A major implication of our research is that these interventions should focus (at least in part) on problems associated with memory. As we have demonstrated and argued, ratings can be no more accurate than the information a rater can recall. Interventions concerning performance appraisal have traditionally been focused on rating errors or rating standards. The latter is surely an important area for an intervention, but organizations have not yet become aware of how important memory processes are for the appraisal process.

Do raters remember specific incidents of performance and combine them to form evaluations, or do they recall a general impression about overall performance and then "remember" the specifics to fit the general impression? This is, of course, the issue of memory-based vs. on-line processing, but the importance of this distinction for practice is quite substantial. If the recall of incidents drives ratings, this should mean that feedback and development should be based on fairly accurate information, but that any decisions made (i.e., merit-pay increases, promotions) are likely to be *less* accurate than they might otherwise be (see Williams *et al.*, 1990). On the other hand, if impressions come first, ratings and decisions based on them are more likely to be accurate, but feedback is likely to be rather meaningless and simply reflect a rater's need to present a consistent justification for the decision reached. Only when organizations come to realize how important these processes are for the way an appraisal system works, will they pay more attention to diary keeping as well as other potential interventions that might aid the memory processes.

Rater training

The impact of cognitive appraisal research on the design of rater training programs has been striking. Although, as I noted earlier, rater training may still not be as common as it should be, when organizations *do* train raters, the emphasis is no longer on ways to eliminate rating errors. Frame of Reference Training (e.g., Pulakos, 1984, 1986) is clearly seen as an improvement over those more traditional training methods. Helping raters to be more expert in their evaluations by providing clear standards and training raters how to use those standards is generally seen as more promising than training raters not to commit halo error, and so simply replacing one response tendency with another.

Borman's (e.g., 1987) work on developing performance models also has implications for rater training. The notion here is that all raters have models of what constitutes good performance (similar to schemata about good performance), and they will rely upon those for making appraisal decisions regardless of what an organization does. But if raters rely upon implicit performance models for making appraisal decisions, and if different raters have different models, it should be possible to determine which models produce ratings that are more accurate, or that meet some other criteria of interest. The next step would be to train raters, not to avoid errors, or even to define clear standards, but to understand and adopt "better" performance models. That is, raters could be trained to develop more useful theories of performance which they would then use to make ratings. An organization could then ensure that all raters used the same model, and that all raters used a model that was consistent with the organization's needs.

The purposes of conducting appraisals

Thirty years ago, Meyer, Kay, and French (1965) wrote a paper in which they decried the common practice of using a single appraisal to make decisions and provide feedback. They argued that this puts the rater in a difficult position since, in many cases, in order to get a ratee the outcomes she or he deserves, they might have to overlook various strengths and weaknesses, thus reducing the effectiveness of the feedback. But research on cognitive processes presents another, and perhaps even more compelling argument for keeping these purposes separate. As I noted above, processes that seem to lead to more accurate decisions (classification accuracy, in Murphy's, 1991, terms), also seem to result in less meaningful and so less effective feedback (behavioral accuracy in Murphy's terms). Is it more important, to an organization, to make the right decisions or to provide meaningful feedback? If the answer is both, then the implication is clearly that there must be two distinct performance appraisals. In one organization where this *is* done ("Texas Transportation" actually), different appraisals are separated by 6 months and are done using different forms with different rating categories. Our research, and the other cognitive appraisal research, would suggest that, not only does using one appraisal for two purposes present motivational problems, but it is also cognitively difficult (if not impossible) for a rater to optimize both goals.

What if the organization can pick one goal over the other? Then they should make it clear what they really want from appraisals, and not try to tell raters that both decisions and feedback are important. Going back to my discussion about rating scales, if decision making is the primary goal, then organizations should use rating scales with relatively simple rating categories and relatively simple rating scales. In fact, in such a system, personnel comparison (ranking) systems might actually work best. If, on the other hand, the primary goal is feedback, then more care needs to be put into the rating dimensions and the rating scales. Everything must make it easier for a rater to give clear, concrete, meaningful feedback to a ratee and, in such cases, some variation of a Behaviorally Anchored Rating Scale may work best.

Criteria for effectiveness

Another clear implication for practice that comes from the research by us and others in this area, relates to the question of the proper criteria for evaluating appraisal effectiveness. Looking at the earlier literature in performance appraisal (and, perhaps, the gap between research and practice *was* smaller than it is now), we can infer that error reduction was a major goal in performance appraisal systems. If so, we can also infer that the effectiveness of an appraisal system was often judged on the basis of whether or not there was evidence of substantial rating errors. Halo error is surely one error that received a great deal of attention, but we cannot overlook the importance of rating distributional problems either. Leniency, especially, was the target of several attempts at improving performance appraisal instruments, and even today my Department Head is concerned that we give too many "A's" in our classes.

One thing cognitive research should have taught us is that, unless we know the true distribution of performance in a work group, it makes no sense to discuss things such as leniency error. And, of course, we *don't* know the true underlying distribution, or we wouldn't need to do performance appraisals. So how many "A's" are too many? Perhaps my students are just very bright, or perhaps I am an excellent instructor. Furthermore, in organizational settings, the stated purpose of performance management systems is to improve employee performance. If such systems are effective, wouldn't an accurate distribution of ratings "look like" leniency? Similar arguments can be made, and have been made, about halo error as well. Unless we know the "true" intercorrelations among rating dimensions, it makes no sense to discuss intercorrelations that are "too high." In the last chapter I discussed the possibility of using information about some of these distributional indices in a different way, and I will take up some future research issues concerning these in the next chapter but, what is clear, is that the presence or absence of any of these "errors" does not constitute a meaningful basis for evaluating the effectiveness of any appraisal system.

What then, of rating accuracy? First, I need to be clear in pointing out that the traditional concern over rating errors was based on the assumption that the presence of these errors was a proxy for the absence of accuracy. Therefore, one could say, organizations (and scholars) have always been interested in rating accuracy. They have simply had problems in developing better proxy measures. But, with the advent of cognitive appraisal research, more direct measures of accuracy became prominent. There have even been proposals for how accuracy *could* be measured in field settings (e.g., Balzer & Sulsky, 1992). At the same time, there has been more interest in the relationship between rating errors and rating accuracy, which has led to the general conclusion that rating errors are either unrelated to rating accuracy, or the relationship is positive such that more errors indicate *greater* accuracy. On the face of it, organizations would be in a dilemma. On the one hand, more and more people are paying attention to rating accuracy but, on the other hand, their traditional proxies for assessing accuracy have been discredited.

But I think the situation is really more positive than that. Our recent field work, along with the suggestions of Ilgen (1993), and Murphy and

Cleveland (1992) would suggest that accuracy is *not* the only, or maybe even the best criterion measure for evaluating effectiveness. I discussed many of these issues in the previous chapter and don't want to repeat them here, but some basic issues are clear. If we consider, yet again, why organizations conduct performance appraisals, it is to make decisions and to provide developmental feedback. In this context, accuracy makes sense as a criterion measure only to the extent that accurate decisions are more likely to lead to greater organizational effectiveness, and accurate feedback is more likely to result in behavioral changes in the desired direction. Let us consider both questions.

Are accurate appraisals more likely to result in better decisions? At one level, of course this will be the case. If the best performers are promoted to positions where they can make even greater contributions to the organization, overall effectiveness should go up. If these individuals are recognized for their contributions by receiving greater pay increases, they should be more motivated to exert effort on the behalf of the organization and, since they are presumably more able than some of their colleagues, this increased motivation is likely to result in greater gains in productivity. But let us look at the situation from the perspective of other employees. We assume that, when the best people are identified, everyone recognizes that they are the best. Employees who are not promoted, or who do not receive pay increases will look at those who do and aspire to bring their performance up to the required level. But what if everyone does not recognize that the best are truly the "best." In cases where performance standards are ambiguous, there may well be disagreements. Some may believe that decisions are based on favoritism or even halo, rather than actual merit. In these cases, accurate decisions are likely to cause problems. Now it is true that the problems will be created with employees who perform below the level of the "top" people, but this is still a problem. Instead, then, let me propose that decisions based on accurate appraisals are most effective when they are perceived by all the employees as being based on *accurate* appraisals. This gets us back to the questions of procedural justice but also suggests that, if perceived fairness and justice must be there in order for accurate appraisals to have their desired effect, then why not simply focus on perceptions of fairness and accuracy? That would get directly to the issue.

Similar arguments apply when we wonder about the effects of accurate appraisals on behavioral change. Feedback concerning strengths and weaknesses are supposed to motivate an employee to work on the weaknesses and improve. But what if the feedback isn't credible? One might argue that it *should* be more credible if it is accurate, and that makes sense. But again, is there any guarantee that accurate feedback will be viewed as the most credible? A large part of the appeal of Realistic Job Previews (see Wanous & Colella, 1990) is that, by telling newcomers the negative aspects of the job, they are more likely to believe the positive ones. Wouldn't the same kind of logic hold here? Wouldn't negative feedback be more acceptable if it were embedded in a discussion where there were clearly both strengths and weaknesses? Wouldn't even positive feedback be more credible if there were areas where the ratee was told he or she needed further development? I think that feedback is likely to be more credible in some situations than in others and, although this may be related to the accuracy of the feedback, I'm not certain how strong a relationship there is (and I will propose some future research questions concerning this relationship in the next chapter). Therefore, why not simply assess the credibility of the feedback directly? If credibility mediates the effectiveness of the feedback, measuring credibility directly would seem to make more sense than measuring accuracy and hoping for credibility as well.

Thus cognitive research on performance appraisal has serious implications for the criteria organizations use to evaluate appraisal effectiveness. Ilgen (1993) proposes looking at other direct measures such as improvement in performance or increased job knowledge. All these suggestions point to the idea that perhaps appraisal accuracy should not be the criterion used. Furthermore, if rating accuracy may not be the optimal criterion then, surely, an imperfect proxy of rating accuracy, such as the presence of rating errors, makes even less sense.

CONCLUSIONS

Cognitive appraisal research, such as the research we have been conducting, has had an impact on both research and practice, and these have been discussed in some detail. Whether appraisal research continues to focus on cognitive processes (and I think it will for at least a while longer) or not, scholars will look back on appraisal research and demarcate research before and after the cognitive era. What is, I believe, somewhat surprising, is the relevance of this research for practice (although, as I will discuss in the next chapter, the future for practice may not be so clear).

Traditionally, the link between research findings and practical applications has not been as strong as all that, and discussion of cognitive variables is not likely to make the link any stronger. But whose fault is it? Surely, if practitioners are not open to seeing how non-traditional research programs might have implications for them, they will dismiss these programs and the results will never be translated to practice. But I think that, in many cases, the fault lies more with the scholars than the practitioners. We write for a scholarly audience and we work to demonstrate the relevance of our work for theory and scholarship. As we begin to work in areas that require more specialized knowledge, we demonstrate that we can contribute to those areas by speaking to others in those areas, rather than to practitioners. When we published our paper in the *Journal of Personality and Social Psychology* (1986), we had to refer to evaluations of multiple targets because, *JPSP* publishes only basic research and, if we called it performance appraisal it would no longer be basic, but applied research. I don't mean to criticize a journal for which I have a great deal of respect, but this story illustrates the problem. To gain acceptance by one group whose opinions we value, we are often forced to adopt jargon and an approach which will move us further away from another group. Therefore, I believe it is the role of cognitive scholars to explain the practical implications of our work. If we wait for practitioners to read our papers about schemata, response time, and non-individuated information, we may have to wait a long time. We may need to use those terms to make our message clear to other scholars or to better place our research into a larger body of literature but, if we expect anyone to act upon any of it, we also need to explain in clear terms exactly what we have to offer to practice.

Chapter 8

Where do we go from here?

As I near the end of this book, I am struck by how far this research program has really come. After reading my description of the simple model that guided my dissertation, and the problems I had in operationalizing any search processes, the reader should not find it strange to learn that I am very pleasantly surprised to be able to write this much about what *was* eventually accomplished. But this chapter is not about how far things came or what was accomplished. It is about where things need to go from here. In the role of someone making suggestions about directions for the future, I will criticize what we have done as well as rely upon it. Through all of this, I will state my belief that cognitive appraisal research will continue to be a viable, vibrant area for research, although I think that the cognitive research in the future will need to be different from the cognitive research in the past. Nonetheless, I will begin to discuss directions for future research that are tied to the major pieces of our original model, before going on to suggest completely different approaches. Finally, I will present some thoughts about things that need to happen for this research to continue to progress, and the potential barriers that need to be overcome. With that as introduction, I will begin by examining issues for future research based on our original cognitive model.

INFORMATION ACQUISITION

Most of the basic work on acquisition processes has been done. We have examined purposeful search strategies and we have shown how patterns of acquisition influence ratings by affecting patterns of organization in memory. We have even demonstrated how such factors as time pressures, purpose of appraisal, ratee gender, and interpersonal affect can influence what is searched for and/or what is attended to. So where do we go next?

The first direction to go with research on acquisition is towards field settings and away from the lab. Virtually all of the studies of information acquisition have been conducted in a laboratory. Even when we try to introduce distractions and competition for attention, we still cannot simulate situations where long-standing relationships, clear schemata, or well- established performance expectations might all influence what a rater feels he or she needs to see about a given ratee. But how do we study information acquisition in the field? Balzer's (1986) study provides the answer. We study acquisition by studying the content of rater diaries. We have tried to analyze some of these data from our own studies of diary keeping, but there are problems. The data are only usable when we can associate a name with performance information, and that is only possible when diaries are organized according to persons. Since that is probably the preferred way to organize diaries (and will probably be the way chosen when raters have a choice) this may not be a problem.

Of course, we can never be sure if raters are recording everything they see or attend to in a diary, so it is not a perfect method, but, by collecting data about performance expectations, affect, etc. and then relating these data to diary entries for those same ratees, we should be able to get a better picture of how raters acquire performance information in the field. Only then will we be able really to answer questions about the effects of the various factors on initial acquisition of information. Alternatively, more intense studies with fewer raters might allow a researcher to follow a rater as he or she carried out their job. This approach has been used to better understand what managers do at work (e.g., Mintzberg, 1973), and it might well work in this context. In this way, we can learn more about what information is sought and what information is encountered, and a trained observer can determine what information is actually available to a rater. Of course, we can never be sure if the rater and the observer will attend to the same information and process it in the same way, but this still represents a viable means of studying information acquisition in the field.

Although this research must move to the field, there is still work to be done in the lab as well. Earlier I mentioned that Banks and Roberson (1983) reported on a lab study where they actually had raters record everything they attended to and reacted to. They presented a great deal of information and were able to get a much richer picture of what raters were acquiring and how. The idea here was to actually describe the detailed level of processing that a rater engaged in while making appraisal decisions (this approach is sometimes referred to as process tracing). I'm not sure the study has ever been published, and it was a great deal of trouble to carry out; and the very act of having raters record each piece of information they attend to and each decision they make at each step in the process, may in fact distort the ways in which raters actually process information. But such an intense study may be easier to carry out in the lab than in the field, and may yield more detail about acquisition processes.

Finally, we need to develop more and richer classification schemes for information used in performance appraisal. Our work began by thinking about information in terms of attributions (i.e., distinctiveness, consensus, and consistency). We have examined information in terms of positive or negative performance information, relevance for one ratee versus another, and relevance for one performance dimension versus another, but none of these seem particularly imaginative. Can we develop models of performance information that get at the diagnosticity of performance information? Trope and Bassok (1982) among others, have studied information diagnosticity (the extent to which a piece of information removes ambiguity and helps to reach a decision) in person perception, and it would seem that a similar approach could be adopted for appraisal information. Whether this is the specific direction to take or not, the general idea still seems valid. If we are going to understand how and why raters acquire and attend to information, we need some model for classifying information, so we can develop a theory of why raters seek the kinds of information they do. The development of such a model or classification would seem an important next step for research on information acquisition.

INFORMATION ORGANIZATION IN MEMORY

Here, too, a great deal of the groundwork has been done already. Nonetheless, we need to better understand how more-expert raters organize information in the field. Our field work has shown that organizing principles such as those we have studied in the lab, can work in the field as well, but are there are other schemes that are used in practice? Again, our approach to this has been quite simple. We have looked at organization according to persons and performance dimensions, and we have considered organization chronologically and according to performance level. But if raters in the field were using much more complex organizing schemes, we might not be able to detect them. Remember, computing an index such as an ARC score requires the researchers to specify beforehand what are the possible organizing principles, and we may not be aware of all the options. For example, when I first encountered wine in any meaningful way, it was either red, white, or rosé. I could surely detect dry and sweet as well, but I was not able to draw upon any finer categories (which may have also been a function of the wine I was drinking). As I became more knowledgeable, I could tell a Merlot from a Cabernet or a Zinfandel, and even learned about tannin. I cannot, however, taste a glass of wine and tell anyone the year or specific *appellation*, but others can. My point is that experts have more, and finer categories available to them to classify performance information. I think it is important that we explore what those categories might look like for more expert raters, and it would seem that developing rater models of performance, such as those developed by Borman (1987) and Borman *et al.* (1995), might aid us in identifying these categories.

INFORMATION PROCESSING

This is an area where we can use a lot more work. We need to know whether raters rely upon on-line or memory-based processing in the field. I discussed some reasons why one might predict either one to dominate in the field, and I am relatively sure that there is some of each taking place, but this is an area of research that simply must be moved to the field. The implications for what kind of information is available to the rater for providing feedback, and how accurately a rater can classify ratees under these two processing models are vast. If raters regularly rely upon on-line processing, we would expect clarification decisions to be accurate, but we would expect feedback to be based on stereotypical and inaccurate information, since the rater would not be able to access the specific performance incidents needed. If, on the other hand, raters relied upon memory-based processing, we would expect feedback to be based on actual performance incidents, but classification to be less accurate. Thus understanding the role of both processing models also has implications for an organization's relative concerns over the two types of accuracy.

Specific areas where research might be useful would be in identifying factors that might influence the relative importance of either processing model. These factors might include environmental factors such as the time pressures put on the rater, the number of ratees to be evaluated, the purpose for the appraisal, or even the relative importance the organization really places on performance ratings. Alternatively, the factors might be related to rater individual differences such as experience of the rater, or even mental ability or something like cognitive complexity, or perhaps something as simple as how good a rater's memory is. Finally, the processing model could be determined by the distribution of performance in the group of ratees, or other personal or work characteristics of the ratees themselves. There is a great deal we do not understand about when and why raters rely on different processing models and, of course, developments in other areas may yet produce other alternative processing models for our consideration.

In addition to these issues that follow directly from our original model, there are a number of other areas where I think future research efforts should be directed that, although not directly related to one portion of our model or another, surely are related to the processes we described.

RATING SCALE RESEARCH

I have stated, several times, that a major implication of the cognitive approach to performance appraisal is that the format of the rating scale is probably less important to the appraisal process than had been previously believed. Nonetheless, I think there are some important directions for future research regarding rating scales. I think the real lesson here has been that it doesn't much matter if we use a Behaviorally Anchored Rating Scale, or a Graphic Rating Scale, but I don't believe this means that rating scale research is irrelevant. It simply needs to be redirected. Can we develop a rating scale, based on what we know about rater cognitive processes, and can it be used effectively in organizations? These are questions that should be answered.

The dimensions for appraisal instruments have traditionally been based upon job analysis or, if an organization wanted to use a single instrument for a wide variety of jobs, it probably developed a scale around traits that someone believed were important for all jobs. But the work on performance models and schemata suggests another possibility. Instead of performing a job analysis, we would have raters describe their performance models, detailing the factors *they* believed contributed to successful performance on the job, and describing their view of what constituted a "good performer." Notice that this is not the same as doing a job analysis (although it is not unrelated) since job analysis is concerned with a description of what someone does on the job. Here we would be more interested in a rater's *implicit* model of how someone performs the job successfully. This will probably involve more traits and behaviors than tasks and outcomes, but there is no reason why it cannot serve as the basis for an appraisal instrument. We would need to determine those aspects of individual performance models that are held in common by all raters, and *these* would provide the dimensions for ratings.

In addition, the actual scales used to make the ratings would also be derived from raters and their performance models. If there was an area of the job where raters could only distinguish among two categories of behavior or performance, then we would have only two. If other areas allowed for more levels or categories, we would use them. We could even allow raters to supply additional categories as they became more familiar with the jobs (similar to what is done when BARS are used in practice). The advantages of such an approach would include having raters able to rely upon their performance models, which they probably do in any case, but they would also be able to base their ratings directly upon that model. This should make appraisals less cognitively demanding, and should also result in raters having more confidence in their ratings, and more faith in the meaningfulness of the entire system. Furthermore, since raters would only need to assign ratees to as many categories as they felt comfortable with, we would expect less random "noise" in ratings, a greater likelihood that raters could and would defend their ratings, and a greater probability of raters being able to provide meaningful feedback to ratees. All of this should increase rater acceptance of the appraisal system, and commitment to the system. It is not clear that this would result in greater ratee acceptance as well, but there is no reason to believe that acceptance by ratees would be less under such a system.

What are the disadvantages of such an approach? There are several. The potential advantage in using such an instrument would only last as long as the group of raters remained intact. If there were an entirely new group of raters, they might not use the same performance models (although see below for an alternative approach). Furthermore, this approach is likely to result in a different appraisal instrument for each distinct job. It is interesting to note that the same criticisms are mentioned concerning the use of BARS, and perhaps these are simply costs that are associated with any instrument developed by raters for specific jobs, instead of by consultants for all jobs. Although these are serious considerations it would seem, on balance, that the potential advantages would outweigh the potential disadvantages.

It is also interesting to speculate, though, on what such an approach might mean for determining performance standards for ratees (see Bobko & Colella, 1994). It is surely desirable to have all ratees judged according to the same standards, and in fact developing consistent standards is one of the goals of Frame of Reference Training. Since different raters might be using different models, even if they shared portions of their models, we might expect different raters to interpret a particular behavior differently. This could present problems for comparing ratings provided by one rater with ratings provided by another. On the other hand, if raters clearly communicated their own standards to their ratees, especially if these could be stated in terms of goals or objectives, this might actually make the appraisal process *less* stressful for the ratee, who would always know what was expected of him or her. In any case, research designed to examine the efficacy of new approaches to rating scale development would surely have to consider the implications of such approaches for issues of rating standards and the perceived fairness of the appraisal process.

In any event, the time has come for research on scales developed in this way. We need to understand what they provide and what they cost, and we need to learn if, by allowing raters to use categories they feel comfortable with, appraisal systems can work more effectively. Related to this, we need to understand better what happens when raters are forced to use scales based on categories they do not believe in. The traditional research on rating scales may not be as useful in the future, but this new, more cognitively oriented research would seem to be important.

Finally, in the previous chapter I mentioned the idea of doing more research on how different types of rating scales might trigger different categories being accessed, or might actually affect the specific processing models used by raters. This is a direction for research that should be pursued in the future. Even if we could establish that one type of rating scale produced ratings that are superior to those produced by a different scale, this information would be of only limited usefulness unless we also understood the processes underlying those differences. Do BARS scales actually result in raters processing information differently than, say, goal-based appraisal systems? For example, BARS, with their use of behavioral anchors, might require raters to recognize which behaviors were exhibited by a ratee, while systems requiring explanations of which goals were reached might require more free recall. This type of research holds promise as a different, and more productive basis for comparing scales. It would be relatively simple research to conduct, and it might produce some interesting findings that would have real implications for the design of appraisal systems in the future.

RATER TRAINING

As I noted in the previous chapter, this is an area where cognitive appraisal research has already had an impact, but there remains at least one additional direction for research on rater training to move following from this research. I discussed how rating scales could (and probably should) be developed to make them consistent with rater performance models or schemata, but I think that these models can form the basis for a different type of rater training as well. When I described how a rating scale might be developed to be consistent with implicit performance models, one issue was that, as raters change, the rating scale would be reflective of a different group's models rather than the models of those presently using the scales.

But what if an optimal performance model could be developed? That is, if an organization would seriously consider what they valued in the performance of their employees, and developed a performance model that reflected not any one person's implicit model of effectiveness, but rather the organization's beliefs about the behaviors, traits, outcomes, etc. that *really* led to organizational effectiveness. For example, Werner (1994) reports that extra-role behaviors are at least as important for supervisory ratings as behaviors which are prescribed by the ratee's role. Perhaps it is exactly these extra-role behaviors, closely related to Organizational Citizenship Behaviors (OCB; e.g., Organ, 1988; Organ & Konovsky, 1989; Smith, Organ, & Near, 1983) that determine who is viewed as a truly outstanding performer, or in this case contributor as well, in the organization. This notion has been explored in the leadership area, where researchers have linked citizenship behaviors with the quality of the Leader–Member Exchange (LMX) and, subsequently to performance ratings as well (e.g., Duarte, Goodson, & Klich, 1994; Wayne & Ferris, 1990; Wayne & Green, 1993).

Not only would research aimed specifically at identifying and specifying the determinants of such a performance model be useful for a general understanding of how raters make decisions about ratings, but once such a model had been identified in an organization, raters could be trained to use it. Thus, rather than simply identifying individual performance models, it might well be possible to identify a corporate model of outstanding performance, and to train raters so that each of them understands and learns how to use that model in making appraisal decisions. This is not unrelated to the ideas driving Frame of Reference Training, but it extends the idea a bit further. The relative success of Frame of Reference Training, though, would further suggest that a training program designed around performance models could work. Nonetheless, this would require research on both the identification of performance models and the effectiveness of programs designed to train raters to use optimal models.

THE ROLE OF INTERPERSONAL AFFECT

I suppose I see further research on the role of interpersonal affect as really being an extension of the ideas I've outlined concerning research on performance models. Our research has led me to question whether interpersonal affect really does develop independent of past performance in the field, but I think the question is still open for debate. The problem is that the laboratory research, in an attempt to isolate the effects of affect, has always involved designs where affect was manipulated independent of performance. Perhaps this is a case where, by borrowing from the social psychologists, appraisal researchers based their studies on an erroneous set of assumptions and took us in the wrong direction. I don't mean to be critical of those studies, since I am commenting in hindsight, but I think we need to accept the distinct possibility that affect develops as a result of past performance rather than functioning only as a determinant of performance ratings.

But if affect *does* develop as a result of past performance, we also need to explore the relationship between interpersonal affect and other behaviors such as citizenship behavior. Perhaps past performance behavior, where a ratee goes beyond what he or she was expected to do, determines both perceptions of citizenship behavior and interpersonal affect. In fact, we can speculate further about a performance model where the most valued employees are those upon whom a supervisor or leader can rely in an emergency. That is, the valued employees are those who will do whatever needs to be done in a pinch, even it goes beyond their normal job assignments or responsibilities. It is interesting to note that most managerial and supervisory (as well as many non-supervisory) job descriptions list a series of duties and responsibilities, and then include a phrase about including whatever else needs to be done at the time. Perhaps outstanding performers are those who excel in that last category of whatever needs to be done, rather than just in those areas that are prescribed. These individuals are those to whom the supervisor can turn and depend upon; they are good citizens, they are well liked, and they consistently received the highest performance ratings *and* have the most positive Leader–Member relationships. For me this is the most exciting direction that cognitive appraisal research can take us in the future, and I believe that it will be these studies of performance models, their determinants, and their effects, that will carry cognitive appraisal research into its next era.

Furthermore, I think that research that extends the ideas tested in the Robbins and DeNisi (1994) paper, would also be useful. Specifically, whether we are discussing bias based on liking, or bias based on gender, race, age, or any other factor, we need to better understand *how* these factors influence ratings. As I mentioned when discussing this research in Chapter 5, there are very different implications for appraisals according to whether bias influences information acquisition and organization, or whether it simply enters the equation at the last step, as one more piece of information to be considered. We found that affect influenced several processes, but not all of them, and also found the effects to be relatively non-cumulative, but this was a single study and more research is needed to better understand how and where bias influences ratings. One area of particular interest, I think, would be to extend the work of Balzer (1986), to examine how affect and any other potentially "biasing" factor influences the nature and numbers of entries made in rater diaries.

RATER MOTIVES

I have made several references to the work on rater goals and motives in performance appraisals. Much of this discussion has come from Murphy and Cleveland (1992), although there has been very little empirical research aimed at identifying these motives and goals, or demonstrating their importance for appraisals (see Cleveland *et al.*, 1986, 1988, 1989; Longenecker & Gioia, 1988; and Longenecker, Sims, & Gioia, 1987, for exceptions to this). Thus there is a need for further research on this issue, but the idea is quite interesting. It suggests that raters have their own goals and motives that determine their appraisal behavior. Some of these goals may be dysfunctional from the organization's perspective, but others are not. That is, in some cases, raters are trying to do the "right thing" but organizational constraints and practices (e.g., forced distributions of ratings) make that difficult, and so the rater must intentionally "fudge" ratings in order to accomplish a rather functional goal.

What exactly are the different goals that might drive rater behavior? The few empirical studies referenced above provide some insights. When will different goals or motives dominate? I don't know of any studies that have examined this question. Are some raters more likely to act on functional motives, while others are more likely to act on dysfunctional motives; do goals and motives interact with appraisal purpose, the nature of the rating task, or ratee characteristics such as race, age, or gender; do any of these processes interact with interpersonal affect? These are just a few of the important research questions that future studies need to address. A real challenge for researchers who pursue these topics, though, will be determining which questions are best answered in the lab and which are best answered in the field. There do appear to be clear trade-offs here.

Raters in field studies may be willing to report motives and goals in an anonymous setting, but will they admit to relying upon these motives (especially if they are dysfunctional from the organization's perspectives) in situations where they must be identified so that the effects on actual ratings can be studied? On the other hand, the laboratory setting would seem unsuited for this type of research because, presumably, many of these goals and motives grow out of needs to manage work groups over time, and depend upon strong feelings about ratees and the organization, as well as clear consequences for ratings. None of these conditions is usually present in a lab study, but it might be possible to study longer-term relationships in work simulations where individuals are actually hired to do work. There are real consequences for ratings, relationships developing over time, and yet the researchers can control various contextual variables, *and* ensure that no rater is punished for disclosing and/or acting upon personal motives. I think this research is critical for us to move ahead in our understanding of rater decision making processes, but I don't think it will be very easy research to conduct.

CRITERIA FOR EVALUATING EFFECTIVENESS

In Chapter 6 I discussed alternative criteria variables to be used for evaluating the effectiveness of appraisal systems and appraisal interventions, and I described a few studies we conducted where we used some of these alternative measures. But this is an area where research is sorely needed, and I believe this will be another important direction for cognition research to take in the future. I believe we have reached the point where there is enough data to question our old assumptions about proxies for rating accuracy, and I think there are enough voices suggesting that accuracy may not be the optimal criterion measure, for us to get serious about what should be the criteria in these cases.

If we are to continue relying upon accuracy measures, it seems clear that we need to make the distinction between behavioral and classification accuracy, rather than among the various components of accuracy described by Cronbach (1955). The problem, as I discussed earlier, is that I believe there is an inherent trade-off between the two types of accuracy and between the two goals of performance appraisal. Therefore, unless an organization consciously decided that one form of accuracy was more important than the other, relying upon either accuracy measure for evaluation would present problems in accomplishing the goals associated with the other measure. Before proceeding, however, let me be clear that this problem is based on some empirical research, and a lot of logical extension and reasoning. Empirical studies that were designed to test this trade-off would be most useful in helping us to move beyond accuracy to consider alternative criteria.

What about rater and ratee reactions as an alternative? We used rater reactions in our field studies, and I argued why this would seem to make sense. I believe that some type of measure of reactions is preferable, but this suggests other directions for future research. We adapted items from Landy, Barnes, and Murphy (1978), and Landy, Barnes-Farrell, and Cleveland (1980), and found four reactions factors to underlie our measure. Dobbins, Cardy, & Platz-Vieno (1990) developed a 12-item measure of satisfaction with appraisal, and found only a single factor. Whatever measures are developed and used, though, it seems that they must reflect reactions to appraisal processes as well as to the ratings themselves. Dipboye and de Pontbriand (1981), for example, found that satisfaction with appraisals was positively related to perceived opportunities by ratees to express their point of view, and the discussion of plans for the future in a review session, as well as to the perceived relevance of the performance dimensions involved. But these authors also reported that 25% of the variance in appraisal satisfaction was explained by the level of ratings received, and others have also reported that ratees are generally more satisfied with appraisals when they receive higher ratings (e.g., Bannister, 1986; Russell & Goode, 1988).

Thus we need more research on developing measures to better assess reactions, and we need research to help us understand where these reactions may come from. It seems clear that any such measure will need to consider aspects of both distributive and procedural justice, but it also seems that we need to understand whether reactions translate to anything more than satisfaction. Recall, that Ilgen (1993) suggested that alternative criteria for evaluating effectiveness should include improvements in job knowledge and productivity. Since we know that the relationship between satisfaction and performance, in general, is not the simple causal one we had hoped for, we need to know if ratees who are more satisfied with their appraisals will then work harder to improve knowledge and performance. We also need to know if raters who feel better about appraisals are more likely to provide meaningful feedback to enable ratees to improve.

Before leaving the topic of reactions as an alternative criterion measure, I want to discuss further the possible relationship between rater and ratee reactions and the distribution of ratings. As noted earlier, there have been a number of studies on correlates and predictors of subordinate attitudes towards appraisals. The presence of clear performance standards and feedback seems to be consistently correlated with satisfaction with appraisals, while most studies also find that the level of appraisal is related to satisfaction (e.g., Dipboye & de Pontbriand, 1981; Kavanagh & Hedge, 1983; Kavanagh, Hedge, Ree, Earles, & DiBiasi, 1985; Landy, Barnes, & Murphy,

1978; Landy, Barnes-Farrell, & Cleveland, 1980; Russell & Goode, 1988; also see review by Dickinson, 1993). Although most studies of acceptability have focused on supervisory evaluations, two studies dealing with peer evaluations reached opposite conclusions (see Cederblom & Lounsbury, 1980; McEvoy & Buller, 1987), and several studies have investigated the relationship between the use of different rating forms and appraisal acceptability (e.g., Dickinson & Zellinger, 1980; Friedman & Cornelius, 1976; Hedge, Teachout, & Dickinson, 1987; Silverman & Wexley, 1984). But, clearly, most of the studies of employee reactions to appraisals have focused upon characteristics of the appraisal interview, noting that more participation, more supervisory support, and more problem-solving are all associated with more positive reactions and attitudes (see Burke, Weitzel, & Weir, 1978; Burke & Wilcox, 1969; Ilgen, Peterson, Martin, & Boeschen, 1981; Kay, Meyer, & French, 1965; Maier, 1958; Nemeroff & Wexley, 1979; Wexley, 1979). But, through all this, we know little or nothing about the relationships between subordinate reactions and characteristics of ratings other than mean levels. Even there, the effects of lower ratings on satisfaction and acceptability seem to be mitigated by constructive feedback and goal setting.

Do ratees (and raters) perceive different distributions of ratings as more or less fair and accurate? Does this make those sets of ratings more acceptable? Will that translate into changes in performance or job knowledge? These would seem to be critical questions to answer. Organizations have traditionally viewed ratings that were normally distributed as being somehow more accurate (or otherwise superior) to ratings that showed a more skewed distribution, and perhaps raters and ratees would react the same way. Traditional concerns over halo error would seem to imply that many believe ratings that vary across different dimensions within a ratee are somewhat more accurate, and perhaps raters and ratees share this view as well. These are issues that could be investigated in both field and laboratory settings, and should provide additional insight into the determinants of reactions to ratings, and how these reactions might relate to changes in behavior.

This brings me to the final consideration in this area. Are there trade-offs among these different criteria? For example, we still don't know if improved acceptability and reactions are associated with a greater likelihood of changes in performance or job knowledge, which is the ultimate question we need to answer here, but there are other interesting questions as well. When discussing distribution indexes, I indicated that I thought these might be worth studying in their own right, regardless of their relationship with accuracy. But what if, as suggested by some of the research discussed in Chapter 6, greater halo error *is* associated with greater accuracy? What if, at the same time, ratees find ratings where there is greater within-ratee discrimination (i.e., less halo) more likely to be accurate and so more acceptable? Would it then be more important for ratings to *be* accurate or to be *perceived to be* accurate?

There are a number of interesting and important questions that must be answered in this area. Once we began to question traditional assumptions about criteria for effectiveness, we opened up other problems that were not even being considered in the past. All of these research questions, though, can be reduced to the one "simple" question that we must ultimately answer: what is the most meaningful criterion measure we can use to evaluate the effectiveness of appraisal systems? Clearly, we have a lot of work to do before we can answer it.

THE FUTURE OF COGNITIVE RESEARCH IN PERFORMANCE APPRAISAL

The cognitive approach to studying performance appraisal began in earnest with Landy and Farr's (1980) review paper, but grew out of the work of several of us who came to the conclusion that past efforts to improve performance appraisal were misdirected. Up until this point, I have been discussing the development of a particular program of research that represented the cognitive approach. I have tried to describe what we found and what it might mean, and I have discussed some implications for future research that grow out of this research. But what does the future hold for cognitive approaches to performance appraisals?

More traditional approaches to performance appraisal were largely abandoned when we believed they could not solve our problems. As I noted throughout, critics of the cognitive approach have suggested the same was true for this research, even before any empirical work had really appeared. Will it really continue? In part, the answer depends on what we label as cognitive research. In their book, Murphy and Cleveland (1992) identify themselves as scholars who do *not* do cognitive research, and who am I to argue with their own self-definition? But I believe their emphasis on rater motives and goals, the role of appraisal as a means of communication, and the entire body of their work, especially Murphy's work on rating accuracy and on-line vs. memory-based processing, suggests that they are interested in cognitive processes and so *do* conduct cognitive research. If their work is cognitive, we will continue to see cognitive research for quite a while. I also believe that scholars such as Feldman and Lord will also continue the cognitive tradition in their work, and I can think of a number of other scholars for whom this is true. Thus I believe that cognitive research will continue to thrive, as long as it accepts the criticism that has been leveled and adapts accordingly.

But cognitive appraisal research, like all HR and I/O psychology research, will have to adapt to changing times. Within the research community, there is more concern that we consider organization-level contextual variables, and even consider the environment beyond the organization when we study HR practices such as appraisals. Thus cognitive processes will have to be considered in these larger contexts, and we will need to incorporate organizational-level variables (and beyond) in trying to understand how raters process performance information and how they arrive at performance ratings. Clearly, HR research is moving away from micro-level research in areas like rater decision making processes. As we approach the millennium, there is more concern over organizational structures, macro-level variables, and relating HR practices to firm performance in such a way that we can describe the characteristics of high performing firms (e.g., Huselid, 1995; Jackson, Schuler, & Rivero, 1989; also see review by Jackson & Schuler, 1995). I don't want to suggest that there is anything wrong with this type of research, in fact it is quite important, but it moves us in a different direction. In these studies, the interest is on systems, the dependent variable is usually firm performance, and there is often little theory to suggest why certain practices should produce gains in productivity. This is quite at odds with cognitive research which has a much more micro orientation, and which is probably more interested in understanding what is going on than in relating anything to firm performance (although clearly both are important). The point here is that cognitive research must reflect these changing interests and considerations if it is to remain a vital force. The *zeitgeist* is to move away from detailed understanding of cognitive processes and towards relating HR practices to organizationally relevant outcomes. Can we show that how raters process information and whether or not they like a ratee relates to firm or work unit productivity? I think perhaps we can, but this means we need to expand the scope of our research, and this need, as much as any problems with measures of rating accuracy, would seem to suggest that we move towards more organizationally relevant outcome measures in evaluating the effectiveness of any appraisal programs.

Finally, there is the real issue that workplaces and how we do work are changing. As organizations restructure and re-engineer themselves, work is no longer defined as it once was. Performance appraisal as we have known it is still based on job analysis. There are defined tasks and/or responsibilities and/or goals for every job, and we can evaluate performance relative to these. But people don't always have clearly defined jobs, they have bundles of tasks that may change on a daily basis, and work is rarely the product of any one individual. Work, jobs, and even organizations are changing every day, and systems that are based on static models of work and the workplace are, or soon will be, outdated. Cascio (1995) echoes these concerns, and also suggests that performance appraisal in the future will have to be adapted to team performance models, and will have to address the problems associated with feedback and evaluations from multiple sources (i.e., 360° appraisals). Does cognitive appraisal research have a place in this changing world of work?

I think it does. Cognitive appraisal research has already led to suggestions for the design of appraisal systems that are based on cognitive processes and *not* upon more traditional job analysis techniques (e.g., Feldman, 1986; Peters & DeNisi, 1990). Models of team performance and team decision making (e.g., Hollenbeck, Ilgen, Sego, Hedlund, Major, & Phillips, 1991; McIntyre & Salas, 1995) are being developed and, although these may result in a different conceptual model of the appraisal process, they will also lead to new and different categories which raters will probably still use to categorize and process ratees, even if the unit of analysis moves from the individual to the team. Finally, although there has not been much research on the appraisal process for peers or subordinates (although the Borman, White, & Dorsey, 1995, paper is surely a start in this direction), there is absolutely no reason why our present cognitive models could not be adapted for use with other types of raters. In fact, consideration of the appraisal process for different groups of ratees may actually help us understand how best to combine the ratings from these different raters to form a single, meaningful evaluation of a ratee.

I think that cognitive researchers will have to adapt to these changes, but I think they can, and that cognitive models still have something to contribute. In fact, I believe that cognitive-oriented research is like the genie that has been let out of the bottle. It may not be as pervasive as it has been, and it may be replaced, even, as the dominant model of appraisal research, but I cannot imagine that it will go away. Once we began to consider raters as decision makers, and began considering how they acquired and processed information to make decisions, how could we ever again conceive of models that ignored the rater as an active participant in the appraisal process? Cognitive appraisal research may change, but I don't believe anyone will again be able to ignore the role of cognition on the appraisal process, as well as on a wide range of organizational processes. That will be the lasting legacy of this research.

Our research program has helped demonstrate that cognitive models can be integrated with "hot" processing models stressing rater affect. We have also provided some evidence that gender bias in appraisals can be studied from a cognitive perspective. Studies in the lab also provided some evidence that rating instruments can play a role in cognitive processing, and data from both the lab and the field have shown that performance diaries can play a critical role in the cognitive processes that operate as part of the performance appraisal process.

Our other field research demonstrated that several of the critical processes we had identified in the lab seemed to operate in the field as well, and that interventions such as structured recall and structured diary keeping influenced recall and ratings in the field much as they did in the lab. In these field studies, of course, we could not use rating accuracy as a dependent variable, and this led us to examine several indices of rating distribution and rater reactions to appraisals and the appraisal process as alternative criteria measures. This work led us to reconsider the central role of accuracy in appraisal research. The work of other scholars in the field had suggested that errors were not related to accuracy in the way that had been assumed and that, in any event, rating accuracy did not guarantee the acceptability of ratings and the resultant behavioral change that appraisals were really designed to effect. These results and these arguments led to a suggestion that a consideration of alternative criterion measures was another area where research was needed in the future.

Thus I hope I have demonstrated that we have learned a lot about the appraisal process, and that our research has implications for future research as well as practice. Furthermore, I hope I have pointed to some of those directions for future research. The future is uncertain, and the future of the way we do, think of, and study work, is quite uncertain. Nonetheless, I hope I have provided some evidence to suggest that cognitively oriented appraisal research *can* play a role in the research we do in the workplace of the future.

SOME FINAL THOUGHTS

It is a pleasant feeling to look back on this research program. Although it did not go entirely as had been planned, it has had a beginning and a middle, although I don't believe it has reached the end quite yet. The very fact that I can refer to this as a research "program", then, is quite important. These were not a series of studies designed to accomplish limited and somewhat unrelated goals. The research was always aimed at understanding rater cognitive processes, and we learned as we moved along. In fact, if I were to think about some things I would like the reader to take away, one of them would be knowledge gained, not only by reading what we did right, but also knowledge gained by reading what we did wrong. I assume that if we could learn from our mistakes, others can as well.

I would also like the reader to take away an appreciation of the benefits of doing systematic research. The thirty or so experiments that we did as part of this research project have had a substantial impact upon the appraisal literature over the 10 year period from 1985 to 1995. Perhaps an equal number of well-designed studies carried out over the same period would have had an equal impact, but I don't think so. During that period our work has been cited almost 200 times (195 according to the Social Science Citation Index, through September of 1995), and our model (DeNisi et al., 1984) has been cited by every leading appraisal scholar for the past ten years.

The ideas and efforts of a large number of people went into this project. They contributed either through direct participation, or by discussing research ideas, or by writing papers that we could use to develop our own ideas. Therefore I have tried to be sure and not take all the credit for this work. Nonetheless, as I write the final page of this book, I am proud to have been an important part of this research program, and I hope this work continues to make a contribution both to research and practice in the area of performance appraisal.

Bibliography

Ajzen, I., Dalton, C., & Blyth, D. P. (1979). Consistency and bias in the attribution of attitudes. *Journal of Personality and Social Psychology, 37,* 1871–1876.

Alexander, E. R., & Wilkins, R. D. (1982). Performance rating validity: The relationship of objective and subjective measures of performance. *Group and Organization Studies, 7,* 485–496.

Anderson, N. H., & Hubert, S. (1963). Effects of concomitant verbal recall on order effects in personality impression formation. *Journal of Verbal Learning and Verbal Behavior, 2,* 379–391.

Anderson, C. A., Lepper, M. R., & Ross, L. (1980). Perseverance of social theories: The role of explanation in the persistence of discredited information. *Journal of Personality and Social Psychology, 39,* 1037–1049.

Atkin, R. S., & Conlon, E. J. (1978). Behaviorally Anchored Rating Scales: Some theoretical issues. *Academy of Management Review, 3,* 119–128.

Arvey, R. D., & Hoyle, J. C. (1974). A Guttman approach to the development of behaviorally based rating scales for systems analysts and programmer/analysts. *Journal of Applied Psychology, 59,* 61–68.

Arvey, R. D., & Jones, A. P. (1985). The use of discipline in organizations: A framework for future research. In L. Cummings & B. Staw (Eds.), *Research in organizational behavior* (Vol. 7). Greenwich, CT: JAI Press.

Balzer, W. K. (1986). Biases in the recording of performance-related information: The effects of initial impressions and centrality of the appraisal task. *Organizational Behavior and Human Decision Processes, 37,* 329–347.

Balzer, W. K., & Sulsky, L. M. (1992). Halo and performance appraisal research: A critical examination. *Journal of Applied Psychology, 77,* 975–988.

Banks, C. G., & Murphy, K. R. (1985). Toward narrowing the research–practice gap in performance appraisal. *Personnel Psychology, 38,* 335–345.

Banks, C. G., & Roberson, L. (1983). Relationship between cognitive schema and rating accuracy. Paper presented at the annual meeting of the American Psychological Association, Anaheim, CA.

Bannister, B. D. (1986). Performance outcome feedback and attributional feedback: Interactive effects on recipient responses. *Journal of Applied Psychology, 71,* 203–210.

Bargh, J. A. (1982). Attention and automaticity in the processing of self-relevant information. *Journal of Personality and Social Psychology, 43,* 425–436.

Barnes-Farrell, J. L., & Couture, K. A. (1983). Effects of appraisal salience on immediate and memory-based judgments. In C. Banks & L. Roberson (Chairs), *Cognitive processes in performance appraisal: New findings.* Symposium presented at the Meetings of the American Psychological Association, Anaheim, CA.

Baron, A. S., & Abrahamsen, K. (1981). Will he – or won't he – work with a female manager? *Management Review*, November, 48–53.

Barrett, R. S. (1966). Influence of supervisor's requirements on ratings. *Personnel Psychology, 19*, 375–387.

Barrett, R. S., Taylor, E. K., Parker, J. W., & Martens, W. L. (1958). Rating scale content: I. Scale information and supervisory ratings. *Personnel Psychology, 11*, 333–346.

Bartlett, C. J., & Sharon, A. T. (1969). Effects of instructional conditions in producing leniency on two types of rating scales. *Personnel Psychology, 22*, 251–263.

Bartlett, F. C. (1932). *Remembering*. New York: Macmillan.

Bayeroff, A. G., Haggerty, H. R., & Rundquist, E.A. (1954). Validity of ratings related to rating techniques and considerations. *Personnel Psychology, 7*, 93–114.

Beatty, R. W., & Schneier, C. E. (1981). *Personnel administration: An experiential/ skill building approach* (2nd Edn.). Reading, MA: Addison-Wesley.

Beauvais, C., & Spence, J. T. (1987). Gender, prejudice, and categorization. *Sex Roles, 16*, 89–100.

Becker, B. E., & Cardy, R. L. (1986). Influence of halo error on appraisal effectiveness. *Journal of Applied Psychology, 68*, 218–226.

Berkshire, J. R., & Highland, R. W. (1953). Forced-choice performance ratings: A methodological study. *Personnel Psychology, 6*, 355–378.

Bernardin, H. J. (1977). Behavioral expectation scales versus summated scales: A fairer comparison. *Journal of Applied Psychology, 62*, 422–427.

Bernardin, H. J. (1978). Effects of rater training on leniency and halo errors in student ratings of instructors. *Journal of Applied Psychology, 63*, 301–308.

Bernardin, H. J. (1979). Rater training: A critique and reconceptualization. *Proceedings of the 39th Annual Meeting of the Academy of Management*, Atlanta, GA.

Bernardin, H. J., Alvares, K. M., & Cranny, C. J. (1976). A recomparison of behavioral expectation scales to summated scales. *Journal of Applied Psychology, 61*, 564–570.

Bernardin, H. J., & Beatty, R. W. (1984). *Performance appraisal: Assessing human behavior at work*. Boston, MA: PWS-Kent Publishing Company.

Bernardin, H. J., & Buckley, M. R. (1981). A consideration of strategies in rater training. *Academy of Management Review, 6*, 205–212.

Bernardin, H. J., Cardy, R. L., & Carlyle, J. J. (1982). Cognitive complexity and appraisal effectiveness: Back to the drawing board? *Journal of Applied Psychology, 67*, 151–160.

Bernardin, H. J., LaShells, M. B., Smith, P. C., & Alvares, K. M. (1976). Behavioral expectation scales: Effects of developmental procedures and formats. *Journal of Applied Psychology, 61*, 75–79.

Bernardin, H. J., Orban, J. A., & Carlyle, J. J. (1981). Performance ratings as a function of trust in appraisal, purpose for appraisal, and rater individual differences. *Proceedings of the Academy of Management Meetings* (pp. 311–315).

Bernardin, H. J., & Pence, E. C. (1980). Rater training: Creating new response sets and decreasing accuracy. *Journal of Applied Psychology, 65*, 60–66.

Bernardin, H. J., & Villanova, P. (1986). Performance appraisal. In E. Locke (Ed.), *Generalizing from laboratory to field settings*. Lexington, MA: Lexington Books.

Bernardin, H. J., & Walter, C. S. (1977). Effects of rater training and diary keeping on psychometric errors in ratings. *Journal of Applied Psychology, 62*, 64–69.

Bingham, W. V. (1939). Halo, valid and invalid. *Journal of Applied Psychology, 23*, 221–228.

Blanz, F., & Ghiselli, E. E. (1972). The mixed standard scale: A new rating system. *Personnel Psychology, 25*, 185–199.

Blau, F. D., & Ferber, M. A. (1987). Occupations and earnings of women workers. In K.S. Doziara, M. H. Moskow, & L. D. Tanner (Eds.), *Working women: Past, present, future*. Washington, D. C.: Bureau of National Affairs.

Blencoe, A. G. (1984). An examination of raters' cognitive processes in performance appraisal: A laboratory investigation. Columbia, SC: Unpublished Ph.D. Dissertation, College of Business Administration, University of South Carolina.

Blumberg, H. H., DeSoto, C. B., & Keuthe, J. L. (1966). Evaluation of rating scale formats. *Personnel Psychology, 19*, 243–260.

Bobko, P., & Colella, A. (1994). Setting performance standards: A review and research propositions. *Personnel Psychology, 46*, 763–780.

Borgida, E. (1978). Scientific deduction – Evidence is not necessarily informative: A reply to Wells and Harvey. *Journal of Personality and Social Psychology, 36*, 477–482.

Borman, W. C. (1975). Effects of instruction to avoid halo on reliability and validity of performance ratings. *Journal of Applied Psychology, 60*, 556–560.

Borman, W. C. (1978). Exploring the upper limits of reliability and validity in job performance ratings. *Journal of Applied Psychology, 63*, 135–144.

Borman, W. C. (1983). Implications of personality theory and research for the rating of work performance in organizations. In F. Landy, S. Zedeck, & J. Cleveland (Eds.), *Performance measurement and theory*. Hillsdale, NJ: Erlbaum.

Borman, W. C. (1987). Personal constructs, performance schemata, and "folk theories" of subordinate effectiveness: Exploration in an Army officer sample. *Organizational Behavior and Human Decision Processes, 40*, 307–322.

Borman, W. C. (1991). Job behavior, performance, and effectiveness. In M. D. Dunnette & L. M. Hough (Eds.), *Handbook of Industrial and Organizational Psychology* (Vol. 2) (2nd Edn.). Palo Alto, CA: Consulting Psychologists Press.

Borman, W. C., White, L. A., & Dorsey, D. W. (1995). Effects of ratee task performance and interpersonal factors on supervisor and peer performance ratings. *Journal of Applied Psychology, 80*, 168–177.

Borman, W. C., White, L.A., Pulakos, E. D., & Oppler, S. H. (1991). Models of supervisory job performance ratings. *Journal of Applied Psychology, 76*, 863–872.

Bransford, J. D., & Franks, J. J. (1971). The abstraction of linguistic ideas. *Cognitive Psychology, 2*, 331–350.

Brown, E. M. (1968). Influence of training method and relationship to halo error. *Journal of Applied Psychology, 52*, 195–199.

Buckley, M. R., & Bernardin, H. J. (1980). An assessment of the components of an observer training program. Paper presented at the Annual Meeting of the Southeastern Psychological Association.

Burke, R. J., Weitzel, W., & Weir, T. (1978). Characteristics of effective employee performance review and development interviews: Replication and extension. *Personnel Psychology, 31*, 903–919.

Burke, R. J., & Wilcox, D. S. (1969). Characteristics of effective employee performance review and development interviews. *Personnel Psychology, 22*, 291–305.

Cafferty, T. P., DeNisi, A. S., & Williams, K. J. (1986). Search and retrieval patterns for performance information. *Journal of Personality and Social Psychology, 50*, 676–683.

Cafferty, T. P., Skedsvold, P. K., & DeNisi, A. S. (1988). Search strategy preference and the processing of patterned performance information. Paper presented at the American Psychological Association Meetings, Atlanta, GA.

Campbell, J. P., Dunnette, M., Arvey, R. D., & Hellervik, L. V. (1973). The development and evaluation of behaviorally based rating scales. *Journal of Applied Psychology, 57*, 15–22.

Capon, N., & Burke, M. (1980). Individual, product class, and task-related factors in consumer information processing. *Journal of Consumer Research*, 7, 314–326.

Cascio, W. F. (1995). Whither industrial and organizational psychology in a changing world of work? *American Psychologist*, 50, 928–939.

Cardy, R. L., Carnikas-Walker, F. C., Sutton, C. L., & Wade, K. J. (1991). Person and system sources of performance variance: Empirical findings. Paper presented at the Annual Meeting of the Society for Industrial and Organizational Psychology, St. Louis, MO.

Cardy, R. L., & Dobbins, G. H. (1986). Affect and appraisal accuracy: Liking as an integral dimension in evaluating performance. *Journal of Applied Psychology*, 71, 672–678.

Cardy, R. L., & Dobbins, G. H. (1994). *Performance appraisal: Alternative perspectives*. Cincinnati, OH: Southwestern Publishing.

Cederblom, D., & Lounsbury, J. W. (1980). An investigation of user acceptance of peer evaluations. *Personnel Psychology*, 33, 567–579.

Chaiken, S. (1980). Heuristic vs. systematic information processing and the use of source vs. message cues in persuasion. *Journal of Personality and Social Psychology*, 39, 752–766.

Christensen-Szalanski, J. J. (1980). A further examination of the selection of problem-solving strategies: The effects of deadlines and analytic aptitudes. *Organizational Behavior and Human Performance*, 25, 107–122.

Cleveland, J. N., Morrison, R., & Bjerke, D. (1986). Rater intentions in appraisal ratings: Malevolent manipulation or functional fudging. Paper presented at the First Annual Conference of the Society for Industrial and Organizational Psychology, Chicago, IL.

Cleveland, J. N., Murphy, K. R., Barnes-Farrell, J. L., & Banks, C.G. (1988). Analyzing appraisal as goal-directed behavior: An alternative approach to performance appraisal research and practice. Unpublished manuscript, Department of Psychology, Colorado State University.

Cleveland, J. N., Murphy, K. R., & Williams, R. E. (1989). Multiple uses of performance appraisal: Prevalence and correlates. *Journal of Applied Psychology*, 74, 130–135.

Cline, M. E., Holmes, D. S., & Werner, J. C. (1977). Evaluations of the work of men and women as a function of the sex of the judge and the type of work. *Journal of Applied Social Psychology*, 7, 89–93.

Cohen, C. E. (1981a). Goals and schemata in person perception: Making sense from the stream of behavior. In N. Cantor & J. F. Kihlstrom (Eds.), *Personality, cognition, and social interaction*. Hillsdale, NJ: Erlbaum.

Cohen, C. E. (1981b). Person categories and social perception: Testing some boundaries of the processing effects of prior knowledge. *Journal of Personality and Social Psychology*, 40, 441–452.

Coombs, B., & Slovic, P. (1979). Newspaper coverage of causes of death. *Journalism Quarterly*, 56, 837–849.

Cooper, W. H. (1981a). Conceptual similarity as a source of illusory halo in job performance ratings. *Journal of Applied Psychology*, 66, 302–307.

Cooper, W. H. (1981b). Ubiquitous halo. *Psychological Bulletin*, 90, 218–244.

Cornelius, E. T., DeNisi, A. S., & Blencoe, A. G. (1984). The PAQ and the shared stereotype hypothesis: Some reservations. *Personnel Psychology*, 37, 453–464.

Craik, F. I., & Lockhart, R. S. (1972). Levels of processing: A framework for memory search. *Journal of Verbal Learning and Verbal Behavior*, 11, 671–684.

Craik, F. I., & Tulving, E. (1975). Depth of processing and the retention of words in episodic memory. *Journal of Experimental Psychology: General*, 104, 268–294.

Crocker, J. (1981). Judgment of covariation by social perceivers. *Psychological Bulletin, 90*, 272–292.

Crockett, W. H., Mahood, S., & Press, A. N. (1975). Impressions of a speaker as a function of variations in the cognitive characteristics of the perceiver and the message. *Journal of Personality, 43*, 168–178.

Cronbach, L. J. (1955). Processes affecting scores on "understanding of others" and "assumed similarity". *Psychological Bulletin, 50*, 177–193.

Cronshaw, S. F., & Lord, R. G. (1987). Effects of categorization, attribution, and encoding processes on leadership perceptions. *Journal of Applied Psychology, 72*, 97–106.

Darley, J. M., & Gross, P. H. (1983). A hypothesis-confirming bias in labeling effects. *Journal of Personality and Social Psychology, 44*, 20–33.

Day, D. V., & Sulsky, L. M. (1995). Effects of frame-of-reference training and information configuration on memory organization and rating accuracy. *Journal of Applied Psychology, 80*, 158–167.

Deaux, K. (1976). Sex and the attribution process. In J. Harvey, W. Ickes, & R. Kidd (Eds.), *New directions in attribution research* (Vol. 11). New York: Wiley.

Deaux, K., & Emswiller, T. (1974). Explanation for successful performance on sex-linked tasks: What is skill for the male is luck for the female. *Journal of Personality and Social Psychology, 29*, 80–85.

DeCotiis, T. A. (1977). An analysis of the external validity and applied relevance of three rating formats. *Organizational Behavior and Human Performance, 19*, 247–266.

DeCotiis, T. A., & Petit, A. (1978). The performance appraisal process: A model and some testable hypotheses. *Academy of Management Review, 21*, 635–646.

DeNisi, A. S. (1977). Sampling strategies and several other factors influencing the accuracy of performance evaluations. West Lafayette, IN: Unpublished Ph.D. Dissertation, Department of Psychological Sciences, Purdue University.

DeNisi, A. S., Cafferty, T. P., & Meglino, B. M. (1984). A cognitive model of the performance appraisal process. *Organizational Behavior and Human Decision Processes, 33*, 360–396.

DeNisi, A. S., Cafferty, T. P., Meglino, B. M., Williams, K. J., & Blencoe, A. G. (1982). Rater information search strategies: A new approach to studying the evaluation process and some preliminary results. Paper presented at the International Congress of Applied Psychology Meetings, Edinburgh.

DeNisi, A. S., Cafferty, T. P., Williams, K. J., Blencoe, A. G., & Meglino, B. M. (1983). Rater information acquisition strategies: Two preliminary experiments. *Proceedings of the Academy of Management Meetings*, Dallas, TX.

DeNisi, A. S., Cafferty, T. P., Williams, K. J., Meglino, B. M., & Blencoe, A. G. (1982). The effects of schema-based expectations and actual performance on performance evaluations. *Proceedings of the American Institute of Decision Sciences Meetings*, San Francisco, CA.

DeNisi, A. S., Cornelius, E. T., & Blencoe, A. G. (1987). A further investigation of common knowledge effects on job analysis ratings: On the applicability of the PAQ for all jobs. *Journal of Applied Psychology, 72*, 262–268.

DeNisi, A. S., Hom, P. W., Bannister, B. D., & Kinicki, A. J. (1980). Behaviorally Anchored Rating Scales for teacher evaluations. Paper presented at the Annual Meeting of the Academy of Management, Detroit, MI.

DeNisi, A. S., & Peters, L. H. (1991). Memory reorganization and performance appraisal: A field experiment. Paper presented at the Academy of Management Meetings, Miami, FL.

DeNisi, A. S., & Peters, L. H. (1992). Diary keeping and the organization of information in memory: A field extension. Paper presented at the Conference of the Society for Industrial and Organizational Psychology, Montreal.

DeNisi, A. S., & Peters, L. H. (in press). The organization of information in memory and the performance appraisal process: Evidence from the field. *Journal of Applied Psychology.*

DeNisi, A. S., Robbins, T. L., & Cafferty, T. P. (1988). Diary keeping and performance appraisal: A basis for structuring information in memory or just taking notes? Paper presented as part of *New directions in appraisal decision making research,* a symposium presented at the Academy of Management Meetings, Anaheim, CA.

DeNisi, A. S., Robbins, T. L., & Cafferty, T. P. (1989). The organization of information used for performance appraisals: The role of diary keeping. *Journal of Applied Psychology, 74,* 124–129.

DeNisi, A. S., Robbins, T. L., & Summers, T. P. (in review). Organization processing, and the use of performance information: A cognitive role for appraisal instruments. *Journal of Applied Social Psychology.*

DeNisi, A. S., Robbins, T. L., & Williams, K. J. (1989). Retrieval vs. computational models: What we remember vs. what we use. Paper presented as part of *The relationship between memory and judgment in performance appraisal,* a symposium presented at the Conference of the Society for Industrial and Organizational Psychology (D. Woehr, Chair), Boston, MA.

DeNisi, A. S., & Summers, T. P. (1986). Rating forms and the organization of information: A cognitive role for appraisal instruments. Paper presented at the Annual Meeting of the Academy of Management,Chicago, IL.

Dewey, B. J. (1994). Changing to skill-based pay. *Compensation and Benefits Review,* January–February, 38–43.

Dickinson, T. L. (1993). Attitudes about performance appraisal. In H. Schuler, J. Farr, & M. Smith (Eds.), *Personnel selection and assessment.* Hillsdale, NJ: Erlbaum.

Dickinson, T. L., & Zellinger, P. M. (1980). A comparison of the Behaviorally Anchored Rating and mixed standard scale formats. *Journal of Applied Psychology, 65,* 147–154.

Dipboye, R. L. (1985). Some neglected variables in research on discrimination in appraisals. *Academy of Management Review, 10,* 116–127.

Dipboye, R. L., & de Pontbriand, R. (1981). Correlates of employee reactions to performance appraisals and appraisal systems. *Journal of Applied Psychology, 66,* 248–251.

Dipboye, R. L., Fromkin, H. L., & Wiback, K. (1975). Relative importance of applicant sex, attractiveness, and scholastic standing in the evaluation of job applicant resumes. *Journal of Applied Psychology, 60,* 39–43.

Dobbins, G. H., Cardy, R. L., & Carson, K. P. (1991). Perspectives on human resource management: A contrast of person and system approaches. In G. Ferris & K. Rowland (Eds.), *Research in personnel and human resources management* (Vol. 9). Greenwich, CT: JAI Press.

Dobbins, G. H., Cardy, R. L., & Platz-Viéno, S. J. (1990). A contingency approach to appraisal satisfaction: An initial investigation of the joint effects of organizational variables and appraisal characteristics. *Journal of Management, 16,* 619–632.

Dobbins, G. H., Cardy, R. L., & Truxillo, D. M. (1986). Effects of ratee sex and purpose of appraisal on accuracy of performance evaluations. *Basic and Applied Social Psychology, 7,* 225–241.

Dobbins, G. H., Cardy, R. L., & Truxillo, D. M. (1988). The effects of individual differences in stereotypes of women and purpose of appraisal on sex differences in performance ratings: A laboratory and field study. *Journal of Applied Psychology*, *73*, 551–558.

Duarte, N. T., Goodson, J. R., & Klich, N. R. (1994). Effects of dyadic quality and duration on performance appraisal. *Academy of Management Journal*, *37*, 499–521.

Ebbesen, E. B. (1981). Cognitive processes in inferences about a person's personality. In E. Higgins, C. Herman, & M. Zanna (Eds.), *Social cognition: The Ontario symposium* (Vol. 1). Hillsdale, NJ: Erlbaum.

Eder, R. W., & Buckley, M. R. (1988). The employment interview: An interactionist approach. In G. Ferris & K. Rowland (Eds.), *Research in personnel and human resources management* (Vol. 6; pp. 75–108). Greenwich, CT: JAI Press.

Einhorn, H. J., & Hogarth, R. M. (1981). Behavioral decision theory: Process of judgment and thought. *Annual Review of Psychology*, *32*, 53–88.

Eisenhardt, K. (1989). Agency theory: An assessment and review. *Academy of Management Review*, *14*, 57–74.

Feldman, J. M. (1981). Beyond attribution theory: Cognitive processes in performance appraisal. *Journal of Applied Psychology*, *66*, 127–148.

Feldman, J. M. (1986). Instrumentation and training for performance appraisal: A perceptual-cognitive viewpoint. In K. Rowland & G. Ferris (Eds.), *Research in personnel and human resources management* (Vol. 4; pp. 148–216). Greenwich, CT: JAI Press.

Feldman, J. M. (1994). On the synergy between theory and application: Social cognition and performance appraisal. In R. Wyer & T. Srull (Eds.), *Handbook of social cognition* (2nd Edn.). New York: Academic Press.

Ferris, G. R., Judge, T. A., Rowland, K. M., & Fitzgibbons, D. E. (1993). Subordinate influence and the performance evaluation process: Test of a model. *Organizational Behavior and Human Decision Processes*, *53*, 325–339.

Fiedler, F. (1967). *A theory of leadership effectiveness*. New York: McGraw-Hill.

Fiedler, K. (1982). Causal schemata: A review and criticism of research on a popular construct. *Journal of Personality and Social Psychology*, *42*, 1001–1013.

Fisher, C. D. (1979). Transmission of positive and negative feedback to subordinates: A laboratory investigation. *Journal of Applied Psychology*, *64*, 533–540.

Fisher, C. D. (1987). Toward a more complete understanding of occupational sex discrimination. *Journal of Economic Issues*, *21*, 113–138.

Fisicaro, S. A. (1988). A re-examination of the relationship between halo error and accuracy. *Journal of Applied Psychology*, *73*, 239–244.

Fisicaro, S. A., & Lance, C. E. (1990). Implications of three causal models for the measurement of halo error. *Applied Psychological Measurement*, *14*, 419–429.

Fiske, S. T. (1980). Attention and weight in person perception: The impact of negative and extreme behavior. *Journal of Personality and Social Psychology*, *38*, 889–906.

Flanagan, J. C. (1949). Critical requirements: A new approach to evaluation. *Personnel Psychology*, *2*, 419–425.

Flanagan, J. C. (1954). The critical incident technique. *Psychological Bulletin*, *51*, 327–358.

Flanagan, J. C., & Burns, R. K. (1955). The employee performance record: A new appraisal and development tool. *Harvard Business Review*, September/October, 95–102.

Folger, R., Konovsky, M. A., & Cropanzano, R. (1992). A due process metaphor for performance appraisal. In L. Cummings & B. Staw (Eds.), *Research in Organizational Behavior*, (Vol. 14, pp. 129–177) Greenwich, CT: JAI Press.

Forgas, J. P. (1981). Epilogue: Everyday understanding and social cognition. In J. P. Forgas (Ed.), *Social cognition: Perspectives on everyday understanding* (pp. 259–270). San Diego, CA: Academic Press.

Foti, R. J., & Lord, R. G. (1987). Prototypes and scripts: The effects of alternative methods of processing information on rating accuracy. *Organizational Behavior and Human Decision Processes*, *39*, 318–340.

Friedman, B. A., & Cornelius, E. T. (1976). Effects of rater participation in scale construction on the psychometric characteristics of two rating scale formats. *Journal of Applied Psychology*, *61*, 210–216.

Frieze, I., & Weiner, B. (1971). Cue utilization and attributional judgments for success and failure. *Journal of Personality*, *39*, 591–605.

Gabrielcik, A., & Fazio, R. H. (1984). Priming and frequency estimation: A strict test of the availability heuristic. *Personality and Social Psychology Bulletin*, *10*, 85–89.

Ganzach, Y. (1994). Theory and configurality in expert and layperson judgments. *Journal of Applied Psychology*, *79*, 439–448.

Garland, H., Hardy, A., & Stephenson, L. (1975). Information search as affected by attribution type and response category. *Personality and Social Psychology Bulletin*, *4*, 612–615.

Gaylord, R. A., Russell, E., Johnson, C., & Severin, D. (1951). The relationship of ratings to production records: An empirical study. *Personnel Psychology*, *4*, 363–369.

Gerhart, B., & Milkovich, G. T. (1993). Employee compensation: Research and practice. In M. D. Dunnette & L. M. Hough (Eds.), *Handbook of industrial and organizational psychology* (Vol. 3) (2nd Edn.). Palo Alto, CA: Consulting Psychologists Press.

Goldstein, I. L. (1993). *Training in organizations* (3rd edn.). Pacific Grove, CA: Brooks Cole Publishing Co.

Gomez-Mejia, L. R., & Balkin, D. B. (1992). *Compensation, organizational strategy, and firm performance*. Cincinnati, OH: Southwestern Publishing.

Gomez-Mejia, L. R., & Welbourne, T. M. (1988). Compensation strategy: An overview and future steps. *Human Resource Planning*, *11*, 173–189.

Gordon, M. E. (1970). The effect of the correctness of behavior observed on the accuracy of ratings. *Organizational Behavior and Human Performance*, *5*, 366–379.

Graesser, A. C., Woll, S.B., Kowalski, D. J., & Smith, D. A. (1980). Memory for typical and atypical action in scripted activities. *Journal of Experimental Psychology: Human Learning and Memory*, *6*, 503–515.

Greenwald, A. G. (1968). Cognitive learning, cognitive response to persuasion, and attitude change. In A. Greenwald, T. Brock, & T. Ostrom (Eds.), *Psychological foundations of attitudes*. New York: Academic Press.

Guilford, J. P. (1954). *Psychometric methods*. New York: McGraw-Hill.

Guion, R. M. (1965). *Personnel testing*. New York: McGraw-Hill.

Gupta, N., Beehr, T. A., & Jenkins, G. D. (1980). The relationship between employee gender and supervisor–subordinate cross-ratings. *Proceedings of the 40th Annual Meetings of the Academy of Management*, Detroit, MI. (pp. 396–400).

Gupta, N., Ledford, G. E., Jenkins, G. D., & Doty, D. (1992). Survey-based prescriptions for skill-based pay. *American Compensation Association Journal*, *1*, 48–59.

Hambrick, D. C., & Mason, P. A. (1984). Upper echelons: The organization as a reflection of its top managers. *Academy of Management Review*, *9*, 193–206.

Hamilton, D. L. (1979). A cognitive-attributional analysis of stereotyping. In L. Berkowitz (Ed.), *Advances in experimental social psychology* (Vol. 12). New York: Academic Press.

Hamilton, D. L., & Huffman, L. J. (1971). Generality of impression formation for evaluative and non-evaluative judgments. *Journal of Personality and Social Psychology*, *20*, 200–207.

Hamilton, D. L., Katz, L. B., & Leirer, V. O. (1980). Cognitive processes in first impression formation. *Journal of Personality and Social Psychology, 39,* 1050–1063.

Hansen, R. D. (1980). Commonsense attribution. *Journal of Personality and Social Psychology, 39,* 969–1009.

Hansen, R. D., & Donoghue, J. M. (1977). The power of consensus: Information derived from one's own and others' behavior. *Journal of Personality and Social Psychology, 35,* 294–302.

Hansen R. D., & Lowe, C. A. (1976). Distinctiveness and consensus: The influence of behavioral information on actors' and observers' attributions. *Journal of Personality and Social Psychology, 34,* 425–433.

Harvey, R. J. (1991). Job analysis. In M. D. Dunnette & L. M. Hough (Eds.), *Handbook of industrial and organizational psychology* (Vol. 2) (2nd Edn.). Palo Alto, CA: Consulting Psychologists Press.

Hastie, R. (1981). Schematic principles in human memory. In E. T. Higgins, E. P. Herman, & M. P. Zanna (Eds.), *Social cognition: The Ontario Symposium* (pp. 39–88). Hillsdale, NJ: Erlbaum.

Hastie, R. (1984). Causes and effects of causal attributions. *Journal of Personality and Social Psychology, 46,* 44–56.

Hastie, R., & Carlston, D. E. (1980). Theoretical issues in person memory. In R. Hastie, T. Ostrom, E. Ebbesen, R. Wyer, D. Hamilton, & D. Carlston (Eds.), *Person memory: The cognitive basis of social perception* (pp. 1–54). Hillsdale, NJ: Erlbaum.

Hastie, R., & Kumar, P. A. (1979). Person memory: Personality traits as organizing principles in memory for behavior. *Journal of Personality and Social Psychology, 37,* 25–38.

Hastie, R., & Park, B. (1986). The relationship between memory and judgment depends on whether the judgment task is on-line or memory-based. *Psychological Review, 93,* 256–268.

Hastie, R., Park, B., & Weber, R. (1984). Social memory. In R. S. Wyer & T. K. Srull (Eds.), *Handbook of social cognition* (Vol. 2). Hillsdale, NJ: Erlbaum.

Hauenstein, N. M. (1992). An information processing approach to leniency in performance judgments. *Journal of Applied Psychology, 77,* 485–493.

Hausmann, S. E., & Strupp, H. H. (1995). Non-technical factors in supervisors' ratings of job performance. *Personnel Psychology, 8,* 201–217.

Hedge, J. W., Teachout, M. S., & Dickinson, T. L. (1987). User acceptance as a criterion for choosing performance measures. In M. Secunda (Chair), *Beyond current performance appraisal research: Acceptability as a new paradigm.* Symposium conducted at the Annual Meeting of the American Psychological Association, New York.

Heilman, M. E. (1980). The impact of situational factors on personnel decisions concerning women: Varying the sex composition of the applicant pool. *Organizational Behavior and Human Performance, 26,* 376–390.

Hemsley, G. D., & Marmurek, H. H. (1982). Person memory: The processing of consistent and inconsistent person information. *Personality and Social Psychology Bulletin, 8,* 433–438.

Heneman, H. G. (1974). Comparison of self and superior ratings of managerial performance. *Journal of Applied Psychology, 59,* 638–643.

Heneman, R. L., Greenberger, D. B., & Annonyuo, C. (1989). Attributions and exchange: The effects of interpersonal factors on the diagnosis of employee performance. *Academy of Management Journal, 32,* 466–476.

Hernstein, J. A., Carroll, J. S., & Hayes, J. R. (1981). The organization of knowledge about people and their attributes in long-term memory. *Representative Research in Social Psychology, 11,* 17–37.

Higgins, E. T., & McCann, C. D. (1984). Social encoding and subsequent attitudes, impressions and memory: Context-driven and motivational aspects of processing. *Journal of Personality and Social Psychology, 47*, 26–39.

Higgins, E. T., Rholes, C. R., & Jones, C. R. (1977). Category accessibility and category formation. *Journal of Experimental Social Psychology, 13*, 131–154.

Hoffman, C., Mischel, W., & Mazze, K. (1981). The role of purpose in the organization of information about behavior: Trait-based vs. goal-based categories in person cognition. *Journal of Personality and Social Psychology, 40*, 211–225.

Hollenbeck, J. R., Ilgen, D. R., Sego, D. J., Hedlund, J., Major, D. A., & Phillips, J. (1991). Multilevel theory of team decision making: Decision performance in teams incorporating distributed expertise. *Journal of Applied Psychology, 80*, 292–316.

Hollman, T. D. (1972). Employment interviewers' errors in processing positive and negative information. *Journal of Applied Psychology, 56*, 130–134.

Hom, P. W., DeNisi, A. S., Kinicki, A. J., & Bannister, B. D. (1982). Effectiveness of feedback from Behaviorally Anchored Rating Scales. *Journal of Applied Psychology, 68*, 568–576.

Horton, D. L., & Mills, C. B. (1984). Human learning and memory. *Annual Review of Psychology, 35*, 361–394.

Howard, J. W., & Rothbart, M. (1980). Social categorization and memory for in-group and out-group behavior. *Journal of Personality and Social Psychology, 38*, 301–310.

Huber, V. L., Neale, M. A., & Northcraft, G. B. (1987). Decision bias in personnel selection decisions. *Organizational Behavior and Human Decision Processes, 40*, 136–147.

Huselid, M.A. (1995). The impact of human resource management practices on turnover, productivity, and corporate financial performance. *Academy of Management Journal, 38*, 635–672.

Ilgen, D. R. (1993). Performance appraisal accuracy: An illusive or sometimes misguided goal? In H. Schuler, J. Farr, & M. Smith (Eds.), *Personnel selection and assessment.* Hillsdale, NJ: Erlbaum.

Ilgen, D. R., & Favero, J. L. (1985). Limits in generalization from psychological research to performance appraisal processes. *Academy of Management Review, 10*, 311–321.

Ilgen, D. R., & Feldman, J. M. (1983). Performance appraisal: A process focus. In B. Staw & L. Cummings (Eds.), *Research in organizational behavior* (Vol. 5). Greenwich, CT: JAI Press.

Ilgen, D. R., & Klein, H. J. (1988). Organizational behavior. *Annual Review of Psychology, 40*, 327–351.

Ilgen, D. R., Peterson, R. B., Martin, B. A., & Boeschen, D. A. (1981). Supervisor and subordinate reactions to performance appraisal sessions. *Organizational Behavior and Human Performance, 28*, 311–330.

Isen, A. M., Johnson, M. M., Mertz, E., & Robinson, G. F. (1985). The influence of positive affect on the unusualness of word associations. *Journal of Personality and Social Psychology, 48*, 1413–1426.

Isen, A. M., Shalker, T., Clark, M., & Karp, L. (1978). Affect, accessibility of material in memory and behavior: A cognitive loop? *Journal of Personality and Social Psychology, 36*, 1–12.

Jackson, S. E., & Schuler, R. S. (1995). Understanding human resource management in the context of organizations and their environments. *Annual Review of Psychology, 46*, 237–264.

Jackson, S. E., Schuler, R. S., & Rivero, J. C. (1989). Organizational characteristics as predictors of personnel practices. *Personnel Psychology, 42*, 727–786.

Jacoby, J., Chestnut, R. W., Weigel, K. C., & Fisher, W. A. (1976). Pre-purchase information acquisition: Description of a process methodology, research paradigm, and pilot investigation. In B. Anderson (Ed.), *Advances in consumer research* (Vol. 3), Proceedings of the Association for Consumer Research Conference.

Jeffery, K. M., & Mischel, W. (1979). Effects of purpose on the organization and recall of information in person perception. *Journal of Personality, 47*, 297–319.

Johnson, D. M. (1963). Reanalysis of experimental halo effects. *Journal of Applied Psychology, 47*, 46–47.

Johnson, D. M., & Vidulich, R. N. (1956). Experimental manipulation of the halo effect. *Journal of Applied Psychology, 40*, 130–134.

Jones, E. E., & Davis, K. E. (1965). From acts to dispositions: The attribution process in person perception. In L. Berkowitz (Ed.), *Advances in experimental social psychology* (Vol. 2). New York: Academic Press.

Jones, E. E., & McGillis, D. (1976). Correspondent inferences and the attribution cube: A comparative reappraisal. In J. Harvey, W. Ickes, & R. Kidd (Eds.), *New directions in attribution research* (Vol. 1). Hillsdale, NJ: Erlbaum.

Jones, E. E., Rock, L., Shaver, K. C., Goethals, G. R., & Ward, L. M. (1968). Patterns of performance and ability attributions: An unexpected primacy effect. *Journal of Personality and Social Psychology, 10*, 317–340.

Jones, E. E., & Thibaut, J. W. (1958). Interaction goals as bases of inference in person perception. In R. Taigiuri & L. Petrullo (Eds.), *Person perception and interpersonal behavior.* Stanford, CA: Stanford University Press.

Kahn, R. L., Wolfe, D. M., Quinn, R. P., Snoek, J. D., & Rosenthal, R. A. (1964). *Organizational stress: Studies in role conflict and ambiguity.* New York: Wiley.

Kahneman, D., & Tversky, A. (1973). On the psychology of prediction. *Psychological Review, 80*, 237–251.

Kane, J. S. (1982a). Evaluating the effectiveness of performance appraisal systems. Unpublished manuscript, University of North Carolina at Greensboro.

Kane, J. S. (1982b). Rethinking the problem of measuring performance: Some new conclusions and a new appraisal method to fit them. Paper presented at the Fourth Johns Hopkins University National Symposium on Educational Research.

Kane, J. S., & Bernardin, H. J. (1982). Behavioral observation scales and the evaluation of performance appraisal effectiveness. *Personnel Psychology, 35*, 635–642.

Kane, J. S., Bernardin, H. J., Villanova, P., & Peyrefitte, J. (1995). The stability of rater leniency: Three studies. *Academy of Management Journal, 38*, 1036–1051.

Kane, J. S., & Lawler, E. E. (1979). Performance appraisal effectiveness: Its assessment and determinants. In B. Staw & L. Cummings (Eds.), *Research in organizational behavior* (Vol. 1; pp. 425–478). Greenwich, CT: JAI Press.

Kanouse, D. E., & Hansen, L. R. (1972). Negativity in evaluations. In E. Jones, D. Kanouse, H. Kelley, R. Nisbet, S. Valins, & B. Weiner (Eds.), *Attribution: Perceiving the causes of behavior.* Morristown, NJ: General Learning Press.

Katz, I., & Glass, D. C. (1979). An ambivalence amplification theory of behavior toward the stigmatized. In W. G. Austin & S. Worschel (Eds.), *The social psychology of intergroup relations* (pp. 201–246). Monterey, CA: Brooks/Cole.

Kavanagh, M. J., & Hedge, J. W. (1983). A closer look at correlates of performance appraisal system acceptability. Paper presented at the Eastern Academy of Management Meetings, Pittsburgh, PA.

Kavanagh, M. J., Hedge, J. W., Ree, M., Earles, J., & DiBiasi, G. L. (1985). Clarification of some issues in regard to employee acceptability of performance appraisals. Paper presented at the Eastern Academy of Management Meetings, Albany, NY.

Kavanagh, M. J., MacKinney, A. C., & Wollins, L. (1971). Issues in managerial performance: A multitrait–multimethod analysis of ratings. *Psychological Bulletin, 68*, 34–49.

Kay, E., Meyer, H. H., & French, J. R. P. (1965). Effects of threat in a performance appraisal interview. *Journal of Applied Psychology, 49*, 311–317.

Kelley, H. H. (1967). Attribution theory in social psychology. In D. Levine (Ed.), *Nebraska Symposium on Motivation*. Lincoln, NE: University of Nebraska Press.

Kinicki, A., & Lockwood, C. A. (1985). The impact of appraisal purpose on rater accuracy and the encoding of performance information. Unpublished manuscript, Department of Management, Arizona State University.

Kingstrom, P. O., & Mainstone, L. E. (1985). An investigation of the rater–ratee acquaintance and rater bias. *Academy of Management Journal, 28*, 641–653.

Kipnis, D. (1960). Some determinants of supervisory esteem. *Personnel Psychology, 13*, 377–391.

Klaas, B., & DeNisi, A. S. (1989). Managerial reactions to employee dissent: The impact of grievance activity on performance ratings. *Personnel Psychology, 32*, 705–717.

Kozlowski, S. W. J., & Ford, J. K. (1991). Rater information acquisition processes: Tracing the effects of prior knowledge, performance level, search constraint, and memory demand. *Organizational Behavior and Human Decision Processes, 49*, 282–301.

Kozlowski, S. W. J., & Kirsch, M. P. (1987). The systematic distortion hypothesis, halo, and accuracy. *Journal of Applied Psychology, 72*, 252–261.

Kozlowski, S. W. J., Kirsch, M. P., & Chao, G. T. (1986). Job knowledge, ratee familiarity, conceptual similarity, and halo error: An exploration. *Journal of Applied Psychology, 71*, 45–49.

Kozlowski, S. W. J., & Mongillo, M. (1992). The nature of conceptual similarity schemata: Examination of some basic assumptions. *Personality and Social Psychology Bulletin, 18*, 88–95.

Kraiger, K., & Ford, K. J. (1985). A meta-analysis of ratee race effects in performance rating. *Journal of Applied Psychology, 70*, 56–65.

Kuiper, N. A., & Rogers, T. B. (1979). Encoding of personal information: Self–other differences. *Journal of Personality and Social Psychology, 37*, 499–514.

Lance, C. E., LaPointe, J. A., & Fisicaro, S. A. (1994). Tests of three causal models of halo rater error. *Organizational Behavior and Human Decision Processes, 57*, 83–96.

Lance, C. E., LaPointe, J. A., & Stewart, A. M. (1994). A test of the context dependency of three causal models of halo rater error. *Journal of Applied Psychology, 79*, 332–340.

Landy, F. J., Barnes, J., & Murphy, K. (1978). Correlates of perceived fairness and accuracy in performance appraisals. *Journal of Applied Psychology, 63*, 751–754.

Landy, F. J., Barnes-Farrell, J., & Cleveland, J. (1980). Correlates of perceived fairness and accuracy in performance appraisals: A follow-up. *Journal of Applied Psychology, 65*, 355–356.

Landy, F., & Farr, J. (1980). Performance rating. *Psychological Bulletin, 87*, 72–102.

Latham, G. P., Fay, C. H., & Saari, L. M. (1979). The development of behavioral observation scales for appraising the performance of foremen. *Personnel Psychology, 30*, 255–268.

Latham, G. P., & Wexley, K. N. (1977). Behavioral observation scales for performance appraisal purposes. *Personnel Psychology, 30*, 255–268.

Latham, G. P., Wexley, K. N., & Pursell, E. D. (1975). Training managers to minimize rating errors in the observation of behavior. *Journal of Applied Psychology, 60*, 550–555.

Lau, R. R., & Russell, D. (1980). Attributions in the sports pages. *Journal of Personality and Social Psychology, 39,* 29–38.

Lawler, E. E. (1967). The multitrait–multimethod approach to measuring managerial job performance. *Journal of Applied Psychology, 51,* 369–381.

Leventhal, G. S., & Michaels, J. W. (1971). Locus of case and equity motivators as determinants of reward allocation. *Journal of Personality and Social Psychology, 17,* 229–235.

Levine, J., & Butler, J. (1952). Lecture vs. group decision in changing behavior. *Journal of Applied Psychology, 36,* 29–33.

Lichtenstein, S., Slavic, P., Fischoff, B., Layman, M., & Coombs, B. (1978). Judged frequency of lethal events. *Journal of Experimental Psychology: Human Learning and Memory, 4,* 551–578.

Liden, R. C., Wayne, S. J., & Stilwell, D. (1993). A longitudinal study of the early development of leader–member exchanges. *Journal of Applied Psychology, 78,* 662–674.

Lingle, J. H., & Ostrom, T. M. (1979). Retrieval selectivity in memory-based judgments. *Journal of Personality and Social Psychology, 37,* 180–194.

London, M., & Hakel, M. D. (1974). Effects of applicant stereotypes, order, and information on interview stereotypes. *Journal of Applied Psychology, 59,* 157–162.

London, M., & Poplawski, J. R. (1976). Effects of information on stereotype development in performance appraisal and interview contexts. *Journal of Applied Psychology, 61,* 199–205.

London, M., & Stumpf, S. A. (1983). Effects of candidate characteristics on management promotion decisions: An experimental study. *Personnel Psychology, 36,* 241–259.

Longenecker, C. O., & Gioia, D. A. (1988). Neglected at the top: Executives talk about executive appraisal. *Sloan Management Review,* Winter, 41–47.

Longenecker, C. O., Sims, H. P., & Gioia, D. A. (1987). Behind the mask: The politics of employee appraisal. *Academy of Management Executive, 1,* 183–193.

Lord, L. G., Ross, L., & Lepper, M. R. (1979). Biased assimilation and attitude polarization: The effects of prior theories on subsequently considered evidence. *Journal of Personality and Social Psychology, 37,* 2098–2109.

Lord, R. G. (1985a). Accuracy in behavioral measurement: An alternative definition based on raters' cognitive schema and signal detection. *Journal of Applied Psychology, 70,* 66–71.

Lord, R. G. (1985b). An information processing approach to social perception, leadership, and behavioral measurement in organizations. In B. Staw & L. Cummings (Eds.), *Research in organizational behavior* (Vol. 7). Greenwich, CT: JAI Press.

Lord, R. G., & Alliger, G. M. (1985). A comparison of four information processing models of leadership and social perceptions. *Human Relations, 38,* 47–65.

Lord, R. G., Foti, R. J., & DeVader, C. (1984). A test of leadership categorization theory: Internal structure, information processing, and leadership perceptions. *Organizational Behavior and Human Performance, 34,* 343–378.

Lord, R. G., Foti, R. J., & Phillips, J. S. (1982). A theory of leadership categorization. In J. Hunt, U. Sekaran, & C. Schrieshiem (Eds.), *Leadership: Beyond established views.* Carbondale, IL: Southern Illinois University Press.

Lord, R. G., & Maher, K. J. (1991). Cognitive theory in Industrial/Organizational psychology. In M. D. Dunnette & L. Hough (Eds.), *Handbook of industrial and organizational psychology* (Vol. 1) (2nd Edn.). Palo Alto, CA: Consulting Psychologists Press.

Lowin, A., & Craig, J. R. (1968). The influence of level of performance on managerial style: An experimental lesson in the ambiguity of correlational data. *Organizational Behavior and Human Performance, 3,* 440–458.

Maier, N. R. F. (1958). *The appraisal interview: Objectives, methods, and skills.* New York: Wiley.

Major, B. (1980). Information acquisition and attribution processes. *Journal of Personality and Social Psychology, 39,* 1010–1023.

Manis, M., Dovalina, I., Avis, N. E., & Cardoze, S. (1980). Base rates can affect individual predictions. *Journal of Personality and Social Psychology, 38,* 231–248.

Markus, H. (1977). Self-schemata and processing information about the self. *Journal of Personality and Social Psychology, 35,* 63–78.

McArthur, L. Z. (1972). The how and what of why: Some determinants and consequences of causal attributions. *Journal of Personality and Social Psychology, 22,* 171–193.

McCall, M. W., & DeVries, D. L. (1976). Appraisal in context: Clashing with organizational realities. Paper presented at the meeting of the American Psychological Association, Washington, D.C.

McCauley, C., & Stitt, C. C. (1978). An individual and quantitative measure of stereotypes. *Journal of Personality and Social Psychology, 36,* 929–940.

McDonald, T. (1990). The effect of dimension content on observation and ratings of job performance. *Organizational behavior and Human Decision Processes, 48,* 252–271.

McEvoy, G. M., & Buller, P. F. (1987). User acceptance of peer appraisals in an industrial setting. *Personnel Psychology, 40,* 785–797.

McGregor, D. (1957). An uneasy look at performance appraisal. *Harvard Business Review, 35,* 89–94.

McIntyre, R. M., & Salas, E. (1995). Measuring and managing for team performance: Emerging principles from complex environments. In R.A. Guzzo & E. Salas (Eds.), *Team effectiveness and decision making in organizations* (pp. 9–45). San Francisco: Jossey-Bass.

Meyer, H. H., Kay, E., & French, J. R. P. (1965). Split roles in performance appraisal. *Harvard Business Review, 43,* 123–129.

Michel, J. G., & Hambrick, D. C. (1992). Diversification posture and top management team characteristics. *Academy of Management Journal, 35,* 9–37.

Miller, G. A. (1956). The magical number seven, plus or minus two: Some limits on our capacity for processing information. *Psychological Review, 63,* 81–97.

Minsky, M. (1980). K-lines: A theory for memory. *Cognitive Science, 4,* 117–133.

Mintzberg, H. (1973). *The nature of managerial work.* New York: Harper & Row.

Mobley, W. H. (1982). Supervisor and employee race and sex effects on performance appraisals: A field study of adverse impact and generalizability. *Academy of Management Journal, 25,* 598–606.

Mohrman, A. M., & Lawler, E. E. (1983). Motivation and performance appraisal behavior. In F. Landy & J. Cleveland (Eds.), *Performance measurement and theory.* Hillsdale, NJ: Erlbaum.

Morash, M., & Greene, J. R. (1986). Evaluating women on patrol: A critique of contemporary wisdom. *Evaluation Review, 10,* 230–255.

Motowidlo, S. (1986). Information processing and personnel decisions. In K. M. Rowland & G. R. Ferris (Eds.), *Research in personnel and human resource management* (Vol. 4; pp. 1–44). Greenwich, CT: JAI Press.

Mount, M. K., & Thompson, D. E. (1987). Cognitive categorization and quality of performance ratings. *Journal of Applied Psychology, 72,* 240–246.

Murphy, K. R. (1991). Criterion issues in performance appraisal research: Behavioral accuracy versus classification accuracy. *Organizational Behavior and Human Decision Processes, 50,* 45–50.

Murphy, K. R., & Balzer, W. K. (1989). Rater errors and rating accuracy. *Journal of Applied Psychology, 74,* 619–624.

Murphy, K. R., Balzer, W. D., Lockhart, M. C., & Eisenman, E. J. (1985). Effects of previous performance on evaluations of present performance. *Journal of Applied Psychology, 70,* 72–84.

Murphy, K. R., & Cleveland, J. N. (1992). *Performance appraisal: An organizational perspective.* Boston: Allyn & Bacon.

Murphy, K. R., & Constans, J. I. (1987). Behavioral anchors as a source of bias in ratings. *Journal of Applied Psychology, 71,* 39–44.

Murphy, K. R., Gannett, B. A., Herr, B. M., & Chen, J. A. (1986). Effect of subsequent performance on evaluations of previous performance. *Journal of Applied Psychology, 71,* 427–431.

Murphy, M. D. (1979). Measuring of category clustering in free recall. In C. R. Puff (Ed.), *Memory organization and structure* (pp. 51–83). New York: Academic Press.

Murray, A. I. (1989). Top management team heterogeneity and firm performance. *Strategic Management Journal, 10,* 125–141.

Nathan, B. R. (1986). The halo effect: It is a unitary concept! A reply to Fox *et al.* (1983). *Journal of Occupational Psychology, 59,* 235–238.

Nathan, B. R., & Lord, R. G. (1983). Cognitive categorization and schemata: A process approach to the study of halo in ratings. *Journal of Applied Psychology, 68,* 102–114.

Nathan, B. R., & Tippins, N. (1990). The consequences of halo "error" in performance ratings: A field study. *Journal of Applied Psychology, 75,* 290–296.

Naylor, J. C., & Wherry, R. J. (1965). The use of simulated stimuli and the JAN technique to capture and cluster the policies of raters. *Educational and Psychological Measurement, 23,* 969–986.

Neisser, V. (1976). *Cognitions and reality: Principles and implications of cognitive psychology.* San Francisco: Freeman.

Nemeroff, W. F., & Wexley, K. N. (1979). An exploration of the relationship between performance feedback interview characteristics and interview outcomes as perceived by managers and subordinates. *Journal of Occupational Psychology, 52,* 25–34.

Newtson, D. (1973). Attribution and the unit of perception of ongoing behavior. *Journal of Personality and Social Psychology, 28,* 28–38.

Newtson, D., Engquist, G., & Bois, J. (1977). The objective basis of behavior units. *Journal of Personality and Social Psychology, 35,* 847–862.

Newtson, D., & Ridner, R. J. (1979). Variability in behavior and ability attribution. *Journal of Personality and Social Psychology, 37,* 1847–1858.

Nieva, V. F., & Gutek, B. (1980). Sex effects on evaluation. *Academy of Management Review, 5,* 267–276.

Nisbett, R. E., & Borgida, E. (1975). Attribution and the psychology of prediction. *Journal of Personality and Social Psychology, 32,* 932–943.

Nisbett, R. E., & Wilson, T. D. (1977). The halo effect: Evidence for unconscious alteration of judgments. *Journal of Personality and Social Psychology, 35,* 250–256.

Northcraft, G. B., Neale, M. A., & Huber, V. L. (1988). The effects of cognitive bias and social influence on human resources management decisions. In G. Ferris & K. Rowland (Eds.), *Research in personnel and human resources management* (Vol. 6; pp. 157–189). Greenwich, CT: JAI Press.

Oltman, P. K., Raskin, E., Witkin, H. A., & Karp, S. A. (1971). *Group embedded figures test* (Manual). Palo Alto, CA: Consulting Psychologists Press.

Organ, D. W. (1988). *Organizational citizenship behavior: The good soldier syndrome*. Lexington, MA: Lexington Books.

Organ, D. W., & Konovsky, M. (1989). Cognitive versus affective determinants of organizational citizenship behavior. *Journal of Applied Psychology, 74*, 157–164.

Ostroff, C., & Ilgen, D. R. (1986). The relationship between cognitive categories of raters and rating accuracy. Paper presented at the Annual Meeting of the Society for Industrial and Organizational Psychology, Chicago, IL.

Ostrom, T. M., Lingle, J. H., Pryor, J. B., & Geva, N. (1980). Cognitive organization of person perception. In R. Hastie, T. Ostrom, E. Ebbesen, R. Wyer, D. Hamilton, & D. Carlston (Eds.), *Person memory: The cognitive basis for social perception*. Hillsdale, NJ: Erlbaum.

Ostrom, T. M., Pryor, J. B., & Simpson, D. D. (1981). The organization of social information. In E. Higgins *et al.* (Eds.), *Social cognition: The Ontario symposium on personality and social psychology*. Hillsdale, NJ: Erlbaum.

Park, O. S., & Sims, H. P. (1989). *Beyond cognition in leadership: Prosocial behavior and affect in managerial judgment*. Paper presented at the Academy of Management Meetings, Washington, D.C.

Payne, J. W. (1976). Task complexity and contingent processing in decision making: An information search and protocol analysis. *Organizational Behavior and Human Performance, 16*, 366–387.

Payne, J. W., Braunstein, M. L., & Carroll, J. S. (1978). Exploring predecisional behavior: An alternative to decision research. *Organizational Behavior and Human Performance, 22*, 17–44.

Peters, D. L., & McCormick, E. J. (1966). Comparative reliability of numerically versus job-task anchored rating scales. *Journal of Applied Psychology, 50*, 92–96.

Peters, L. H., & DeNisi, A. S. (1990). An information processing role for appraisal purpose and job type in the development of appraisal systems. *Journal of Managerial Issues, 2*, 160–175.

Peters, L. H., O Connor, E. J., & Weekley, J. (1984). Sex bias in managerial evaluations: A replication and extension. *Journal of Applied Psychology, 69*, 349–352.

Pfeffer, J. (1983). Organizational demography. In L. Cummings & B. Staw (Eds.), *Research in organizational behavior* (Vol. 5; pp. 299–357). Greenwich, CT: JAI Press.

Posner, M. I., & Snyder, C. R. (1975). Attention and cognitive control. In R. L. Solso (Ed.), *Information processing and cognition: The Loyola symposium*. Hillsdale, NJ: Erlbaum.

Press, A. N., Crockett, W. H., & Delia, J. G. (1975). Effects of cognitive complexity and perceiver's set upon the organization of impressions. *Journal of Personality and Social Psychology, 32*, 865–872.

Pryor, J. B., & Ostrom, T. M. (1981). The cognitive organization of social information: A converging operations approach. *Journal of Personality and Social Psychology, 41*, 628–641.

Pryor, J. B., Ostrom, T. M., Dukerich, J. M., Mitchell, M. L., & Hernstein, J. A. (1983). Preintegrative categorization of social information: The role of persons as organizing categories. *Journal of Personality and Social Psychology, 44*, 923–932.

Pulakos, E. D. (1984). A comparison of two rater training programs: Error training versus accuracy training. *Journal of Applied Psychology, 69*, 581–588.

Pulakos, E. D. (1986). The development of different training programs to increase accuracy with different rating tasks. *Organizational Behavior and Human Decision Processes, 38*, 76–91.

Pulakos, E. D., Schmitt, N., & Ostroff, C. (1986). A warning about the use of the standard deviation across dimensions within ratees to measure halo. *Journal of Applied Psychology, 71*, 29–32.

Pulakos, E. D., & Wexley, K. N. (1983). The relationship between perceptual similarity, sex, and performance ratings in manager–subordinate dyads. *Academy of Management Journal, 26*, 129–139.

Renwick, P. A., & Tosi, H. L. (1978). The effects of sex, marital status, and educational background on selection decisions. *Academy of Management Journal, 21*, 93–103.

Reyes, R. M., Thompson, W. C., & Bower, G. H. (1980). Judgmental biases resulting from differing availability of arguments. *Journal of Personality and Social Psychology, 39*, 2–12.

Robbins, T. L. (1991). The influence of affect on the cognitive processes in performance evaluations. Unpublished Ph.D. Dissertation, College of Business Administration, University of South Carolina.

Robbins, T. L., & DeNisi, A. S. (1991). The influence of affect on the cognitive processes in performance evaluation. *Proceedings of the Southern Management Association Meetings* (pp. 385–387).

Robbins, T. L., & DeNisi, A. S. (1993). A cognitive look at sex bias in the performance appraisal process. *Journal of Management, 19*, 113–126.

Robbins, T. L., & DeNisi, A. S. (1994). A closer look at interpersonal affect as a distinct influence on cognitive processing in performance evaluations. *Journal of Applied Psychology, 79*, 341–350.

Roenker, D. L., Thompson, C. P., & Brown, S. C. (1971). Comparison of measures for the estimation of clustering in recall. *Psychological Bulletin, 76*, 45–48.

Rosch, E. (1975). Cognitive representations of schematic categories. *Journal of Experimental Psychology: General, 104*, 192–233.

Rosch, E. (1977). Principles of categorization. In N. Warren (Ed.), *Studies in cross-cultural psychology*, (Vol. 1). New York: Academic Press.

Rose, G. L., & Andiappan, P. (1978). Sex effects on managerial hiring decisions. *Academy of Management Journal, 21*, 104–112.

Ross, L., Lepper, M. R., Strack, F., & Steinmetz, G. (1977). Social explanation and social expectation: Effects of real and hypothetical explanations on subjective likelihood. *Journal of Personality and Social Psychology, 35*, 817–839.

Ross, M., & Sicoly, R. (1979). Egocentric biases in availability and attribution. *Journal of Personality and Social Psychology, 37*, 322–336.

Rothbart, M. (1980). Memory processes and social beliefs. In D. L. Hamilton (Ed.), *Cognitive processes in stereotyping and intergroup behavior*. Hillsdale, NJ: Erlbaum.

Rothbart, M., Evans, M., & Fulero, S. (1979). Recall for confirming events: Memory processes and the maintenance of social stereotypes. *Journal of Experimental Social Psychology, 15*, 343–355.

Rothbart, M., Fulero, S., Jensen, C., Howard, J., & Birrell, P. (1978). From individual to group impressions: Availability heuristics in stereotype formation. *Journal of Experimental Social Psychology, 14*, 237–245.

Rothe, H. F. (1946a). Output rates among butter wrappers: I. Work curves and their stability. *Journal of Applied Psychology, 30*, 199–211.

Rothe, H. F. (1946b). Output rates among butter wrappers: II. Frequency distributions and hypotheses regarding the "restriction of output." *Journal of Applied Psychology, 30*, 320–327.

Rothe, H. F. (1949). The relation of merit ratings to length of service. *Personnel Psychology, 2*, 237–242.

Rothe, H. F. (1951). Output rates among chocolate dippers. *Journal of Applied Psychology, 35,* 94–97.

Rothe, H. F. (1978). Output rates among industrial employees. *Journal of Applied Psychology, 63,* 40–46.

Ruble, D. N., & Feldman, N. S. (1976). Order of consensus, distinctiveness, and consistency information and causal attribution. *Journal of Personality and Social Psychology, 34,* 930–937.

Rudd, H. (1921). Is the rating of human character predictable? *Journal of Educational Psychology, 12,* 425–438.

Russell, J. S., & Goode, D. L. (1988). An analysis of managers' reactions to their own performance appraisal feedback. *Journal of Applied Psychology, 73,* 63–67.

Saal, F. E., Downey, R. G., & Lahey, M. A. (1980). Rating the ratings: Assessing the quality of ratings data. *Psychological Bulletin, 88,* 413–428.

Schank, R., & Abelson, R. (1977). *Scripts, plans, goals, and understanding.* Hillsdale, NJ: Erlbaum.

Schmidt, F. L., & Johnson, R. H. (1973). Effect of race on peer ratings in an industrial setting. *Journal of Applied Psychology, 57,* 237–241.

Schneier, C. E. (1977). Operational utility and psychometric characteristics of behavioral expectations scales. *Journal of Applied Psychology, 62,* 541–548.

Schneider, W., & Shiffrin, R. M. (1977). Controlled and automatic human information processing: I. Detection, search, and attention. *Psychological Review, 84,* 1–66.

Schul, Y. (1983). Integration and abstraction in impression formation. *Journal of Personality and Social Psychology, 44,* 45–54.

Scott, W. E., & Hamner, W. C. (1975). The influence of performance profiles on the performance evaluation process: An examination of the validity of the criterion. *Organizational Behavior and Human Performance, 14,* 197–215.

Sentis, K. P., & Burnstein, E. (1979). Remembering schema-consistent information: effects of balance schema on recognition memory. *Journal of Personality and Social Psychology, 37,* 2200–2211.

Severin, D. (1952). The predictability of various kinds of criteria. *Personnel Psychology, 5,* 93–104.

Sharon, A. T., & Bartlett, C. J. (1969). Effect of instructional conditions in producing leniency on two types of rating scales. *Personnel Psychology, 22,* 252–263.

Sherman, R. C., & Titus, W. (1982). Covariation information and cognitive processing: Effects of causal implications on memory. *Journal of Personality and Social Psychology, 43,* 989–1000.

Shiffrin, R. M., & Schneider, W. (1977). Controlled and automatic human information processing: II. Perceptual learning, automatic attending, and a general theory. *Psychological Review, 84,* 127–190.

Silverman, S. S., & Wexley, K. N. (1984). Reaction of employees to performance appraisal interviews as a function of their participation in rating scale development. *Personnel Psychology, 37,* 703–710.

Sisson, E. D. (1948). Forced choice: The new Army rating. *Personnel Psychology, 1,* 365–381.

Slovic, P., & Lichtenstein, S. (1971). Comparison of Bayesian and regression approaches to the study of information processing in judgments. *Organizational Behavior and Human Performance, 6,* 649–744.

Smith, C. A., Organ, D. W., & Near, J. P. (1983). Organizational citizenship behavior: Its nature and antecedents. *Journal of Applied Psychology, 68,* 653–663.

Smith, D. E. (1986). Training programs for performance appraisal: A review. *Academy of Management Review, 11,* 22–40.

Smith, J., & Hakel, M. D. (1979). Convergence among data sources, response bias, and reliability and validity of a structured job analysis questionnaire. *Personnel Psychology, 32*, 677–692.

Smith, K. H. (1973). Effects of exceptions on verbal reconstructive memory. *Journal of Experimental Psychology, 97*, 119–139.

Smith, P. C., & Kendall, L. M. (1963). Retranslation of expectations: An approach to the construction of unambiguous anchors for rating scales. *Journal of Applied Psychology, 47*, 149–155.

Snyder, M. (1981). Seek and ye shall find: Testing hypotheses about other people. In E. Higgins, C. Herman, & M. Zanna (Eds.), *Social cognition: The Ontario symposium* (Vol. 1). Hillsdale, NJ: Erlbaum.

Snyder, M., & Cantor, N. (1979). Testing hypotheses about other people: The use of historical knowledge. *Journal of Experimental Social Psychology, 15*, 330–342.

Snyder, M., & Uranowitz, S. (1978). Reconstructing the past: Some cognitive consequences of person perception. *Journal of Personality and Social Psychology, 36*, 941–950.

Spool, M. D. (1978) Training programs for observers of behavior: A review. *Personnel Psychology, 31*, 853–888.

Srull, T. K. (1981). Person memory: Some tests of associative storage and retrieval models. *Journal of Experimental Psychology: Human Learning and Memory, 7*, 440–463.

Srull, T. K. (1983). Organizational and retrieval processes in person memory. *Journal of Personality and Social Psychology, 44*, 1157–1170.

Srull, T. K., & Brand, J. F. (1983). Memory for information about persons. *Journal of Verbal Learning and Verbal Behavior, 22*, 219–230.

Srull, T. K., & Wyer, R. S. (1979). The role of category accessibility in the interpretation of information about persons: Some determinants and implications. *Journal of Personality and Social Psychology, 37*, 1660–1672.

Srull, T. K., & Wyer, R. S. (1980). Category accessibility and social perception: Some implications for the study of person memory and interpersonal judgments. *Journal of Personality and Social Psychology, 38*, 841–856.

Staelin, R., & Payne, J. W. (1976). Studies of the information seeing behavior of consumers. In J. Carroll & J. Payne (Eds.), *Cognition and social behavior*. Hillsdale, NJ: Erlbaum.

Steiner, D. D., Dobbins, G. H., & Trahan, W. A. (1991). An attributional model of training. *Journal of Organizational Behavior, 12*, 271–286.

Stevens, G. E., & DeNisi, A. S. (1980). Women as managers: Attitudes and attributions for performance by men and women. *Academy of Management Journal, 23*, 355–361.

Stigler, G. J. (1961). The economics of information. *Journal of Political Economy, 69*, 213–225.

Stockford, L., & Bissell, H.W. (1949). Factors involved in establishing a merit rating scale. *Personnel, 26*, 94–116.

Stone, E. F. (1979). Field independence and perceptions of task characteristics: A laboratory investigation. *Journal of Applied Psychology, 64*, 305–310.

Stumpf, S. A., & London, M. (1981). Capturing rater policies in evaluating candidates for promotion. *Academy of Management Journal, 24*, 752–766.

Sulsky, L. M., & Day, D. V. (1992). Frame-of-reference training and cognitive categorization: An empirical investigation of rater memory issues. *Journal of Applied Psychology, 77*, 501–510.

Sulsky, L. M., & Day, D. V. (1994). Effects of frame-of-reference training on rater accuracy under alternative time delays. *Journal of Applied Psychology, 79*, 535–543.

Swann, W. B., Stephenson, B., & Pittman, T. (1981). Curiosity and control: On the determinants of the search for social knowledge. *Journal of Personality and Social Psychology, 40,* 635–642.

Taylor, E. K., & Hastman, R. (1956). Relationship of format and administration to the characteristics of graphic rating scales. *Personnel Psychology, 9,* 181–206

Taylor, E. K., Parker, J. W., & Ford, G. L. (1959). Rating scale content: IV. Predictability of structured and unstructured scales. *Personnel Psychology, 12,* 247–266.

Taylor, S. E., & Crocker, J. (1981). Schematic bases of social information processing. In E. Higgins, C. Herman, & M. Zanna (Eds.), *Social cognition: The Ontario symposium* (Vol. 1). Hillsdale, NJ: Erlbaum.

Taylor, S. E., & Fiske, S. T. (1978). Salience, attention, and attributions: Top of the head phenomena. In L. Berkowitz (Ed.), *Advances in experimental social psychology* (Vol. 11). New York: Academic Press.

Taylor, S. E., Crocker, J., Fiske, S. T., Sprinzen, M., & Winkler, J. (1979). The generalizability of salience effects. *Journal of Personality and Social Psychology, 37,* 357–368.

Taylor, S. E., & Falcone, H. (1982). Cognitive bases of stereotyping: The relationship between categorization and prejudice. *Personality and Social Psychology Bulletin, 8,* 426–432.

Taylor, S. E., Fiske, S. T., Close, M., Anderson, C., & Ruderman, A. (1977). Solo status as a psychological variable. Los Angeles: Unpublished manuscript, Dept. of Psychology, UCLA, CA.

Thorndike, E. L. (1920). A constant error in psychological ratings. *Journal of Applied Psychology, 4,* 25–29.

Tornow, W. (Ed.) (1993). *Human Resource Management Journal, 32.* (Special Issue on 360° Degree Feedback).

Tosi, H., & Tosi, L. (1986). What managers need to know about knowledge-based pay. *Organizational Dynamics, 14,* 52–64.

Trope, Y., & Bassok, M. (1982). Confirming and diagnosing strategies in information gathering. *Journal of Personality and Social Psychology, 43,* 22–24.

Trost, M. R., Kinicki, A. J., & Prussia, G. E. (1989). Chronic category accessibility and mood influences accuracy of appraisal ratings. Paper presented at the Academy of Management Meetings, Washington, D.C.

Tsui, A. S. (1983). An analysis of social structure and managerial reputational effectiveness. *Proceedings of 43rd Annual Meeting of the Academy of Management,* Dallas, TX.

Tsui, A. S., & Barry, B. (1986). Interpersonal affect and rating errors. *Academy of Management Journal, 27,* 619–635.

Tsui, A. S., & Gutek, B. A. (1984). A role set analysis of gender differences in performance, affective relationships, and career success of middle managers. *Academy of Management Journal, 27,* 619–635.

Tudor, N. L., (1980). The effect of the sexual composition of a group on discrimination against women and sex-role attitudes. *Psychology of Women Quarterly, 5,* 292–310.

Tulving, E. (1974). Recall and recognition of semantically encoded words. *Journal of Experimental Psychology, 102,* 778–787.

Tversky, A., & Kahneman, D. (1973). Availability: A heuristic for judging frequency and probability. *Cognitive Psychology, 5,* 207–232.

U.S. Department of Labor, Bureau of Labor Statistics (1991). *Employment and earnings,* 38(7), 76. Washington, D.C.: U.S. Government Printing Office.

Varma, A., DeNisi, A. S., & Peters, L. H. (1993). Interpersonal affect in performance appraisal. Paper presented at the Annual Conference of the Society for Industrial and Organizational Psychology, San Francisco, CA.

Varma, A., DeNisi, A. S., & Peters, L. H. (1996). The role of interpersonal affect in performance appraisal: A field study. *Personnel Psychology, 49*, 341–60.

Walsh, J. P. (1988). Selectivity and selective perception: An investigation of managers' belief structures and information processing. *Academy of Management Journal, 31*, 873–896.

Wanous, J. P., & Colella, A. (1990). Organizational entry research: Current status and future directions. In G. Ferris & K. Rowland (Eds.), *Organizational entry* (pp. 253–313). Greenwich, CT: JAI Press.

Wayne, S. J., & Ferris, G. R. (1990). Influence tactics, affect, and exchange quality in supervisor–subordinate interactions: A laboratory and field study. *Journal of Applied Psychology, 75*, 487–499.

Wayne, S. J., & Green, S. A. (1993). The effects of leader–member exchange on employee citizenship and impression management behavior. *Human Relations, 46*, 1431–1440.

Weiss, H. M., Ilgen, D. R., & Sharbaugh, M. E. (1982). Effects of life stress on information search behaviors of organizational members. *Journal of Applied Psychology, 67*, 60–68.

Wells, G. L., & Harvey, J. H. (1977). Do people use consensus information in making causal attributions? *Journal of Personality and Social Psychology, 35*, 279–293.

Werner, J. M. (1994). Dimensions that make a difference: Examining the impact of in-role and extra-role behaviors on supervisory ratings. *Journal of Applied Psychology, 79*, 98–107.

Wexley, K. N. (1979). Performance appraisal and feedback. In S. Kerr (Ed.), *Organizational behavior* (pp. 241–259). Columbus, OH: Grid.

Wexley, K. N., & Klimoski, R. (1984). Performance appraisal: An update. In K. Rowland and G. Ferris (Eds.), *Research in personnel and human resources* (Vol. 2). Greenwich, CT: JAI Press.

Wexley, K. N., & Latham, G. P. (1981). *Developing and training human resources in organizations* (Ch. 3; 2nd Edn.). New York: Harper-Collins.

Wexley, K. N., Sanders, R. E., & Yukl, G. A. (1973). Training interviewers to eliminate contrast effects in employment interviews. *Journal of Applied Psychology, 57*, 233–236.

Wexley, K. N., Yukl, G. A., Kovacks, S. Z., & Sanders, R. (1972). The importance of contrast effects. *Journal of Applied Psychology, 56*, 45–48.

Wherry, R. J. (1952). The control of bias in ratings: A theory of rating. Columbus, OH: Ohio State Research Foundation.

Wherry, R. J., & Bartlett, C. J. (1982). The control of bias in ratings: A theory of ratings. *Personnel Psychology, 35*, 521–532.

Whitlock, G. H. (1963). Application of the psychophysical law to performance appraisal. *Journal of Applied Psychology, 47*, 15–23.

Williams, K. J. (1982). Attributional mediation of schema and change. Unpublished M.S. thesis, Department of Psychology, University of South Carolina.

Williams, K. J. (1984). Appraisal salience and the need to reprocess information: Effects on organization, recall, and rating of performance information. Unpublished Ph.D. Dissertation, Department of Psychology, University of South Carolina.

Williams, K. J., & Alliger, G. M. (1989). Affect and the cognitively active rater: Examining the role of affect in performance decisions. Paper presented at the Academy of Management Meetings, Washington, D.C.

Williams, K. J., Cafferty, T. P., & DeNisi, A. S. (1990). Effects of appraisal salience on recall and ratings. *Organizational Behavior and Human Decision Processes, 46*, 217–239.

Williams, K. J., DeNisi, A. S., Blencoe, A. G., & Cafferty, T. P. (1985). The role of appraisal purpose: Effects of purpose on information acquisition and utiliztion. *Organizational Behavior and Human Decision Processes, 36*, 314–339.

Williams, K. J., DeNisi, A. S., Meglino, B. M., & Cafferty, T. P. (1986). Initial judgments and subsequent appraisal decisions. *Journal of Applied Psychology, 71*, 189–195.

Williams, K. J., & Keating, C. W. (1987). Affect and the processing of performance appraisal information. Paper presented at the Second Annual Conference of the Society of Industrial and Organizational Psychology, Atlanta, GA.

Williams, K. J., Wickert, P., & Peters, R. D. (1985). Appraisal salience: II. Effects of instructions to subjectively organize information. *Proceedings of the Southern Management Association Meetings*, Kissiminee, FL.

Woehr, D. J. (1994). Understanding frame-of-reference training: The impact of training on the recall of performance information. *Journal of Applied Psychology, 79*, 525–534.

Wong, P. T., & Weiner, B. (1981). Why people ask "Why" questions and the heuristics of attributional search. *Journal of Personality and Social Psychology, 40*, 650–663.

Wright, P. (1974). The harassed decision maker: Time pressures, distractions and the use of evidence. *Journal of Applied Psychology, 59*, 555–562.

Wyer, R. S., & Hinkle, R. L. (1976). Informational factors underlying inferences about hypothetical people. *Journal of Personality and Social Psychology, 34*, 481–495.

Wyer, R. S., & Srull, T. K. (1981). Category accessibility: Some theoretical and empirical issues concerning the processing of social stimulus information. In E. T. Higgins, C. P. Herman, & M. P. Zanna (Eds.), *Social Cognition: The Ontario symposium* (pp. 161–197). Hillsdale, NJ: Erlbaum.

Wyer, R. S., Srull, T. K., & Gordon, S. (1984). The effects of predicting a person's behavior on subsequent trait judgments. *Journal of Experimental Social Psychology, 20*, 29–46.

Wyer, R. S., Srull, T. K., Gordon, S. E., & Hartwick, J. (1982). Effects of processing objectives on recall of prose material. *Journal of Personality and Social Psychology, 43*, 674–688.

Zajonc, R. B. (1980). Feeling and thinking: Preferences need no inferences. *American Psychologist, 35*, 151–175.

Zedeck, S. (1986). A process analysis of the assessment center method. In L.L. Cummings and B. Staw (Eds.), *Research in organizational behavior* (Vol. 8; pp. 259–296). Greenwich, CT: JAI Press.

Zedeck, S., & Cascio, W. F. (1982). Performance appraisal decisions as a function of rater training and the purpose of the appraisal. *Journal of Applied Psychology, 67*, 752–758.

Zedeck, S., & Kafrey, D. (1977). Capturing rater policies for processing evaluation data. *Organizational Behavior and Human Performance, 18*, 269–294.

Zuckerman, M. (1978) Actions and occurrences in Kelley's cube. *Journal of Personality and Social Psychology, 36*, 647–656.

Name index

Carlston, D.E. 76
Carlyle, J.J. 56, 129
Carroll, J.S. 32, 47, 59
Cascio, W.F. 56, 186
Cafferty, T.P. 13
Cederblom, D. 185
Chaiken, S. 35
Chao, G.T. 126–7, 157
Chen, J.A. 112
Chestnut, R.W. 32, 47
Christensen-Szalanski, J.J. 35
Clark, M. 112
Cleveland, J.N. 3–4, 11, 14, 19, 21, 30–1, 41, 97, 121, 128–9, 159, 169, 181, 183–5
Cline, M.E. 108
Close, M. 108
Cohen, C.E. 35, 38, 77
Colella, A. 42, 170, 178
Conlon, E.J. 44
Constans, J.I. 83
Coombs, B. 74
Cooper, W.H. 4, 12, 24, 126–7
Cornelius, E.T. 125, 160, 184
Couture, K.A. 73, 76
Craig, J.R. 148
Craik, F.I. 39, 71
Cranny, C.J. 6, 125
Crocker, J. 32, 38–9
Crockett, W.H. 35–6, 38
Cronbach, L.J. 182
Cronshaw, S.F. 113, 155
Cropanzano, R. 129, 166

Dalton, C. 38
Darley, J.M. 91
Davis, K.E. 25, 41
Day, D.V. 44, 83, 126, 163
Deaux, K. 104
DeCotiis, T.A. 12–15, 21, 31, 34, 111, 125, 126
Delia, J.G. 36, 38
DeNisi, A.S. 3, 11, 13–15, 18, 21, 23–4, 28–31, 33–4, 40, 42, 44–6, 49–51, 55, 57–8, 61, 65, 67, 70, 75–6, 82–3, 87–8, 91, 94, 98, 101–3, 107–8, 110–11, 113, 117, 123, 129, 131, 133, 140, 145–6, 149, 155, 159, 160–62, 181, 187–8
de Pontbriand, R. 183
De Soto, C.B. 5
DeVries, D.L. 35
Dewey, B.J. 1

DiBiasi, G.L. 183
Dickinson, T.L. 6, 129, 184
Dipboye, R.L. 42, 107, 111, 183
Dobbins, G.H. 3, 8, 42, 111, 145–6, 153, 159, 183
Donoghue, J.M. 42
Dorsey, D.W. 187
Doty, D. 1
Downey, R.G. 122, 125
Duarte, N.T. 179
Dukerich, J.M. 59, 112
Dunnette, M.D. 6

Earles, J. 183
Ebbesen, E.B. 34
Eder, R.W. 161
Einhorn, H.J. 31
Eisenhardt, K. 1
Eisenman, E.J. 34, 111
Emswiller, T. 104
Engquist, G. 155
Evans, M. 38

Falcone, H. 108
Farr, J. 3, 6–8, 11–16, 20–1, 23–4, 42, 107, 151–2
Favero, J.L. 64, 96, 121, 157
Fay, C.H. 6
Fazio, R.H. 74
Feldman, J.M. 3, 13, 16–18, 20, 24, 28, 30, 38, 43–4, 83, 101–2, 157, 161, 163, 185, 187
Feldman, N.S. 99
Ferber, M.A. 107
Ferris, G.R. 117, 149, 179
Fiedler, F. 34
Fiedler, K. 111
Fischoff, B. 74
Fisher, C.D. 11, 35, 109
Fisher, W.A. 32, 47
Fisicaro, S.A. 126–7
Fiske, S.T. 34, 39, 43, 108
Fitzgibbons, D.E. 117
Flanagan, J.C. 6
Folger, R. 129, 166
Ford, G.L. 91
Ford, K.J. 42, 157
Forgas, J.P. 111–12
Foti, R.J. 19, 27, 38
Franks, J.J. 71
French, J.R.P. 18, 35, 127, 168, 184

Subject index

ability attributions 105
acceptability, performance appraisal 152, 177, 184
accuracy: behavioral 127, 138, 168, 171; classification 127, 168; as criterion of effectiveness 168–71, 182–5; decision making 127, 168, 170; definition 68, 126–7; differential 126; distributional 184; elevational 126; and error 125–30, 149–51, 163, 169; high 131; importance 188; measurement 68, 169–71; observational 27, 156; rating 1, 3–4, 7, 12, 14, 20, 25–7, 31, 43–6, 59, 64–5, 74, 77, 79, 81–2, 84–5, 93, 95, 108, 126, 129, 132, 141, 150–1, 156–7, 164, 169–70, 184–5, 187; recall 59, 64, 73, 84–5, 90; stereotype 126; *see also* true performance
acquisition, of information 1, 12, 21, 25–6, 28, 31–4, 48, 70, 97, 173–5; activities 37, 56; and affect 114; bias 181; casual 37, 65, 68; constraints 49–55; field studies 173–4; and memory 59; patterns of 27, 44, 58–60, 63, 65, 118; preconceptions 33–4, 39; purpose 34–5, 39, 64–5, 71, 76, 118; rater 49–50, 65, 164, 187; and rating scale 6, 11, 13–15, 20, 28, 30, 33, 36–7, 39, 41, 44, 58–64, 82–6, 133; role of 44; strategies of 27, 46, 48–9, 57–8, 65; under time pressure 35, 48
adaptability, of ratee 134, 142
adjusted ratio of clustering (ARC) 60–2, 77, 89, 134, 136, 142–3, 175
affect: bias 111–12, 117, and cognitive processes 111–12, 116–17, 119, 122,
153, 157; consistency 113–16; diary keeping 146–8, 162; interpersonal 110–16, 146–9, 159, 162, 180–1; job related 116; measures 146; negative 115–16; past performance 115–17, 146, 149; positive 115–16, 146, 148; ratee 108, 111–12, 117; rater 97–8, 112, 119, 151, 153; rating 147–8, 151, 153, 161, 163–4, 186, 187; social 114
agency theory 1
anchors *see* behaviorally anchored rating scales
applications, of research 163–72
appraisal: *see* cognitive appraisal; performance appraisal
assessment centers 160
attention, division of *see* competing tasks
attitude 84; positive 183–4
attribution theory 17, 25–6, 28, 32–3, 41–2, 50, 53–5; patterns 103–6
automatic processing 17, 18, 20, 102
average performance 103

base-rate information *see* consensus
behavior: changes 184; extra-role 179; observation 20, 31–2, 37
behavioral: accuracy 127, 138, 168, 171; discrimination scales 10; observation scales (BOS) 6, 36, 123
behaviorally anchored rating scales (BARS) 6, 36, 113, 123, 166, 168, 177–9
between-ratee discriminability 134, 137, 139, 142–5
bias 1, 10, 38, 40, 42–3, 46, 50, 91, 97, 123, 149, 159, 181; and affect 111–12,